PENGUIN BOOKS

BELIEVERS

Jeffery L. Sheler is an award-winning journalist who reported for *U.S. News & World Report* for twenty-four years, fifteen as the religion editor. He authored thirty-five cover stories and is now a contributing editor for the magazine. He is also the author of *Is the Bible True?*, which was named one of the top ten religious books of 2000 by *Christianity Today*. Sheler is an occasional correspondent for PBS's *Religion & Ethics NewsWeekly*. He lives in Virginia.

# BelieveRs

## A JOURNEY INTO
## EVANGELICAL AMERICA

Jeffery L. Sheler

PENGUIN BOOKS

PENGUIN BOOKS

Published by the Penguin Group

Penguin Group (USA) Inc., 375 Hudson Street, New York, New York 10014, U.S.A.
Penguin Group (Canada), 90 Eglinton Avenue East, Suite 700, Toronto,
Ontario, Canada M4P 2Y3 (a division of Pearson Penguin Canada Inc.)
Penguin Books Ltd, 80 Strand, London WC2R 0RL, England
Penguin Ireland, 25 St Stephen's Green, Dublin 2, Ireland
(a division of Penguin Books Ltd)
Penguin Group (Australia), 250 Camberwell Road,
Camberwell, Victoria 3124, Australia (a division of Pearson Australia Group Pty Ltd)
Penguin Books India Pvt Ltd, 11 Community Centre,
Panchsheel Park, New Delhi – 110 017, India
Penguin Group (NZ), 67 Apollo Drive, Rosedale, North Shore 0632,
New Zealand (a division of Pearson New Zealand Ltd)
Penguin Books (South Africa) (Pty) Ltd, 24 Sturdee Avenue,
Rosebank, Johannesburg 2196, South Africa

Penguin Books Ltd, Registered Offices:
80 Strand, London WC2R 0RL, England

First published in the United States of America by Viking Penguin,
a member of Penguin Group (USA) Inc. 2006
Published in Penguin Books 2007

10   9   8   7   6   5   4   3   2   1

Copyright © Jeffery L. Sheler, 2006
All rights reserved

A portion of this book appeared in *America's Best Colleges*, 2004 edition,
U.S. News & World Report. Used by permission of the publisher.

ISBN 978-0-14-311267-9
CIP data available

Printed in the United States of America

*For Doreen,*
*the love of my life,*
*who makes the journey worthwhile*

# Contents

# Believers

# Prologue

It was Monday morning, March 23, 1987, and members of the national staff of *U.S. News & World Report* were filing into a small glass-walled conference room on the sixth floor of the magazine's modern redbrick office building in Washington, D.C., to begin planning the cover story for that week's issue.

Over the weekend, all hell had broken loose in the lofty pulpits of the nation's electronic church. Television evangelist Jim Bakker had resigned in disgrace from his $130 million a year PTL (Praise the Lord) ministry after confessing to an illicit sexual encounter with Jessica Hahn, a Long Island church secretary, in a Florida hotel room, and then allegedly paying her hush money from PTL coffers. Tattling to church elders about Bakker's misconduct—calling it a "cancer on the body of Christ"—was fellow Assemblies of God preacher Jimmy Swaggart, himself a fast-rising star of TV evangelism, who was accused by Bakker and others of plotting to take over Bakker's South Carolina–based television network and Christian theme park. Rebuking Swaggart—"Satan has put something in your heart"—was still another TV preacher, Oral Roberts, who a few days earlier had retreated to the top of his Tulsa prayer tower and told his own viewers that God would "call me home" unless he raised $8 million within three weeks. Meanwhile, a fourth tel-evangelist, *Old-Time Gospel Hour* preacher and Moral Majority founder Jerry Falwell, had stepped in as temporary caretaker of the PTL empire and immediately gone on the air to exhort Bakker's flock—many of whom were suspicious of Falwell's intentions—to "close ranks and prevent the Devil from having a field day" amid the chaos.

A soap opera scriptwriter couldn't have concocted a more sordid plot. It had all the tantalizing elements of a made-for-TV melodrama: sex, deception, betrayal, cover-up, recrimination. It was a delicious scandal, and my *U.S. News* colleagues found it hilarious. Someone in the room dubbed it "Pearlygate."

But *U.S. News* was a serious magazine, and its editor at the time, David Gergen, a former adviser to presidents Nixon, Ford, and Reagan, thought the story needed to go beyond the titillating sins of the preachers. The fact that Bakker had been exposed as a scoundrel did not seem all that surprising. After all, the *Elmer Gantry* archetype of preacher as huckster was almost a cliché. So Bakker was a con man. What else was new?

What Gergen and others in the room found more fascinating was the size of the televangelists' following, the fact that millions of Americans apparently found this campy religious shtick inspiring and appealing to the point that they were willing to send money, despite—and, in some cases, in response to—the preachers' absurd on-air antics.

What did we know about Bakker's followers?

"I think we're talking mainly here about evangelicals," someone offered. Several people nodded and others chimed in—"born agains ... fundamentalists ... holy rollers ... snake handlers." One reporter explained to the rest of us that evangelicalism was a rather rustic brand of Christianity that appealed mainly to undereducated rural folk in the South and Midwest. It didn't have much traction in the more urbane and enlightened precincts of the Northeast and the West Coast. Another staffer who had grown up in the Deep

South noted that Jimmy Swaggart and bad-boy piano pounder Jerry Lee Lewis were cousins. Both were born and raised in rural Louisiana. "Jerry Lee found fame in the honky-tonks and night-clubs and Jimmy Lee found it in the pulpit," he drawled. "Folks down there still like to argue about which one is the better showman."

The discussion quickly degenerated into a babel of quips, snickering, and unintelligible side chatter. Gergen tried to get the discussion back on track.

Maybe the story needed to include a profile of the TV preachers' followers—who they are and why they seem to be so easily and willingly taken in. That prompted more snide commentary on reports of the Bakkers' opulent lifestyle—rumors of gold bathroom fixtures, multiple homes and Mercedes-Benz luxury cars, an air-conditioned dog house—all paid for by hundreds of thousands of viewers, many of them retirees or low-income wage earners who dutifully sent in their monthly checks as PTL Partners or put their donations on credit cards.

To my colleagues around the table, all of this was simply unfathomable. It was as if the TV evangelists and their followers existed in some bizarre parallel universe with no discernible points of contact with intelligent life on earth.

"Why would anyone *do* that? Are these people gullible or just plain stupid?"

"They've got to be fanatics—how else can you explain it?"

"Who *are* these people?"

The questions were left hanging in the air.

My face suddenly felt flush, and I nervously glanced around the room to see if anyone had noticed. I knew the answer—or at least I thought I did. Over the years I had personally known people who had been faithful viewers of Bakker or Swaggart or some other flamboyant televangelist, and who sometimes even sent them money. And I knew even more people who lived unapologetically within the broader evangelical subculture, sharing at least some of the basic tenets of the TV preachers' folksy brand of Christian faith.

But the evangelical Christians I knew bore little resemblance to the simplistic and shallow caricature my colleagues were conjuring up. They were not fanatics, and they certainly were not stupid. I knew this from personal experience.

After all, for most of my life I had considered myself one of them.

I was saved as a teenager in 1963 at a fundamentalist Baptist church in Grand Rapids, Michigan. It was a week or two after Easter, near the end of a Sunday evening service, sitting in a simple and unadorned cement-block sanctuary that smelled faintly of Pine-Sol and floral perfume, when I offered up a simple silent prayer: "Lord Jesus, I know I'm a sinner and that you died on the cross for me. I ask you to forgive me and come into my heart."

According to the Baptist understanding of things, having prayed that childlike prayer, and believing that God had heard and answered it, I could rest assured from that day forward that when I died I would spend eternity in heaven. By the grace of God I'd been saved from sin and from hell—not by baptism or by joining the church, or by any other ritual or good deed. It was in accepting Jesus by faith as my personal savior that I had become a child of God.

That was the crux of the gospel as it was preached week after week at Maplelawn Baptist Church and, as I would learn later, at thousands of other churches throughout the country that subscribed to a brand of conservative Protestantism that today is loosely characterized as evangelical Christianity. Evangelical wasn't a term we used very often at Maplelawn. We considered ourselves fundamentalists, a label that did not yet carry all of the negative baggage it would accrue a few decades later, when it would be used to describe radical Muslims or hardliners of just about any religion.

For the next three years that little Baptist church would become my spiritual home. The people were earnest and friendly, a good mix of young and old, with lots of families whose breadwinners worked at the nearby General Motors plant or the Steelcase furniture factory. Many lived in the neighborhood in inexpensive tract houses built for returning veterans of World War II. Their faith was simple and sure: The Bible was God's word, inspired and infallible from cover to cover, and it pointed to Jesus as the only way of salvation.

The church's pastor was an intense man with penetrating eyes, crooked teeth, and dark wavy hair parted high in a style reminiscent of the 1930s crooner Rudy Vallee. Pastor Smith—like most Baptist ministers, he didn't take to being called Reverend—seemed to know everything there was to know about the Bible. He could quote it from memory effortlessly, chapter after chapter. In his sermons his standard practice was to dissect Bible passages word by word, sometimes analyzing verb tenses in the original Greek and Hebrew in order to make his point. And his point, more often than not, was that people needed to get right with God or face eternal punishment in hell. Except for an occasional rant against godless communism, he never preached about politics or social issues, even though the civil rights movement was in full swing and many of the nation's clergy were becoming actively engaged. If people wanted to hear about that stuff, he said, there were plenty of liberal churches downtown that had nothing better to offer. Ours was a Bible-believing church, and our mission was to save souls.

That being so, Pastor Smith tended to end every service in pretty much the same manner. After finishing his sermon he would bow his head and offer a prayer, which he would conclude with the phrase "in Jesus' name." But instead of signing off with the traditional "Amen," he would continue on without breaking cadence.

"I want every head bowed and every eye closed—no one looking around. If you know you are a sinner tonight and you have never asked Jesus to save you, I want you to raise your hand."

It didn't always produce results. But fairly often, after a few minutes of relatively mild cajoling, at least one or two in the congregation would lift their hands. "Yes, I see that hand there in the back. You may put it down. Thank you. Anyone else? Yes, I see that hand. Yes."

Generally, people who responded to the pastor's invitation were not regular attenders. If they had been they would have known what was coming next and might have thought it better to keep their hands neatly folded in their laps like the rest of us.

"We're going to stand and sing a closing hymn, and as we sing, if you raised your hand, I want you to come forward and meet me here at the front of the church. You need Jesus tonight. You may never have another chance. Don't leave here without him. You come, and we'll have someone pray with you and show you how you can be saved tonight."

He did this at every service, even at funerals—although with some modification. "We're thankful today that our dear departed brother knew the Lord, and we can rejoice knowing that he has gone on to receive his heavenly reward. But what about you? If you were to die today, do you know where you'd spend eternity? I want every head bowed and every eye closed ..."

Occasionally there were complaints, usually from out-of-town relatives of the deceased who questioned the propriety of proselytizing mourners fresh in their grief. Obviously these people weren't saved or they would have known that inviting people to accept Jesus always trumps the rules of etiquette. What better time to get people to think about the eternal fate of their souls than when they're gazing into an open casket?

For his part, Pastor Smith not only took the criticism in stride; he wore it like a badge of honor. As Christians, he would remind us, we are not called to please men, but God. And God expected all of us to spread the gospel of salvation without fail and without apology. People all around us were dying and going to hell. We had the answer. We were obligated to share it. Those of us who were not preachers were not let off the hook. We were expected to "witness"—to engage people one-on-one in order to persuade them to accept Jesus as their personal savior.

Getting people to accept Jesus was the focus of almost everything we did at Maplelawn. We called it being born again—a New Testament term that in the early 1960s hadn't yet worked its way into the cultural vernacular and so made a handy code word to use when witnessing: "Have you been born again?" It made a great opening line. If the question elicited a look of puzzlement, as it usually did, you had your answer. If a person didn't know the lingo, they obviously didn't know Jesus. It was perfect for sorting out true Christians from pretenders.

As important as we knew it was, truth be told, witnessing was something that few of us really relished. In fact, to many of us it was downright intimidating. As a fourteen-year-old kid with acne, the thought of walking up to complete strangers on the street, let alone people I actually knew at school, and talking to them in a personal way about Jesus and sin and the fate of their immortal souls—I couldn't imagine anything more daunting.

But there were powerful incentives. "The Bible tells us that someday we'll stand before the judgment seat of Christ and give an account of the opportunities we've been given here on earth. What will you say on that day? How many souls will be writhing in hell because you didn't take time to tell them about Jesus?" Pastor Smith was not a flamboyant man. He seldom raised his voice when he preached. He didn't have to. When he said things like that it was usually in calm, measured tones accompanied by lots of direct eye contact—which made it all the more disturbing. It was enough to give a kid nightmares.

There were positive incentives as well. The pastor assured us that when we got to heaven, if we'd been good and faithful servants we'd receive a golden crown to place at the feet of Jesus. And for every soul who accepted Jesus as a result of our efforts, we'd receive a star in our crown.

Now *that*, I thought, was cool. I wanted a golden crown when I got to heaven. And for me, no plain old crown would do. I wanted stars—lots of them.

So I threw myself into Christian fundamentalism with all the zeal I could muster. I practically lived at church: Sunday school, Sunday morning and evening services, Wednesday night prayer meeting, youth group—whenever the doors were unlocked, I was there. I started carrying a pocket-sized Bible to school, and mustered up enough courage to begin witnessing to my classmates. I wrote and talked about my faith in English and social studies classes, and got into heated arguments with classmates who went to churches that didn't interpret the Bible correctly, as we Baptists did. At one point, along with another student who went to my church, I considered running for student council on a platform of banning school dances. We knew we wouldn't succeed, but at least we'd have made our stand for Christ—without apology.

I suppose, in a way, my fundamentalist faith also functioned as my teenage rebellion—a relatively benign but effective way of declaring independence and finding my own way in the adult world. My mother and father were honest, moral people who believed in God but were not regular churchgoers, and who made no pretense of being saved. They drank beer and smoked cigarettes and enjoyed hanging out at the local Amvets club. Obviously they were bound for hell.

I, on the other hand, had chosen a different road—the right road. I caught them completely off guard when I walked into our smoky little house one day and announced that I had become a Christian and consequently would no longer be attending movies or school dances, listening to rock-and-roll music, or participating in family card games. Oh and by the way, I added, if you were to die tonight, do you know where you would spend eternity?

My parents were on the receiving end of my first fumbling attempts at witnessing. Usually they took my ham-handed assaults with amazing composure.

My mother always listened patiently as I thumbed through my Bible, laying out my case, carefully following notes I had written to myself: "All have sinned and come short of the glory of God ... the wages of sin is death ... but God so loved the world that he gave his only begotten Son ... if you confess with your mouth the Lord Jesus Christ and believe in your heart that God raised him from the dead, thou shalt be saved ..."

She would listen, nod her head, and agree with everything I said. But whenever I would try to close the deal, she would slip away.

"I'm not ready."

Not ready? Why not?

"I'm just not, but you keep doing what you're doing. You keep going to church. Maybe some day you'll be a minister." I never knew what to say to that. I always suspected she was just happy I wasn't out carousing.

My father was a different story entirely. He was a self-educated man, a World War II veteran who had loaded bombs for the Army Air Corps in France, come home, gotten married, and taken up the sheet-metal trade. He knew exactly what he believed and what he didn't, and he was as combative as I was.

"Who says I need to be saved?"

It's in the Bible.

"So who wrote the Bible?"

God. It's inspired by God.

"It's inspired by something, alright." I could get nowhere with him.

Of course, I wanted my parents to be saved, but when they refused to capitulate to the obviously superior logic of my Scripture-supported arguments, it only served to reaffirm in me the rightness of my chosen path and the wrongness of theirs. I wasn't about to give up trying to convert them. My parents would remain the ultimate challenge of my personal evangelism. But by then I had been a Christian for several weeks and I had yet to win a convert. My crown was starless. I decided it was time to move on to an easier target.

My little sister, Nancy, would be no match for my battle-tested skills of pious persuasion. She was a precocious and mischievous eight-year-old, and even though she hadn't yet reached the "age of accountability"—twelve, according to Pastor Smith—I knew she needed Jesus. So with my Bible and notes in hand, I went into her room one evening just after she'd been tucked in, sat down on the edge of her bed, and proceeded to explain that she was a sinner on her way to hell. She listened with rapt attention as I told her how she could be saved. Then I asked her if she wanted to accept Jesus as her savior, and she said yes. And we prayed together.

As I left her room and closed the door, I smiled, knowing that somewhere in heaven's vast storehouse of eternal rewards a freshly minted crown of gold just my size suddenly glistened with the brilliance of a bright new star.

By the end of high school my infatuation with fundamentalism had run its course. I stopped going to the Baptist church, where I had come to be viewed as a backslider. I had mellowed in my faith, having learned that there was more to being a Christian than rigid rules and pushy witnessing.

I began attending the Church of the Nazarene, a relatively small but fast-growing evangelical denomination that was part of the holiness movement. In many ways the Church of the Nazarene was as conservative as the Baptists. They too had strict rules against drinking, dancing, going to the movies, or using tobacco. But all things considered, I found them to be much more laid-back than the Baptists and not nearly as contentious. I attended a Nazarene college just long enough to get engaged, and then went off to a state university to pursue a career in journalism.

While in college I married my high school sweetheart, who had been raised a Nazarene. We went to Nazarene churches during most of our child-rearing years. It was a good place for families, with lots of activities for kids. Our church became our extended family and our primary social circle.

But as time went on my wife and I found ourselves growing estranged from the Nazarene church and from the evangelical ethos in general. Among other things, we were put off by the informal style of worship that seemed to us utterly disconnected from the mainstream of Christian tradition. We felt drawn to a more liturgical and sacramental form of worship that we knew had nurtured and sustained Christians through the ages, even though evangelicals tended to dismiss it as dead ritualism.

Once our daughters were grown we left the Nazarene church and became mainline Presbyterians, attending a fairly conservative congregation in Washington, D.C., that introduced us to the lectionary, the liturgical calendar, and other historic elements of the Christian faith that we had never known about as evangelicals. It was exactly what we needed and wanted. We felt enriched, connected, and at home.

I had moved on in my journey of faith. My basic beliefs had not changed dramatically, but it was a different season and I was in a different place. And even though I no longer considered myself an evangelical in the traditional sense, I continued to have an affinity for the people and the movement I had known and been a part of for so many years. We shared a history. They were an important part of who I had been and who I had become. That would never change.

So I was confident that I had the answers to my colleagues' questions. I felt I knew all about evangelical Christians, and I knew they were not the rubes and fanatics that my coworkers seemed to think they were. I knew this from personal experience, from having been among them. And I knew that I needed to set the record straight.

But as the cover meeting wore on, the tone of the discussion had become increasingly derisive, not only toward the miscreant ministers but also toward the hapless followers who eagerly supplied the cash that kept the televangelists on the air and in expensive clothes, cars, and jewelry. I suspected there was nothing positive to be gained by openly challenging the prevailing mood of the room and offering a defense of evangelicals based primarily on my personal experience. I wasn't likely to change any minds merely by vouching for them. And frankly, I didn't want the derision directed at me. So I kept silent.

As the discussion wound down the broad outlines of the cover story were beginning to take shape. The main piece would focus on the PTL scandal and the related intrigue involving the other TV preachers. The phrase "pulpit wars" had been bandied about as a possible cover line, but the story would go beyond that and attempt to shed light on the televangelists' followers as well, providing some context for the scandals at the top. Gergen announced that Mel Elfin, the magazine's new national editor and the former Washington bureau chief for *Newsweek*, would cobble together a tentative shooting script and parcel out reporting and writing assignments after lunch. And with that the meeting adjourned.

A few minutes later I tapped on the door of Elfin's corner office and was invited in. Mel was a high-energy, no-nonsense kind of editor, in his early sixties, with short gray hair and black-rimmed glasses. He ran the news operation like a crusty drill sergeant. He was quick to make a joke, but also quick to explode in a blistering tirade if he detected incompetence or sloth.

I told him I thought I could help shed some light on the TV preachers and their followers. Without going into detail, I explained that I was familiar with the basic landscape of the evangelical world, having briefly attended an evangelical college in the late

1960s, and had some contacts inside a few of the major ministry organizations.

"Terrific!" he said. "Can you tell the difference between fundamentalists and Pentecostals?" I think so. "We'll have you do a glossary then, a sort of lexicon of born agains." He also wanted me to assemble a "who's who" of TV evangelists, briefly sketching the key players and how they operated. Those would be sidebars to the main piece. He asked that I also keep an eye on the main story as it developed during the week, specifically watching for any inaccuracies that might creep into the reporting and writing, and keep him posted. Of course, I was more than happy to oblige.

This had gone better than I had hoped. I left Mel's office determined and confident that our cover package would be accurate and fair. I had no interest in protecting the preachers or soft-pedaling the scandal. The story needed to be factual and hard-hitting. If crimes had been committed, and it appeared that there had been, then let the guilty pay. If the preachers' followers had been less than vigilant in demanding accountability, then the facts would speak for themselves. Most of all, I wanted to help the magazine paint an accurate and properly nuanced portrait of evangelical Christians, a people who defied the kinds of easy labels that too often were attached to them.

Despite my worst fears coming out of the Monday cover meeting, the reporting proved to be quite solid and the final package turned out strong. It was a good example of journalism done right.

Yet as successful as that *U.S. News* story turned out to be, it had little discernible impact on the general public literacy level regarding evangelicals. In the ensuing years I would continue to see them stereotyped and maligned in the press and the public arena. In 1993, a writer in the *Washington Post* described evangelicals as "poor, uneducated, and easily led." Others have tried to define them on the basis of barren polling data or sociological studies. Seldom have such efforts ventured beyond the superficial.

But from my vantage point as a journalist and, now, an outsider, I also began to see a strange and disturbing new face put forward from inside the movement, one that didn't square at all with my own experience.

The 1980s and 1990s saw the rise of the religious right and the emergence of evangelicals in the modern political arena. It marked a dramatic departure from the principled disengagement of the 1960s, exemplified so well by Pastor Smith and the people I had encountered at Maplelawn Baptist Church. The religious fervor evangelicals once reserved for worship and soul winning, it seemed to me, now was being applied to winning votes and influencing government policy. Slick pamphlets and voting guides were being mass-produced and disseminated in churches, defining the "Christian" stand on issues ranging from abortion and school prayer to taxes and foreign policy. There was an abundance of demagoguery and a casting of political opponents not merely as rivals but as enemies of God. More than once I heard people in the pews question how anyone could vote Democrat and presume to call themselves Christians. Evangelicals were on their way to becoming an auxiliary of the Republican Party. Like Esau in the book of Genesis, they were selling their birthright for a bowl of pottage. This was not the evangelicalism I remembered.

And then there was the ongoing melodrama on the Christian airwaves—the radio talk-show hosts and TV personalities whose intemperate and sometimes bizarre remarks assaulted the sensibilities of most ordinary Americans, including many evangelicals I knew.

On one hand, it was easy to dismiss the self-serving rants of Pat Robertson, who announced to the six-million-plus viewers of his *700 Club* early in 2004 that he'd been "hearing from the Lord" that President Bush would win reelection "in a walk." It really didn't matter what the president did "good or bad" during the remainder of his term, Robertson explained, because "he's a man of prayer and God's blessing him." This was nearly as mind-boggling as Robertson's taking credit a few years earlier for having prayed a hurricane away from the southeastern Virginia coast, where his TV studios are located.[1]

But there were other self-appointed Christian commentators in some smaller radio and TV markets who, for whatever reason— true belief? to pump up ratings?—fed their listeners a steady diet of partisan propaganda, paranoia, and pop theology that seemed designed to sow fear and distrust of anyone outside the evangelical camp. Their favorite targets: big government, the liberal media, and public education. Did people really buy into these diatribes? Again, I was inclined to give ordinary evangelicals the benefit of the doubt. Surely these broadcast zealots didn't speak for mainstream evangelicalism. But how did they stay on the air unless people were listening—and agreeing?

This period also saw seismic shifts inside some of the nation's major Christian denominations. None were more dramatic or consequential than what some called a fundamentalist takeover of the sixteen-million-member Southern Baptist Convention. Although the conservatives' revolution began in 1979, it was consolidated throughout the 1980s, as moderates were systematically purged from the church's leadership and academic institutions. The takeover was quickly followed by a series of regrettable actions by Southern Baptist leaders that reeked of arrogance and narrowminded intolerance, beginning with a brash pronouncement by the denomination's new president in 1980 that "God Almighty doesn't hear the prayer of a Jew." Later these Baptists launched a campaign to convert American Jews during the Jewish high holy days, and then they mounted similar crusades to proselytize Muslims and Hindus during their holy seasons. These confrontational tactics were widely denounced by other Christian groups, including some evangelicals. But these Baptists had plenty of defenders within the movement. It was not evangelicalism's finest hour.

The right-wing resurgence in the Southern Baptist Convention spawned a counterrevolution during the late 1980s that gave birth to the so-called evangelical left, a curious constellation of religious activists who championed the causes of peace, the poor, and the environment along with the more traditional evangelical emphases on biblical morality and personal salvation. While they were unquestionably evangelical in their theology, they found themselves more often allied with the agendas of the liberal mainline than with their fellow evangelicals and, consequently, struggled to establish a strong base of support within the movement. So far, they haven't succeeded.

As I considered these and other developments it became increasingly clear to me that the evangelical movement that I once had regarded as my home had become a stranger to me. In a relatively short span of years it had grown, evolved, and diversified into something almost unrecognizable, an accelerating stream of American spirituality that had exploded into a churning torrent of confusing crosscurrents—engagement and isolation, innovation and retrogression, action and reaction, one step forward and two steps back.

So the question that I once found so cynical and disconcerting when posed by my *U.S. News* colleagues now has become my own. Who *are* these sixty million Americans who call themselves evangelical Christians? What are their motives, aspirations, and agendas? Who speaks for them, and who does not? What is their vision for America, and what might it mean for the rest of us?

This book is my search for the answers.

As I set out to explore the landscape of modern evangelical America, I embarked on what would become, on the one hand, a pilgrimage to rediscover my own spiritual roots—to revisit and critically reassess some of the teachings and traditions that had shaped my own faith journey, from the strident fundamentalism of my youth to whatever it is that I am today, and perhaps, in the process, to reclaim that which for me is authentic, reasonable, and true.

Yet this is far more than a personal spiritual exercise or an attempt to exorcise some lingering demons from my own past. As my wife is fond of telling me whenever she thinks I'm taking the vicissitudes of life too personally: It's not about me. The significance of this quest goes beyond merely satisfying my personal curiosity. More than anything else it is a journalistic journey to discover the heart and soul of a people I thought I knew—people all of us should now know.

ONE

# Awakening

Virginia Beach, Virginia

The midweek prayer and praise service at Rock Church wasn't scheduled to officially get under way for another fifteen minutes, but Ralph Haddock, a lay minister and one of eight assistant pastors at the five-thousand-member Pentecostal megachurch, already was working up a sweat as he warmed up the assembling crowd of worshipers. A stocky middle-aged man in a crisp gray suit and carefully combed blond hair, Haddock paced back and forth on the blue-carpeted platform, his eyes squeezed shut, a microphone in one hand, the other hand raised high, waving and batting the air as he prayed aloud.

"Oh Lord, we just want to thank you and praise you tonight. You are a holy and merciful God, and we thank you Jesus! Thank you, Jesus!"

Each sentence was punctuated by shouts of "Amen!" and "Yes, Lord!" from the crowded front rows of the modern fan-shaped auditorium where some three hundred worshipers—a well-blended mixture of men and women, young and old, white, black, Hispanic, and Asian—were on their feet, some swaying back and forth, arms lifted upward, their voices rising and falling in an unintelligible cacophony of simultaneous prayer. Some whispered softly in English. Others warbled in an ecstatic "prayer language"—common in charismatic and Pentecostal churches—that sounded like a strange mixture of Native American and Middle Eastern chant: "*Oh-la-la-fa-la-rasha ... Oh-fa-la-ra-la-shana ...* Thank you, Jesus ... Thank you, Jesus."

In one corner of the platform two guitarists, a drummer, and a keyboardist began playing a slow, jazzy gospel melody as worshipers continued to trickle in, quickly setting their Bibles down and joining in the sacred revelry. The 5,200-seat auditorium was less than one-tenth filled. Still, it was a relatively good turnout for a Wednesday night service. And what the crowd may have lacked in number it more than compensated for in enthusiasm.

On this third of November 2004, one day after American voters handed President George W. Bush a second term in office and strengthened Republican control of Congress, the people of Rock Church seemed clearly in a mood to celebrate. Behind the platform a long white banner stretched across the polished granite wall spelled out in bold green letters: RETURN, AMERICA, TO THE LORD YOUR GOD. It was an adaptation of the Old Testament prophet Hosea's exhortation to the ancient Israelites, who had fallen into idolatry and sexual impurity, to forsake their wicked ways "for you have stumbled because of your iniquity."[1] Could it be, on this chilly November night, that the prayers of the people at Rock Church and of millions of other evangelical Christians throughout the country had been answered—that an America they saw as wayward and obstinate, stumbling in its own defiance of godly values and biblical morality, had finally begun to awaken to the call of God by returning to the White House a man of faith whom evangelicals had come to embrace as one of their own?

"You are a holy and righteous God, and we thank you for your long-suffering patience and your great faithfulness," Haddock prayed, his eyes wide open as he looked upward at the bright vaulted ceiling. "We thank you for blessing our nation. We thank you for hearing our prayers. *Ha-rasha-fa-la-shona.* Thank you, Jesus. Thank you, Jesus. "

*"Yes Lord!"*

*"Amen!"*

Up to this point no one had directly mentioned the election, let alone invoked the president's name. And it is no doubt true that on any given Wednesday night the people of Rock Church have no difficulty finding reasons to thank and praise the Almighty with just about as much energy and enthusiasm as I was witnessing. Yet whatever doubts I may have had about exactly what was behind the spirited jubilation and all the fervent God thanking on this particular night were about to be dispelled.

As the prayers subsided and the music faded, the people took their seats and the church's founder, Bishop John Gimenez, stepped to the microphone. Looking dapper in a navy pin-striped suit, red tie, and suspenders, his hair dyed dark brown and combed back, Gimenez, at age seventy-four, appeared to have lost little of the style and energy that had made him a national voice and something of a legend in the Pentecostal wing of American evangelicalism.

A former drug addict from Spanish Harlem, Gimenez spent his teenage and young adult years in and out of New York prisons before he accepted Christ at a Pentecostal church in the South Bronx in 1963. He became a preacher shortly thereafter, and met and married Anne Elizabeth Nethery, a fiery preacher in her own right from Corpus Christi, Texas. Together they traveled the country, holding Holy Ghost revival meetings in tents and small auditoriums and ministering to drug addicts. In 1968 they founded Rock Church in an abandoned church building in Norfolk, Virginia. Within three years they had built a congregation of several hundred and erected a new sanctuary in nearby Virginia Beach. The flock continued to multiply, thanks in part to a weekly television broadcast of the church's spirited Sunday services. By the mid 1970s the church had added a Christian academy and a Bible institute for the training of pastors and missionaries. And twice during the next two decades it would outgrow its sanctuary and build bigger ones. The Gimenezes' ministry included a growing network of satellite churches, many of them planted and led by ministers trained at Rock's Bible institute. Today the Rock Ministerial Family Fellowship counts more than six hundred congregations throughout the world that look to Bishop Gimenez as their overseer and apostle.

During those early years of building a ministry and a national reputation, Gimenez developed a close friendship with Christian broadcaster Pat Robertson, whose television studios are located on a sprawling campus just a few miles down the road. Gimenez was a frequent guest on Robertson's daily television program, *The 700 Club*. Like Robertson, Gimenez had developed a keen interest in Washington politics, and he became a vocal critic of government policies that he believed had contributed to a moral decline in the nation. Chief among his concerns were Supreme Court rulings legalizing abortion and banning school prayer, the government's lax enforcement of antiobscenity laws, and policies that Gimenez saw as promoting a "homosexual agenda" that he considered a direct assault on the traditional family.

Eager to fight back, Gimenez organized a Washington for Jesus rally in 1980 that drew some two hundred thousand evangelical Christians to the nation's capital to pray for a spiritual revival among government leaders and a renewed national embrace of biblical standards of morality. Although it was billed as a nonpartisan event, and no political candidates were endorsed or allowed to speak, Gimenez and others later would declare that the election of President Reagan that November was a clear and direct answer to those fervent prayers.[2] Gimenez followed up with similar rallies in 1988 and 1996, although those events drew much smaller crowds than the first. In his most recent effort, just eleven days before the 2004 election, Gimenez expanded his sights, summoning believers to a rally that this time was billed as "America for Jesus."

About twenty-five thousand people showed up at the Washington mall to hear Gimenez, entertainer Pat Boone, National Association of Evangelicals president Ted Haggard, and a host of others call the nation to repentance and to pray that America would return to its moral roots. "We did what God called us to do," Gimenez said at the close of the event. "The rest is up to him."

And now, as Gimenez looked out over his congregation, he smiled and nodded.

"I know some of you were anxious yesterday because you wanted your man to win, and now you must be feeling better."

"*Yes!*"

"*Praise the Lord!*"

"But I want to remind you, my friends, that the Lord is sovereign. It's the Lord who chooses who wins the election. The president didn't win because of the Republican Party. He won because of a group of people who went to the polls who believe in God, who believe in prayer, and who believe in moral values. He won because of the church, because of people who don't follow a party but who follow a man, the man Jesus Christ."

"*Amen!*"

"*Glory to God!*"

As self-congratulatory as it may have sounded, the bishop's triumphal assessment of the election was not without merit. The precise role that conservative Christians played in Bush's relatively narrow victory would be explored and analyzed by pollsters and pundits for months after the election. But on this day after the vote, news commentators were astonished (and some were aghast) by reports of a heavy turnout of evangelical voters, especially in key battleground states like Ohio and Florida, and by exit polls that showed "moral values" to be the single most pressing issue of the campaign—ahead of jobs and the economy, ahead of the fighting in Iraq, even ahead of the war on terrorism.[3] The same polls found that three out of four of the so-called values voters went for Bush.[4] It was enough to prompt the Associated Press to declare later in the week that Bush's victory, along with the passage of anti-gay-marriage amendments in eleven states, "showed the power of churchgoing Americans in this election."[5] The *Washington Post*'s veteran political analyst David Broder concluded that "the mobilization of religious conservatives, those who are normally more conscientious about going to church than about voting," had been crucial to Bush's win.[6] And a *Chicago Tribune* writer called the president's reelection "the fruit of the Bible ballot."[7]

While later analyses would show that Bush also gained important ground among traditionally Democrat-leaning Roman Catholic and African American voters, it was clear that conservative Protestants like Gimenez's flock had contributed mightily to Bush's narrow margin of victory. A little postelection merrymaking probably was justified. But the bishop would have none of it.

"You may feel like celebrating now," Gimenez said, wagging his finger, his face suddenly stern. "But I must warn you that we dare not go to sleep. We dare not rest on our laurels. We've got to maintain the righteousness of God, because we know that four years from now the enemy will raise his head once again and attack this nation."

I looked up from my note taking. As far as I knew I was the only journalist in the auditorium. But it struck me how alarming the bishop's last remark would have sounded to some of my colleagues in the press, and how inflammatory it would have appeared in print in the morning newspaper. A conservative Christian minister casting his political opponents as the enemy was just the sort of polarizing, over-the-top rhetoric that many in the media had come to expect from the more strident voices of the religious right, and that many nonevangelical Americans had found so disturbing. Never mind that the use of such overheated rhetoric had been soundly criticized from within evangelicalism during the quarter century since the Reverend Jerry Falwell's Moral Majority first charged into the political arena with zealous abandon.[8] Over the years, mostly through trial and error, many conservative Christian activists had discovered that they stood a much better chance of advancing their cause in Washington by embracing the traditional rules of political engagement, such as respect for opposing views and the importance of compromise, than by demonizing the opposition. So it was a little jarring to hear from a megachurch minister in the year 2004 what sounded like a throwback to the bellicose language of those early skirmishes of the culture wars.

But I had been around conservative Christians enough to know that in the common jargon of the evangelical pulpit, "the enemy" has a very specific *spiritual* meaning that has little to do directly with politics, and that most congregants would pick up on it quite naturally, even if most journalists would not. It is, of course, a popular euphemism for Satan, the enemy of God and tempter of mortals, whose literal existence most evangelical Christians take as an article of faith. They base their belief on biblical passages depicting the devil as "the evil one"[9] and "the prince of this world"[10] who deceives and seduces the unwary. The apostle Paul had the devil in mind when he warned the Ephesians that "we wrestle not against flesh and blood, but against principalities, against powers, against the rulers of the darkness of this world, against spiritual wickedness in high places."[11] Taking such passages quite literally, as they do, many evangelicals believe Satan to be as real and as personal as God—not God's equal, but a supernatural power at work in the present age.

So that, at least, is what I assumed the bishop meant by the enemy. My guess was that he was not talking about John Kerry, the Democratic Party, the ACLU, or even Hillary Rodham Clinton—at least not directly. Rather, he was warning his flock to stay on guard against attacks from the spiritual enemy whose aim is to foil God's purposes and ensnare God's people.

But by doing so in a political context the bishop seemed to be ascribing cosmic and eternal significance to the otherwise mundane partisan struggles that lay ahead. More than a mere debate over public policy or even a clash of competing worldviews, what the bishop seemed to envision over the next four years was the continuation of spiritual warfare between the forces of good and evil. It was a thought that echoed the fighting words of James Dobson, influential head of Focus on the Family and easily one of evangelicalism's most politically assertive figures. "When we oppose hardcore and violent pornography, the killing of unborn babies, the provision of immoral advice to teenagers, the threat of euthanasia, and so on," Dobson wrote in *Christianity Today* magazine in 1995, "we are engaged in a battle—not primarily with our philosophical opponents, but against Satan, 'who leads the whole world astray.'"[12]

Yet if Gimenez and Dobson believed that their struggle over abortion and other moral issues was primarily a struggle against Satan, then it seemed an obvious corollary that anyone who happened to disagree with them on those issues was, wittingly or not, in cahoots with the devil. To this way of thinking, while liberals and Democrats may not actually *be* the enemy, it was clear that they were doing the enemy's bidding. Gimenez and Dobson seemed to be giving a very literal meaning to the word "demonize." Obviously they had missed the memo about making nice with the loyal opposition.

The bishop went on.

"The enemy will attack, but the people of God won't sit still for it," Gimenez said, his voice rising now and its cadence quickening.

"We won't lie back. We're going to stand up and we're going to overcome the enemy!"

"*Amen!*"

"We're going to recover everything we've lost in this country. We're going to stop the killing of babies. We're going to put prayer back in our schools. We're going to protect the family. We're going to turn away from the sins that beset us as a nation."

"*Yes!*"

"*Amen!*"

*"Praise the Lord!"*

The congregation was on its feet, applauding, waving, and shouting its agreement with the bishop's rousing exhortation. The agenda Gimenez laid out was ambitious, to say the least. Abortion, school prayer, defending traditional marriage—these were hot-button issues that Christian activists had been raging about for decades, with relatively little to show for it. But this was a room full of true believers. In the election campaign the people of Rock Church had witnessed a political awakening of evangelicals across America, and had seen what in their minds amounted to a providential triumph of good over evil. But now they were being told the real battle lay ahead, and the real victory—restoring righteousness and godliness to a wayward nation—was within their grasp. To the Rock Church congregation, reveling in postelection euphoria and Pentecostal bliss, nothing on this night seemed beyond the reach of God's invigorated army.

And so it also seemed to the decidedly more secular-minded sages of the national news media. Political pundits already had breathlessly begun to assess the ramifications of the unexpectedly strong "morality vote" and to pronounce America's evangelicals a formidable new powerhouse in Washington. Over the next several weeks a writer for the *New York Times* would report that conservative Christian leaders, exulting in their role in the election, "immediately turned to staking out mandates for an ambitious agenda," including banning same-sex marriage, remaking the Supreme Court, and overturning the court's decisions in support of abortion rights.[13] *U.S. News & World Report*, in a lengthy profile of Dobson, would declare that evangelicals "haven't stood as much chance of molding Washington since they began organizing politically in the wake of Roe v. Wade."[14] And on the eve of Bush's course-charting State of the Union speech at the outset of his second term *Time* magazine would devote a cover story to identifying the "25 Most Influential Evangelicals in America," and ask in an accompanying article, "What does Bush owe them?" (*Time*'s implicit answer: plenty.)[15]

The singular message in all of this was clear: the religious right was back, and it was stronger than ever. Evangelicals had solidified their status as a key constituency of the Republican Party, and now were in a powerful position to put their conservative stamp on government policies, the federal judiciary, and American culture. It was a prospect that scared the bejabbers out of liberal critics and others who worried aloud that given their way, conservative Christians would turn back the clock on decades of social and economic progress and send the country skittering down the road to theocracy. Just days after the election Barry Lynn, executive director of Americans United for the Separation of Church and State, predicted bold new incursions against the church-state wall by the invigorated Christian right, and warned that "the culture war may go nuclear" as a result.[16]

Strident speeches like the one I had just heard would do little to assuage such fears. Neither would the widely reported rumblings of evangelical media stars like Dobson, Robertson, and Florida pastor and TV evangelist D. James Kennedy (head of a crusade to "reclaim America for Christ") who wasted little time after the election putting Republicans on notice that they as well as Democrats would pay a price in 2006 and beyond if they failed to deliver on the religious right's agenda.[17] Whether it was mostly bluster or whether these self-anointed leaders were actually capable of directing the political behavior of tens of millions of evangelical voters was of little consequence at that moment. The demands for payback succeeded in getting the attention of the media and of important segments of official Washington. To what ultimate end would remain to be seen. For now it was the illusion of power that mattered.

And so America's evangelicals were back in the national spotlight. Their motives and methods were being explored once again by news organizations whose interest had been rekindled by the election and who consequently tended to perceive evangelicals foremost in political terms, as a people driven by a highly politicized social agenda and led by a handful of ambitious and intemperate spokesmen. Yet it was a perception that my experience both as a religion journalist and a former evangelical told me was questionable, to say the least. To ascribe such monolithic motives and behavior to such a large and diverse population—some fifty million people of voting age—seemed to me a gross oversimplification that ignored—or was oblivious to, or perhaps uninterested in—the varied experience and complexity of the evangelical movement. Evangelical Christians had never shown themselves in modern times to be a particularly politically minded people. They had, indeed, turned out at the polls in greater numbers in 2004 than in 2000, and 78 percent of them had voted for Bush. But voting in a presidential election hardly makes one a political activist. And America's evangelicals clearly were not a political monolith. After all, nearly seven million of them had voted for Kerry, and nineteen million hadn't voted at all.[18]

That said, I knew from history that from time to time there are cataclysmic moments of change, the so-called tipping points when people and nations suddenly, and for reasons that are not always immediately apparent, find themselves propelled by events or circumstance in some bold new direction. Could the 2004 election have been a tipping point for evangelicals? Had a confluence of social issues—abortion, pornography, same-sex marriage, euthanasia—and an apparent crystallization of views on those issues within the two political parties, provided the spark that would ignite some new level of political energy and cohesion within their ranks?

Sitting in the Rock Church auditorium I found myself wondering what would happen once the news cameras and microphones were turned off and all the TV ads and campaign rhetoric faded. Once the winners were sworn in and the rest of America went on with their lives, would evangelicals continue to be politically engaged in ways and to degrees that they never had been before? Would they stand out as some politically hyperactive subculture bent on remaking America in their own image while the rest of the nation slumbered? Or, having done their civic duty and cast their votes along with the rest of the country, would they fall back into old routines? With the election over, what now would energize, consume, and define them as a people of faith? And as for the clearly more politicized public figures among them—people like Dobson, Robertson, Kennedy, and Gimenez—I wondered how many months would pass before they and the rest of us would realize just how little or how much they had actually won.

I returned to Rock Church a couple of months later to visit Gimenez in what I assumed would be a less politically charged atmosphere. I hoped to learn what passions, if any, consumed the bishop and his flock now that the heat of the campaign and the triumphal afterglow of Bush's reelection had begun to fade. Was life returning to normal? And what exactly *was* normal? I wanted a chance to see beyond the Pentecostal preacher's combative public veneer, if that's what it was, in order to catch a glimpse of the person of faith beneath and, from that, perhaps to gain some new insight into the spiritual motivations of his coreligionists within the broader evangelical movement.

I knew, of course, that Rock Church was just one of tens of thousands of evangelical congregations in the United States, and that as a Pentecostal church—one that emphasizes Holy Spirit baptism and experiencing the "gifts of the spirit" such as faith healing, prophesying, and praying in tongues—it was representative of a limited segment of American evangelicalism, albeit an important one. How typical it was in having mixed major doses of politics with traditional ministry during the 2004 campaign was difficult to gauge.

Anecdotally I was aware that like Rock Church hundreds if not thousands of evangelical congregations throughout the country had distributed voter guides and encouraged members to register and vote according to their Christian values. The Southern Baptist Convention, the nation's largest Protestant denomination with some sixteen million members, claimed that during the five months preceding the election it alone had signed up more than one hundred thousand new voters and passed out nearly four hundred thousand pieces of literature in at least twenty states as part of its "I Vote Values" campaign. I also was aware anecdotally that many evangelical pastors had carefully avoided any direct public talk about partisan politics and had not permitted the dissemination of campaign literature at church. "We try to reach out to a diverse community," one Illinois pastor explained to me after the election. "If there was ever a hint that we considered ourselves a Republican or a Democratic stronghold, people just wouldn't come back."

But whether or not Rock Church was typical of evangelical churches in its political involvement, it certainly was not unusual. And given Gimenez's own high visibility, his personal orchestration of the Washington prayer rally, and his apparent penchant for polemical rhetoric, it was probably fair to include him in the ranks of the more political of evangelical clergy. If anyone was likely to keep the pressure on his people long after the election to stay engaged—praying, giving, organizing, lobbying their elected representatives to move on the religious right's agenda—it was Gimenez.

When I arrived at the church one Friday morning in February the auditorium was empty and silent except for a lone custodian vacuuming the platform. The bold banner exhorting America to return to God was nowhere in sight. A bulletin from the previous Sunday that had been left on a rear pew seat listed events for the week ahead—men's and women's prayer breakfasts, a children's choir rehearsal, a Hispanic ministry meeting, a senior citizens' luncheon, sign-ups for men's and women's softball teams—and solicited volunteers for the church's "24-hour Prayer Team" and for its food pantry. Bishop Gimenez had preached that morning on the power of God's word, and in the Sunday evening service Anne Gimenez had delivered a sermon entitled "The Blood of Jesus." No signs of overt politicking so far.

I was fifteen minutes early for my appointment with the bishop, so I took my time as I headed down the long floral-carpeted hallway toward his study, stopping along the way to wander through the church's bookstore and to take in a gallery of photographs and other items displayed on the corridor walls. Clustered in one large section of the hallway were dozens of framed photographs of ministers of various nationalities who serve at Rock churches in India, Africa, the United States, and elsewhere. A few feet away, in an elaborate wooden frame, the smiling faces of John and Anne Gimenez gazed out from a carefully matted clipping from a local newspaper; the headline was "How Did a New York Street Punk and a Gal From Texas Build the Region's Most Famous Mega Church? The Story May Surprise You."

Across the hall—under a sign asking "How Can I Get Involved?"—stood a large literature rack loaded with colorful pamphlets touting volunteer opportunities in the church's ministries to children, the elderly, prison inmates, and the poor. One pamphlet solicited recruits to the God Squad—a team of street-corner evangelists who apparently descend on area shopping centers on weekends to try to convert "those destined for hell." To be a God Squad member, according to the pamphlet, one must be a "tithing member in good standing" and attend special training classes to learn the ins and outs of effective witnessing for Jesus. There certainly seemed to be no shortage of ministry outlets for church members desiring to be active. Most of them were of the soul-saving and Bible-teaching variety.

I arrived at the bishop's outer office and was ushered into his spacious sun-drenched study. The next day Gimenez was to fly to India to deliver $50,000 in relief aid raised by the Rock Ministerial

Family Fellowship for victims of the tsunami that had swept the south Asian coast on December 26, 2004, killing more than 140,000. While there he planned to dedicate a medical clinic and help distribute medical supplies in the riverfront town of Rajahmundry in hard-hit Andhra Pradesh state, where sixty-one churches affiliated with the Rock fellowship had been destroyed and hundreds of church families dislocated by the raging floodwaters. Gimenez would be away for ten days, and no doubt had plenty of last-minute preparations to attend to. But he was eager to sit and talk about the evangelical movement, his ministry's place in that movement, and some of the issues—spiritual and political—that he believed were tearing at America's soul.

"The evangelical church," the bishop began to explain, facing me across a small wooden conference table, "is just a group of ordinary people, made up of every race and nationality, who have had an encounter with God—not just a religious experience, but a real personal encounter with God. And they want to live it and express it to the fullest extent possible, without compromise.

"In doing that we sometimes are perceived as fanatics because we read things in the Bible and say, 'This is what God said.' Now, we're not perfect in our understanding, because anything we get from God has to pass through this human filter," he tapped his temple, "and oftentimes it comes out looking more human than like God. But as best we can we try to explain what God has said in his word, and then we try to adjust, first, ourselves, and then the people we shepherd, and then the community at large. We do this because we're not called just to Jerusalem but also to Judea and to Samaria and to the uttermost parts of the world. In other words, we believe the gospel we preach is to cover the entire world, because that's what Jesus said."

The bishop had just paraphrased what I knew to be three of the central tenets of the evangelical faith: that the Bible is God's inspired and inerrant word; that having a personal faith relationship with Jesus Christ is the only way of salvation; and that Christians are obligated to share the gospel—the good news of salvation—with others. While there are other important teachings, these three taken together form the definitive core of evangelical identity. They also underlie some corollary beliefs and attitudes that many non-evangelicals often find rigid and more than a little arrogant. If the Bible is infallible, for example, then its teachings on everything from marriage to sexual mores are nonnegotiable. If there is "no other name" but Jesus by which humankind can be saved, then faith in anyone or anything else is futile. So it was refreshing to hear the bishop sound a note of humility—by acknowledging that evangelicals were fallible mortals who do not always interpret the Bible correctly.

On tenets beyond those three, from eschatology (doctrines relating to the Second Coming of Christ) to modes of baptism (to sprinkle or to dunk?), evangelicals often differ widely, and sometimes vigorously, something Gimenez knew from personal experience. "I've had other Christians tell me, 'If you don't believe exactly like we do, then you're going to hell,'" he said with a dismissive chuckle. "Well, I was in a lot of hell before I got saved. I was a drug addict in the streets of New York, and God delivered me and saved me. Hell could be right here for some people. But there is another hell, an eternal one. The Bible says, 'What does it profit a man if he gains the whole world and in the end loses his own soul?' We consider the soul more important than the gain. And that's why we are compelled to preach the gospel."

I mentioned the pamphlets I had seen in the hallway and the notices I had read in the Sunday bulletin promoting the church's ministries. I also mentioned my earlier visit to the church and reminded him of his remarks on the night after the election. On one hand, I said, Rock Church seemed heavily focused on traditional ministry—the kinds of religious activities that helped produce its phenomenal growth. Yet he had passionately implored his flock that night to stay politically engaged—a potentially polarizing objective, it seemed to me, that could easily detract from the church's ministry. Could a church do both effectively? Should it even try?

Gimenez answered by ticking off some of the major projects conducted and paid for by the Rock Church congregation: roughly a million dollars a year spent on schools, clinics, and church buildings, mainly in India and Africa, and establishing "cities of refuge" for victims of natural disasters; thousands of dollars more spent providing financial support for Bible students and educational resources for Rock churches around the world. All of this, he said, was in addition to the local ministries and weekly services I had read about in the hallway. "Now," he said, "ask me how much do we spend on political causes. Zero. How much do we spend on political propaganda? Not a penny. We're doing what the gospel says, and if you do what the gospel says, God blesses you."

Technically, the bishop probably was telling the truth about the church's spending. The election-focused America for Jesus rally he led in Washington a few weeks before the presidential vote had been funded by a separate Rock-related entity called One Nation Under God, Inc., which solicited donations through a link from the church's Web site. A fund-raising letter appearing online and signed by Anne Gimenez claimed that more than $1.5 million had been needed for the event to cover staging, sound and lighting equipment, and other unspecified expenses. The same online site offered an assortment of merchandise for sale: $10 T-shirts, $20 golf shirts, and $10 baseball caps emblazoned with the America for Jesus slogan. So it was probably true that no funds directly from Rock Church or its worldwide fellowship had gone into the event. Yet without the fund-raising muscle of John and Anne Gimenez and the volunteer work of other Rock Church staff, the rally clearly would not have happened.

"As you can see," the bishop continued, "we're doing God's work. Our time and our resources go into spreading the gospel and ministering to people's needs. But part of doing God's work is being a good citizen. We love America. And now we are seeing that America has a cancer, and so we make it a matter of prayer. When we went to Washington it was to pray. Some people said it was political. Well," he threw up his hands in feigned surrender, "if you think talking to God is political then, amen, I guess it's political. But we didn't pray 'Lord, put in George Bush.' We prayed 'Lord, bring righteousness to this nation.' And God looks around and sees there's not much to choose. You've got these two candidates, and one speaks of God and prays to God. The other one, it's an abomination what's all around him—the abortion crowd, the homosexual crowd. When most people in the country looked and saw what has taken over the Democratic Party, it didn't leave a choice. They had no choice.

"Did the Lord answer our prayer? I believe he did, but we still have a distance to go. For some time we've been heading downward morally in this country. But now there seems to be a slight momentum, a breeze that's lifting us up again."

It was clear that Gimenez was not hampered in his ministry or in his personal worldview by the perplexing nuances of trying to sort out the sacred from the secular. When it came to dealing with issues like abortion, pornography, and homosexuality Gimenez saw no distinction between the religious and political realms. In his view these were not fundamentally political issues but moral ones addressed in Scripture. So to speak out against abortion from the pulpit or to exhort church members to support a Marriage Protection Amendment was not being political but was a way of encouraging his flock to give legs to their biblically based convictions, to put their faith into action. He reflected what I knew was a common way of thinking among evangelicals: A Christian's values should be integrated holistically into every sphere of life.

That had been the rationale behind the Southern Baptists I Vote Values campaign—that Christians should choose candidates who best reflect their values. Presumably that's what all voters do in deciding how to cast their ballots. Where problems arise, of course, is when a leader—religious or otherwise—attempts to define for an entire group which issues and values are paramount. There had been plenty of Christian voters in 2004, many of them evangelicals, for whom issues of war and peace, the environment, and economic justice were the preeminent moral issues of the campaign. When they voted their values it was not for President Bush.

We talked a while longer—about the church, his own conversion, the influence his late father, a Methodist minister, had had on his decision to go into the ministry, and more about the moral challenges confronting the nation. When our conversation ended I picked up my notebook and recorder and the bishop walked me to the door. In the outer office he stopped and picked up a copy of a book he had written in 1993 entitled *God the Boxer*. "It's all about spiritual warfare," he explained. "I think you might enjoy reading it." He took out a pen and signed an inside page.

"You know," he said, handing me the book, "Bob Dylan sang a song a while back, 'You Gotta Serve Somebody.' Well, America is going to serve somebody. Who's it going to be? Here we are, trying to be this pluralistic, humanistic, no-name, no-God, no-nothing nation. But we have to have a destiny and we have to have a purpose. And if our purpose doesn't start out In God We Trust, then in what will we trust?"

We said good-bye, and when I got to my car I opened the book and read the inscription.

*To Jeff.*
*Remember, God always wins!*
*John Gimenez*

# TWO

# Roots and Branches

Boston, Massachusetts

For an investment of twelve dollars and about two hours' time visitors to Boston can take a guided tour of the Freedom Trail, a walking pilgrimage past historic landmarks in the saga of American independence such as Bunker Hill, Faneuil Hall, the U.S.S. *Constitution* ("Old Ironsides"), and the home of midnight rider Paul Revere. One of the sixteen stops along the winding 2.5 mile route is Park Street Church, a formidable red-brick edifice with a towering white steeple built in 1809 adjacent to the Boston Common and the old Granary Burying Ground, where Revere and fellow revolutionaries John Hancock and Samuel Adams are interred.

Though not as famous, perhaps, as Boston's Old North Church—where two signal lanterns were hung to alert Revere that the British army was approaching by sea—Park Street Church, as costumed guides from the Freedom Trail Foundation are eager to point out, is no less rich in history. Here the abolitionist firebrand William Lloyd Garrison delivered his first antislavery speech in 1829, arguing not only for the abolition of slavery but for equal citizenship for African Americans. Here, too, the patriotic hymn "America" ("My Country 'Tis of Thee") by Samuel Francis Smith, was sung for the first time by a children's choir in 1831. In the early decades of the new republic the cobblestone intersection where the church stands was known as Brimstone Corner both for the fiery sermons emanating from the church's pulpit and for the gunpowder stored in its basement during the War of 1812. Over the years it would continue to be venerated as an important shrine to American freedom.

Park Street Church also holds an esteemed place in the history of the American evangelical movement. One of the oldest continuously active evangelical congregations in the country, it was founded by a small group of expatriates from the nearby Old South Church as a bulwark of biblical orthodoxy against a tide of Unitarianism that began to sweep New England churches in the late eighteenth century. To advance biblical literacy and Trinitarian belief it launched the nation's first Sunday school in 1818, and a year later sent the first Protestant missionaries to Hawaii, then called the Sandwich Islands, demonstrating its evangelical commitment to spreading the gospel throughout the world.

Even the church's prominent location holds historical significance for evangelicals. It is within sight of the spot in Boston Common where in 1740 the Great Awakening revivalist George Whitefield preached to a crowd of more than twenty-three thousand—more than the entire population of Boston, and one of the largest public gatherings in the colonies up to that time. A little more than two centuries later an heir to Whitefield's revivalist legacy, a young Baptist preacher named Billy Graham, would conduct one of his first evangelistic rallies on the very same spot, drawing a crowd of forty thousand on a wet and chilly day in 1950 to hear a message not unlike Whitefield's—a simple plea to come in faith to Jesus. Graham and Park Street's pastor at the time, the Reverend Harold J. Ockenga, along with a handful of other conservative Protestant clergy and theologians, would go on to become leading lights in the emergence of evangelical Christianity as a robust movement and a potent cultural force in the second half of the twentieth century.

If one were looking for the birthplace of modern evangelicalism in America, one might think to look no farther than Park Street Church.

I decided to make my pilgrimage there after conferring with Mark Noll, a history professor at Wheaton College in Illinois and one of the most knowledgeable people on the planet regarding evangelical origins.[1] An evangelical himself, Noll has written more than twenty-five books and dozens of articles on the history of evangelicalism and of early American Protestantism in general. I had spoken with him many times over the years as religion writer for *U.S. News & World Report* and had always found him to be helpful and patient in explaining things in a way that even a journalist could understand.

So when I telephoned and told him I was looking for the place where it all began, I knew I could count on him to steer me to just the right spot. Noll responded to my query as any distinguished scholar would when asked to summarize a lifetime of academic work in a three-second sound bite. He chuckled.

"There really is no such place."

After a brief silence and a cough, I asked him to explain.

"The evangelical movement—some people think 'tradition' may be a better word—cannot be traced to a single place or time," he began. "There is no single founder or instigator as such—no one like Martin Luther for the Protestant Reformation or Joseph Smith for the Mormons."

Evangelicalism, after all, he explained, was not a denomination or even much of a cohesive movement in the way that some social, political, or even religious causes in the past have been—the abolition and temperance movements in the nineteenth century, for example, or the pietist movement among Lutherans in Europe during the seventeenth century. The evangelical movement was more "a confluence of a multiplicity of sectarian and denominational streams," each with its own unique history and setting.

That said, he continued, there were certain defining events, trends, leaders, beliefs, and practices around which the people we call evangelicals eventually coalesced, and from which the movement would take its shape. Some of those important elements were associated with places like Park Street Church that, in Noll's opinion, ranked high among significant historical sites. But there were other noteworthy locations: the home of Jonathan Edwards, the great eighteenth-century preacher and theologian, in Stockbridge, Massachusetts; a crypt beneath a Presbyterian church in Newburyport, Massachusetts, where George Whitefield is buried; the site of Methodism founder John Wesley's missionary parsonage in Savannah, Georgia; Azusa Street in Los Angeles, where revival meetings in 1906 gave birth to modern Pentecostalism; among others.

"If you trace the roots back to Europe," he said, "you can find even more. There's just a tremendous amount of history, and there are plenty of historical places that connect in one way or another to the evangelical movement. But there is no birthplace. Sorry."

I told him that what I really had hoped to find was a historical reference point—a place to begin to explore and to better understand what I knew was a large and diverse movement, one that, in many ways, was puzzling to a lot of people, me included.

In my own experience evangelicalism had seemed largely disconnected from what I thought I knew about historic Christianity. I had been to the Vatican on reporting assignments. I had visited churches in Rome and in Jerusalem that dated to the fourth century. The lineage of belief and practice in the Roman Catholic and Eastern Orthodox churches, I knew, reached back many centuries, perhaps to the days of the apostles. Libraries are filled with their history. I understood how the Protestant Reformation, beginning in the sixteenth century, flowed out of that stream. The Church of the Nazarene, which I joined as a young adult, on the other hand, began in Pilot Point, Texas, in 1908. The Baptist church I attended as a teenager was part of an association that was organized in the 1930s. Some independent evangelical churches I knew about were started last week. How did they fit into the big picture?

It was not that I expected to find one neat strand of history that suddenly would put everything that was important to know about evangelicals into clear perspective. Nor was I particularly interested in exploring history for history's sake. What I hoped I would begin to find, though, were satisfactory answers to seemingly simple questions that have been asked over and over since the mid-1970s, when evangelicals first appeared on the national media's radar screen: Who are these people? Where did they come from? What do they want? The fact that people persisted in asking such questions three decades later was probably less an indication of some cognitive deficiency on their part—or so I hoped, since I included myself among them—than of the considerable diversity within the evangelical movement that makes discerning an all-encompassing answer a not so simple task.

The tens of millions of Americans who march under the evangelical banner today, after all, come from a wide variety of Protestant traditions, from conservative Baptists and Dutch Reformed Calvinists to pacifist Mennonites and tongues-speaking Pentecostals. Some bear familiar denominational labels like Methodist, Presbyterian, Congregationalist, and Lutheran. Others are part of lesser known denominations like the Evangelical Free Church or the Christian and Missionary Alliance. Vast numbers are associated with independent and nondenominational churches of assorted shapes and sizes. Their worship styles run the gamut from traditional and liturgical to contemporary praise and charismatic. And they often differ with one another, sometimes vehemently, on doctrinal matters such as baptism, rules of ordination, charismatic gifts such as speaking in tongues and faith healing, and the meaning of the Lord's Supper. With such an apparent lack of uniformity one might reasonably wonder how evangelicalism can be considered a movement at all.

What loosely unites evangelicals and sets them apart from other Christian traditions, as Noll once explained, is "a shared set of convictions, attitudes, and emphases," many of which grew out of revival movements in Europe and the colonies during the seventeenth and eighteenth centuries. British historian David Bebbington summarizes those common features as: conversionism, an emphasis on being born again, which evangelicals believe occurs when a person accepts Christ as savior and enters into a personal relationship with God; biblicism, a reliance on the Bible, as opposed to church tradition or the pronouncements of church officials, as the ultimate religious authority; activism, the responsibility of all believers, including laypeople, to be engaged in sharing the gospel and converting others to the Christian faith; and crucicentrism, a focus on the redemptive death and resurrection of Jesus Christ as the only source of eternal salvation.[2]

While other Christian traditions may embrace one or more of those characteristic beliefs, the combination represents a distinctly evangelical outlook and forms the gravitational center for what Noll describes as "a large family of churches and religious enterprises" that together make up the evangelical movement.

Exactly how large of a family, I knew, was a question that is not easily answered. I had seen published estimates of their number, based on public opinion surveys, that ranged from 5 percent to 45 percent of the U.S. population—from about fourteen million to well over one hundred million people. Such huge discrepancies reflect the apparent difficulty in defining evangelicals. Since 1976, for example, the Gallup Organization has tried to estimate the number by simply asking people if they identify themselves as born again or evangelical Christians, using the terms synonymously. Gallup's findings have fluctuated from a low of 33 percent in 1987 and 1988, the height of the televangelist scandals, to a high of 47 percent in 1998.[3]

Some experts question whether self-identification alone is the best way of counting the evangelical population. They note that those who describe themselves to pollsters as born again often include a number of Roman Catholics and others who do not otherwise match the traditional characteristics of evangelicals. At the same time, some people who are active participants in evangelical churches—some Southern Baptists, for example—choose for whatever reason not to identify themselves to survey takers as evangelicals. Consequently, some pollsters have begun using a combination of measuring sticks that include self-identification, agreement with core evangelical beliefs such as those on Bebbington's list, and affiliation with churches or denominations known to be evangelical.

Applying those more finely tuned methods, some recent surveys have put the number of evangelicals at about 25 percent of the adult population, or roughly sixty million people—numbers that seem to have gained broad acceptance in the scholarly world. One such survey commissioned in 2004 by *U.S. News & World Report* and the PBS program *Religion & Ethics NewsWeekly* also found that the evangelical population is spread virtually evenly throughout the country with slightly larger concentrations in the Deep South and the upper Midwest. And it found that evangelicals are more likely to live in suburbs, smaller towns, and rural areas than in large cities; are just slightly older and slightly less educated than the general population; and are overwhelmingly Caucasian.[4] Even though many African American Protestants hold evangelical beliefs, the heritage of segregation in this country and the unique history of African American denominations have kept most African Americans from identifying with the evangelical movement or participating in its causes.[5] Despite signs of progress in breaking down historic racial and ethnic barriers in some evangelical venues, for most of the movement the old maxim still holds true—that 11:00 A.M. on Sunday is the most segregated hour of the week.

Being a historian Noll naturally thought I was on the right track in looking to the past for a better understanding of today's evangelicals. He assured me that the historical disconnect I had perceived in my own experience was not as it appeared, that there were clear paths connecting the modern evangelical movement with the broad sweep of Christian history. Exploring those paths, he averred, I was sure to discover that evangelicals' distinctive beliefs, their personal and experiential approach to faith, their seemingly intense desire to convert others, and even their attitudes about social and political involvement were firmly rooted in the experience of Christians through the centuries, and most notably in the revivals of the eighteenth and nineteenth centuries.

In a sense, the history of evangelicalism has been an almost continuous process of revival and reclamation, of a people carving out and maintaining a religious identity over some other group or set of beliefs and practices that they considered to be out of synch with a proper understanding of the gospel. It is a corrective impulse that goes back to the start of the Reformation, and to even earlier purifying movements in Christianity.[6]

Protestantism had begun with Martin Luther's "rediscovery of the gospel"—his embrace of essential New Testament teachings that he felt had been obscured by corrupt practices in the Roman Catholic Church. Chief among those practices was the selling of indulgences, or pardons, to penitent sinners as a means of escaping punishment for sin. To Luther, God's grace was the sole basis of salvation for the sinner, and was to be appropriated through faith alone *(sola fide)*, unmediated by the church, as revealed through the Bible alone *(sola scriptura)*, the only infallible authority on matters of faith. Those central tenets of the Protestant Reformation would remain key elements of modern evangelical belief.

Roughly a century after Luther nailed his ninety-five theses to the cathedral door at Wittenberg, a corrective movement arose within the new Protestant churches of Europe that would further define the evangelical trajectory. During the early decades of the Reformation theologians throughout the continent spent tremendous amounts of energy debating and refining their emerging doctrines. Sermons expounding on dogmatic fine points became standard fare in the pulpits—to the growing consternation of some German and Dutch churchmen, who felt that the inner life of faith was being smothered by a cold rationalism and a pallid religious formalism. The dissenters raised their voices, calling for a return to individual piety and to "true religion" of the heart. And they found many who were eager to respond.

By the end of the seventeenth century the pietist movement, as it had become known, had spread throughout the Lutheran and Reformed churches of continental Europe, and its influence was being felt in England. Its distinguishing beliefs and practices closely resembled those that would come to characterize modern evangelicalism: an emphasis on personal repentance and spiritual regeneration, as opposed to mere intellectual assent to doctrines or participation in church rituals; regular study of the scriptures by laypeople, especially in small-group gatherings; the practice of "heartfelt love" for fellow Christians and unbelievers alike; and the importance of spreading the gospel through foreign and cross-cultural missions.

In England, pietist influences would have a profound impact on Anglican ministers John Wesley, the founder of Methodism, and George Whitefield, who, along with Congregationalist preacher Jonathan Edwards in Massachusetts, would become important figures in the rise of evangelical Christianity in America.

During a missionary voyage to the Georgia colony in 1735 Wesley became acquainted with a group of Moravian pietists aboard ship, and was immediately impressed by their serenity, especially during storms at sea. He discovered that the Moravians possessed a firm assurance of divine acceptance and forgiveness of sins that Wesley, even though he was an ordained clergyman, did not. That discovery led Wesley to question the efficacy of his own faith, prompting him to write at the end of his Georgia mission, "that I who went to America to convert others was never myself converted to God."

When Wesley returned to London he began meeting regularly

with a group of Moravians for prayer and Bible study. During one such gathering, on Aldersgate Street on May 24, 1738, as he would famously record, during a reading of Martin Luther's preface to the Epistle to the Romans: "I felt my heart strangely warmed. I felt I did trust in Christ, Christ alone for salvation; and an assurance was given me that he had taken away *my* sins, even *mine,* and saved *me* from the law of sin and death."[7]

Wesley's palpable experience of conversion would become the ideal for many evangelicals today who, like the Moravian pietists, consider salvation a gift from God to be received with assurance by repenting and placing one's faith in Jesus Christ as savior. As with Wesley and the pietists, many evangelicals believe one's salvation is confirmed experientially when, in the words of St. Paul, "the Spirit bears witness with our spirit that we are the children of God."[8] That settling of the question of the fate of one's eternal soul continues to be for many, as it was for Wesley, an important and attractive feature of the evangelical gospel.

Empowered by his revitalized faith, Wesley went on to travel extensively in England and the colonies, preaching a gospel of warm-hearted piety based on the good news of salvation by faith. On both sides of the Atlantic he and his associates established hundreds of Methodist Societies—small groups that followed a methodical study of the Bible and pious devotion. In America those societies eventually would be organized into the Episcopal Methodist Church, precursor of the modern Methodist denominations.

At roughly the same time that Wesley was preparing for his first fateful missionary voyage to the colonies, a young George Whitefield was undergoing a similar life-changing experience. Two years earlier, as a student at Oxford, Whitefield had undertaken a personal quest for God not unlike Wesley's, spurred on in part by pietist writings. He had come to recognize that "though I had fasted, watched and prayed, and received the Sacrament long, yet I never knew what true religion was." But by the spring of 1735 Whitefield's spiritual search was coming to an end. "About this time," he wrote, "God was pleased to enlighten my soul, and bring me into the knowledge of His free grace, and the necessity of being justified in His sight by *faith only*."[9] He would later point to that realization as his moment of conversion.

A year after leaving Oxford Whitefield was ordained a deacon in the Church of England, and he began a career as an itinerant preacher, exhorting listeners throughout the British Isles, and later in the colonies, to receive new life in Christ. His unconventional message and methods would stir both revival and controversy on both sides of the Atlantic.

Whitefield was a powerful orator with a sonorous voice and a dramatic flair. He was known for his ability to hold an audience spellbound with his theatrical delivery, using vivid word imagery to pluck at the emotions of his listeners. Among the enthralled was the famous English actor David Garrick, who once declared: "I would give a hundred guineas if I could only say 'Oh!' like Mr. Whitefield."[10] As Whitefield's reputation grew, so did his audiences. He soon took to speaking outdoors in order to accommodate the thousands who were turning out to hear him. This was quite an innovation, and one that did not sit particularly well with his fellow Anglican clergy. They accused him of undermining church order by refusing to obtain permission to speak in their parishes and by fostering "enthusiasm"—emotional outbursts—among his listeners. Whitefield eventually found himself shut out of many Church of England pulpits.

Late in 1737 Whitefield accepted an invitation from Wesley to join him in the colonies, where seeds of revival were beginning to sprout. It would be the first of seven preaching tours that would take Whitefield to every major town from Georgia to New Hampshire, and would ignite the Great Awakening—one of the most formative events in American history.

The revival fires in the colonies had been kindled a few years earlier by the young Congregationalist minister Jonathan Edwards. A learned theologian in the Puritan tradition, Edwards, like Whitefield and Wesley, recently had become convinced of the necessity of the new birth for one's eternal salvation. In 1734 he preached a series of spirited sermons on Justification by Faith Alone that caused many at his church in Northampton, Massachusetts, to suddenly grasp a heartfelt and all-consuming faith in "the excellency of Jesus Christ and his sufficiency," as Edwards would later record, "and to be much weaned in their affections from the world."[11] The spiritual stirring began to ripple through other churches in nearby towns, and word of it soon spread to the other colonies and to England.

By the time Whitefield arrived in 1738 the New England revival had begun to fade, but Edwards continued to preach and to write powerfully on the theological themes that had sparked it. He also expounded on the psychology of conversion and defended a preaching style that played on the emotions—that struck terror, if necessary, even among children—in order to save doubting souls from the fires of hell. It was an approach Edwards applied with dramatic effect in his most famous sermon, "Sinners in the Hands of an Angry God," and one that would become a staple of evangelical revivalism.

But it was Whitefield who would fan the smoldering embers of revival back into the roaring fire that swept the American colonies in the early 1740s. From the Boston Common and Philadelphia's Society Hill to the town squares and rural fields of the Carolinas, people gathered by the thousands to hear the famous preacher and his egalitarian message of salvation by grace through faith in Jesus Christ. And, as had happened in England, he was confronted at nearly every stop by fellow Anglican clergy who labeled him a troublemaker. Nonetheless, before his tours of the colonies were complete, notes one Whitefield biographer, "virtually every man, woman, and child had heard the 'Grand Itinerant' at least once. So pervasive was Whitefield's impact in America that he can justly be styled America's first cultural hero. Indeed, before Whitefield it is doubtful any name, other than royalty, was known equally from Boston to Charleston."[12]

The Great Awakening would have a lasting impact on evangelicalism and on the course of Christianity in general in the United States. The eighteenth-century revivals, as Noll points out, promoted "a new style of leadership—direct, personal, popular, and dependent much more on a speaker's ability to draw a crowd than upon that speaker's place in an established hierarchy."[13] It is a style that would be emulated by modern stars of the evangelical pulpit, from itinerant evangelists Billy Sunday in the early 1900s and Billy Graham a half century later, to broadcast personalities like Jimmy Swaggart, Jerry Falwell, and Pat Robertson—all of whom would use their formidable skills as communicators and innovators to build a religious following independent of denominational ties.

The early revivals also undercut traditional church authority by simplifying the essentials of the Christian faith into a message with mass appeal that could be easily disseminated beyond the walls and without the approval of the churches. While "ecclesiastical life remained important" to evangelicals, says Noll, it became "not nearly as significant as the decision of the individual" to hear and accept the good news of salvation.[14] That democratization of Protestant Christianity resonated powerfully in the colonies during the decades leading up to the American Revolution, and continues to do so among evangelicals today.

A second wave of revivals later in the eighteenth century would bring more changes. The Second Great Awakening, as it would become known, erupted on three fronts—New England, the Cumberland Valley, and western New York—between the mid-1780s and the 1820s, with different ramifications in each locale. In the Cumberland Valley and in eastern Kentucky the revivals grew out of a series of camp meetings, where thousands gathered for several days of spirited and sometimes raucous preaching services. Where the first awakening had been led by Congregational and Anglican clergy, the camp-meeting preachers were mostly Baptists and Methodists, and the fervor they inspired helped to establish those denominations—and evangelical Christianity—in the South.

In New England the revival was more cerebral, sparked in part by a renewal of biblical commitment against the perceived heresies of Unitarianism and universalism. It also gave rise to new missionary agencies and to church involvement in social causes such as abolition, temperance, child welfare, and prison reform—demonstrating a concern for the betterment of society that would characterize evangelical Protestantism through most of the nineteenth century.

The awakening in western New York, meanwhile, was largely the work of revivalist preacher Charles Grandison Finney, a Presbyterian minister whose carefully staged services produced thousands of converts in Rochester, and later in other eastern cities. Unlike Jonathan Edwards, who considered revival "a surprising work of God," Finney believed revival could be deliberately induced with careful planning, innovation, and lots of publicity—strategies that would become commonplace in modern evangelistic campaigns. Finney also emphasized the role of human volition in the salvation process, that individuals had the ability to "choose God," and thereby to take control of their own spiritual destiny.[15] That view would become a standard feature of modern American evangelicalism.

Out of the two Great Awakenings, American Protestantism emerged as a powerful culture-shaping force in the nineteenth century, and its character was overwhelmingly evangelical. While there were pockets of liberal dissent and some important doctrinal and regional differences—slavery being the most divisive—nearly all of the major Protestant denominations and their institutions were guided with varying degrees of intensity by a commitment to conversion, biblical authority, missionary outreach, and benevolent activism—all hallmarks of evangelicalism.

It was a type of evangelicalism, as Noll describes it, "infused with postmillennial optimism"[16]—a mind-set that considered social reform to be an important part of the church's mission. By both saving souls *and* fighting social ills, evangelicals believed they could make the world a better place and thereby usher in the Second Coming of Christ. Their outlook was considered postmillennial because it was based on the popular belief that Christ would return after the millennium, a thousand-year period of peace and righteousness predicted in the book of Revelation. Largely as a result of that social-reforming impulse, the number of charitable organizations in New England exploded during this period, growing from about fifty at the time of the War of Independence to nearly two thousand in 1820. Most of them were founded by Protestants, many of them of the evangelical variety.[17]

But by midcentury evangelical optimism found itself facing supreme challenges. The slavery debate had opened deep fissures in antebellum Protestantism. Many northern evangelicals had become zealous abolitionists, and many of their southern counterparts were staunch defenders of the "peculiar institution." Both sides appealed to scripture to make their cases. The sectional conflict split several denominations, creating institutional schisms that in some cases still exist.[18] And as the conflict erupted into a bloody and protracted war, embattled evangelicals in the South turned increasingly inward, embracing an insularity that foreshadowed changes awaiting the broader evangelical movement just a few decades later.

The nation that emerged from the Civil War was, in the minds of most American Protestants, a Christian nation. As religion historian George Marsden has observed, while there were "many Roman Catholics, sectarians, skeptics, and non-Christians [who] had other views of the matter, Protestant evangelicals considered their faith to be the normative American creed."[19] The nineteenth century, after all, had brought successive advances to their cause. They had passed through the refining fire of an apocalyptic war that had posed "the greatest test of American evangelical civilization" up to that time.[20] And the Union victory, in the northern perspective at least, had brought vindication—confirming, as one Presbyterian put it, that "we as individuals, and as a nation, are identified with the kingdom of God among men, which is righteousness, and peace, and joy in the Holy Ghost."[21] American evangelicals were on the march, eager to convert the world to Christ, and they saw nothing on the horizon that could stop them.

But neither the renewed optimism or the apparent cultural predominance of evangelical Protestantism would prevail much longer. The decades after the war brought seismic changes to the American social and economic landscape. Industrialization and immigration hastened the nation's shift from an agrarian to an urban society, creating both new diversity and intractable social problems. Crowded cities blighted by crime, poverty, and disease posed a vexing challenge to the Protestants' belief that they were establishing the biblical millennium. By the 1880s, notes Columbia University professor Randall Balmer, "teeming, squalid tenements populated by immigrants, most of them non-Protestant, hardly looked like the precincts of Zion" that evangelicals had previously envisioned.[22] So they adjusted their theology to reflect what was becoming a decidedly more pessimistic cultural reality.

From about 1870 onward evangelicals increasingly embraced a doctrine known as premillennial dispensationalism. It was an imaginative scheme of interpreting the Bible that held, among other things, that the Second Coming would occur *before* the millennium, and that world conditions until then would grow steadily worse. The doctrine was drawn from the teachings of John Nelson Darby, a nineteenth-century English theologian who believed that history was divided into seven ages, or dispensations, that would culminate in the Final Judgment and the end of the world. Based on a literalistic reading of the Old Testament prophecy books of Ezekiel, Zechariah, and Daniel and the New Testament book of Revelation, Darby came up with a detailed scenario for the end times that would be embellished and updated over the years by his theological successors.

According to the dispensationalist script Christians one day will be snatched out of the world suddenly in a miraculous event called the Rapture, leaving nonbelievers behind to face the Great Tribulation, a seven-year period of turmoil and suffering, during which the world will be ruled by the Antichrist. At the end of that period the world's major powers will be drawn into a Middle East war and face off in the Battle of Armageddon. At the climax of the battle Christ will return to defeat the evil forces and to set up his earthly kingdom of a thousand years—the biblical millennium. After that: the Final Judgment, hell for the wicked and eternal bliss for believers.

That dispensationalist view of the Second Coming would become the default position for a wide swath of evangelicals in the twentieth century, and would be popularized in the bestselling *Left Behind* novels in the 1990s. But late in the nineteenth century the doctrine's growing appeal had an important twofold impact. The belief that the Rapture could occur at any moment, rather than at the end of some elusive Golden Age, prompted many Protestant churches to redouble their missionary and evangelism efforts in order to save as many souls as possible before time ran out.[23] Meanwhile, for many evangelicals, the conviction that the world was beyond human repair and would continue to degenerate until Christ's return made social reform seem futile. While some conservative Christians would continue battling social ills with no less fervor than before, the motivation for doing so had changed: "No longer was the goal to build a 'perfect society,'" as historian Marsden explains. "At best it was to restrain evil until the Lord returned."[24]

The wrenching cultural changes that gave rise to premillennial pessimism sparked an altogether different kind of response among more liberally minded Protestants. Rather than abandoning social reform, as many evangelicals had done, some northern critics of evangelical revivalism saw the dismal plight of the cities as reason to expand efforts on behalf of the poor and downtrodden. For them, sinful institutions—greedy corporations that abused workers and corrupt governments that permitted slumlords and sweatshop owners to operate with impunity—were as much in need of salvation as were sinful individuals. By the end of the century their renewed dedication to social progress acquired distinct theological underpinnings that emphasized ethics and social action over spiritual conversion. The social gospel, as it became known, attracted a strong following in New York and other major northern cities, giving voice to a growing liberal movement that soon would challenge the evangelical dominance of most Protestant denominations.[25]

Even before the rise of the social gospel movement the stage had been set for a clash between theological liberals and conservatives by two paradigm-altering developments coming out of Europe in the middle of the nineteenth century. The publication of Charles Darwin's *The Origin of Species* in London in 1859 had gone virtually unnoticed by American churchmen during the run-up to the Civil War. After the war, however, the theological implications of Darwin's evolutionary theory began to sink in, and many evangelicals saw it as an attack on the truth of the Bible and its account of creation. Meanwhile, a more direct assault on the scriptures had come across the Atlantic in the form of higher criticism—a body of mainly German scholarship that used rationalistic arguments and methods of scientific inquiry to challenge the Bible's origins, historical accuracy, and accounts of the supernatural. Though it had stirred heated debate in the churches of Europe since the 1850s, higher criticism was largely dismissed by evangelicals in this country as irrelevant and inconsequential. But as the century neared its end the antiliteralist and antisupernaturalist claims of the higher critics found a growing audience among liberal Protestants, and along with the social gospel, gained a firm foothold in the major denominations.

Finally aroused from their complacency, evangelicals reacted with passion. By the 1880s conservative theologians were fiercely defending the inspiration and inerrancy of scripture against the skeptical arguments of the modernists, who were seen as questioning not only the Bible's inspiration but such core Christian doctrines as the divinity of Jesus, the Virgin Birth, and the Resurrection. In one famous summation of the conservative position that still reflects the thinking of many evangelicals today, two Princeton Theological Seminary professors, A. H. Hodge and B. B. Warfield, asserted in a Presbyterian journal in 1881 that "the Scriptures not only contain, but *are the words of God,* and hence ... all their elements and all their affirmations are absolutely errorless, and binding [on] the faith and obedience of men."[26]

In virtually every major denomination conservative leaders rose up in an attempt to enforce orthodoxy. Liberals at several prominent seminaries were brought up on heresy charges, trials were held, and some were dismissed. In the South modernist tendencies at places like Methodist-run Vanderbilt University in Nashville and the Southern Baptist Seminary at Louisville, Kentucky, were quickly snuffed out. But in the North, as historian Marsden observes, "Conservative victories turned out to be largely illusory. Liberalism continued to grow as if the trials had never taken place."[27] By the turn of the century it was clear that the era of evangelical hegemony in American Protestantism had come to an end.

But the battle was far from over. In 1909 two California oil tycoons put up $250,000 to publish a twelve-volume series of booklets entitled *The Fundamentals* to enunciate what conservatives saw as essential Christian doctrines, and to draw a line in the sand against the modernists. Written by an array of American and British scholars, the series identified those fundamental truths as biblical inerrancy, the Virgin Birth, Christ's substitutionary atonement (his death on the cross to pay the penalty of sin for mankind), his bodily resurrection, and the authenticity of his miracles. The booklets also included a scathing critique of the liberalizing trend in the Protestant churches and called for a renewal of evangelical commitments to soul winning and personal piety.[28]

Between 1910 and 1915 some three million copies of *The Fundamentals* were printed and distributed to pastors, missionaries, theology professors, seminarians, Sunday school superintendents, and other influential Protestants throughout the English-speaking world. The massive publishing effort would have little immediate impact on the modernist advance. But within a few years a militant conservative movement would arise that would draw both its name and its theological bearings from the contentious pamphlets.[29]

By the end of World War I growing alarm over liberal influence in the churches and moral degeneracy in the culture prompted evangelical dissenters to begin to forge new alliances. In 1919 the World Christian Fundamentals Association met in Philadelphia to rally resistance to "the Great Apostasy [that] was spreading like a plague throughout Christendom."[30] Some six thousand people showed up for that first interdenominational gathering. Smaller conferences were held around the country later that year. At the same time coalitions of "fundamentalists"—as they had begun to call themselves—were organizing within the northern Baptist, Presbyterian, and other denominations to defend biblical orthodoxy in the churches and to battle the "false apostles" of "false science" who were promoting evolution and other "damnable heresies."[31]

While not all evangelicals accepted the fundamentalist label, and while internal disputes prevented it from becoming as effective and cohesive a movement as it might have been, fundamentalism soon came to represent the evangelical vanguard in the battle against religious modernism. Through the early 1920s, fundamentalist preachers railed against doctrinal error and crumbling social mores that, in their estimation, went hand in hand. Condemnation of worldly habits and amusements—smoking, drinking, dancing, card playing, attending movies, and so on—became commonplace in fundamentalist pulpits and publications. As a pastor in Michigan declared at the time: "[T]he people who indulge in these worldly things are always loose in doctrine.... The two go together."[32]

No subject illustrated that connection more dramatically to fundamentalists than Darwinism. To them the theory of evolution was a "lie of Satan" that encouraged atheism and moral degeneracy by denying the literal truth of Scripture: that God created man in His image. If humans were no more than evolved animals, they reasoned, what need was there for God? Liberal Protestants, who rejected biblical literalism, had much less difficulty accepting Darwin's theory.

As the power struggles in the northern denominations intensified—and as the tide increasingly shifted against them—fundamentalist leaders threw themselves into a roiling national debate over whether evolution should be taught in public schools. Modeling their efforts on the successful campaign for Prohibition a few years earlier, they mobilized their flocks and lobbied state legislatures to pass laws banning evolution from the classroom. Between 1923 and 1928 five southern states adopted such laws, and bills were introduced in at least eleven others.[33] But it was a hollow and short-lived victory. The apparent show of fundamentalist strength set the stage for a dramatic legal confrontation that would seal the movement's ultimate decline as a potent cultural force.

In July 1925, John T. Scopes, a twenty-four-year-old high school science teacher, was put on trial in Dayton, Tennessee, accused of violating the state's recently enacted prohibition against teaching "any theory that denies the story of the Divine Creation of man as taught in the Bible."[34] There was never any real doubt that Scopes had broken the law. He had done so deliberately at the request of the American Civil Liberties Union in order to test the statute that he, the ACLU, and many other people around the country believed was unconstitutional. To defend Scopes the ACLU brought in Clarence Darrow, an acerbic and irreverent defense lawyer of national renown, while the famed orator William Jennings Bryant, a three-time Democratic nominee for president and a fundamentalist himself, led the prosecution. For eight sultry days in a circuslike atmosphere, in a stuffy courtroom packed with reporters from around the world, the two legal titans clashed over the legitimacy of scientific inquiry and the literal interpretation of scripture.

Scopes was found guilty and was fined one hundred dollars, although his conviction was overturned later on a technicality. But in the court of public opinion Bryant and the fundamentalists had suffered a humiliating defeat. Throughout the trial Darrow and the assembled press succeeded in portraying them as uneducated, narrow-minded bumpkins whose literalistic religion defied rational thinking. Bryant had made the job easier by submitting to cross-examination and stumbling over Darrow's derisive questions regarding the believability of biblical episodes such as the creation of Eve from Adam's rib, Jonah being swallowed by a fish, and the sun standing still in the sky. As historian George Marsden has observed: "This bizarre episode, wired around the world with a maximum of ballyhoo, would have far more impact on the popular interpretation of fundamentalism than all the arguments of preachers and theologians."[35] The unflattering caricature would stick in the public mind, and "fundamentalist" would become for many a derogatory label.

In the aftermath of the Scopes trial the political momentum to prohibit the teaching of evolution collapsed. Having lost the denominational battles, and perceiving that the culture had turned against them, fundamentalists withdrew from public life and from the Protestant mainstream.

But they did not disappear or sit idle. For the next two decades, largely unnoticed by the media, they began pouring their energy and resources into building their own subculture of churches, denominations, Bible colleges, seminaries, missionary societies, publishing houses, bookstores, and broadcast stations. For fundamentalists in the 1930s, note Professors David Gushee and Dennis Hollinger, "the good life was the separated life hunkered down against a corrupt world, and a rancorous spirit was targeted toward the perceived evils of their day: liberalism, the Social Gospel, Communism, and general worldliness in lifestyle and morals."[36] At the same time a renewed focus on revivalism and missionary work saw conservative denominations like the Southern Baptist Convention, the Assemblies of God, and the Church of the Nazarene grow more rapidly than the country's population.[37]

Yet discontent was brewing within the fundamentalist ranks. By the end of the 1930s, observes Christian Smith, sociology professor at the University of North Carolina–Chapel Hill, it was clear that "much of conservative Protestantism—under the banner of fundamentalism—had evolved into a somewhat reclusive and defensive version of its 19th-century self." And while the movement continued to grow organizationally, some participants began to see its "factionalist, separatist, judgmental character [as] an insurmountable impediment" to spreading the gospel. "The conditions were ripe," says Smith, "for a countermovement from within."[38]

As the nation went off to war in Europe and the Pacific, the desire for a more irenic, cooperative, and culturally engaged evangelicalism began to take hold. In New England, Philadelphia, the Upper Midwest, and California during the 1940s, a new generation of leaders stepped forward to chart a new and more moderate course. Among them were the Reverend Harold Ockenga of Park Street Church in Boston, theologian and journalist Carl F. H. Henry, and a young evangelist named Billy Graham. Although they were mostly fundamentalists in doctrine, the "neo-evangelicals"—as they would call themselves—sought to counteract the antiintellectualism and insularity associated with militant fundamentalism. As a result of their efforts a new constellation of organizations and alliances soon would arise that would help bring about an evangelical resurgence in the final third of the twentieth century.

An important first step came in 1942 when Ockenga and a member of his congregation, J. Elwin Wright, spearheaded a drive to organize the National Association of Evangelicals. Conceived as an alternative to the liberal Federal Council of Churches (later to become the National Council of Churches), and modeled after a

New England church network led by Wright, the NAE brought together a diverse mix of traditions, from conservative Presbyterians and Congregationalists to Anabaptist and Pentecostal denominations like the Mennonite Brethren and the Assemblies of God. Under the NAE umbrella moderate fundamentalists for the first time would have the means by which to speak with a unified voice to the broader culture and to coordinate their efforts to advance the gospel. With a potential constituency of fifteen million at its official launch in 1943, and with Ockenga as its first president, the NAE set out to bring revival to the nation and inaugurate "a new era in evangelical Christianity."[39]

But not everyone was eager to embrace the NAE's vision for unity and moderation. A small cluster of militant separatists led by New Jersey radio preacher Carl McIntire had organized the American Council of Christian Churches to be "the voice of evangelical Christians." But its voice was a belligerent and confrontational one, reflecting the old fundamentalist ways rejected by the neo-evangelicals. After briefly butting heads, the two groups mutually agreed to maintain their separate orbits.[40]

More consequential to the NAE and to evangelical unity was the decision of the Southern Baptist Convention to stand apart. A conservative and aggressively evangelistic denomination with five million members in 1940 (more than sixteen million today), it would have added considerable heft to the fledgling NAE.[41] But the Southern Baptists had a tradition of sectional pride and denominational self-sufficiency. With their own well-established agencies, colleges and seminaries, and publishing concerns, and having melded a "fractious movement of independent congregations" into an expansive religious empire, they saw little to be gained by entering into "entangling alliances with Yankee fundamentalists, holiness come-outers, immigrants, and tongues-speakers."[42]

Without the Southern Baptists and a handful of other conservative denominations that also decided to stay out, the NAE would fall short of becoming the voice of a united movement. Five years after its founding it counted fewer than a million members.[43] (Today the NAE represents some thirty million people, roughly half of the evangelical population.)

Nonetheless, the NAE would succeed early on as a "convener, catalyst, and confidence builder"[44] for the neo-evangelical movement. In 1944 it organized the National Religious Broadcasters to look out for the interests of evangelical radio ministries, a Chaplains Commission to assist evangelical chaplains in the military, and a War Relief Commission, which would eventually become a subsidiary known as World Relief, the NAE's humanitarian assistance arm. The following year it created the Evangelical Foreign Missions Association (now the Evangelical Fellowship of Mission Agencies, the largest missionary association in the world), and established regional offices in Detroit, Minneapolis, Portland, and Los Angeles to promote the cause locally and to keep in touch with the grassroots.[45]

The founding of the NAE was just the beginning. After the war the new evangelical movement gathered momentum on other fronts. In 1946 Carl Henry, a newly ordained northern Baptist minister, published *Remaking the Modern Mind*, which argued that evangelicalism should engage the intellectual life as well as the larger culture.[46] A year later Ockenga and popular California radio evangelist Charles Fuller teamed up to found Fuller Theological Seminary in Pasadena, California. It was to be, in the words of the founders, the "Cal Tech of modern evangelicalism,"[47] producing first-rate scholarship and Christ-centered theological training. Ockenga, Fuller's first president, invited Henry to serve on its faculty. Within a few decades it would become the evangelical flagship and the largest nondenominational seminary in the world.

Meanwhile, Billy Graham, who catapulted to national prominence as a crusade evangelist in the early 1950s, had begun sounding the call for a new evangelical periodical to rival the liberal

Protestant journal *The Christian Century*. Graham envisioned a magazine that would "restore intellectual respectability" to evangelical Christianity while reaffirming with an irenic spirit "the power of the Word of God to redeem and transform" lives.[48] In 1956, with the financial support of petroleum magnate J. Howard Pew, he launched *Christianity Today* and lured Henry, a former newspaper reporter, away from the Fuller seminary to be its first editor. Today the magazine remains the leading voice of mainstream evangelicalism.

Graham's crusade ministry was just one of several "parachurch" organizations to sprout and flourish during the postwar years. Independent, entrepreneurial, innovative, and singularly focused on evangelism, they set a pattern for successful evangelical ministries for the remainder of the century. But no one would match Graham's personal stature as both a symbol and guiding light of the modern evangelical movement. In many respects his rise to prominence paralleled that of the movement itself.

After graduating from Wheaton College, a small Christian liberal arts school near Chicago, in 1943, and after a brief stint as a pastor in a Chicago suburb, Graham signed on as an itinerant evangelist with Youth for Christ, a parachurch ministry aimed at converting high school students. He traveled the country, honing his preaching skills at youth rallies and citywide revival meetings. In 1949, at the age of thirty, he launched a three-week tent crusade in Los Angeles where his dynamic style and simple Bible message, tinged with anticommunist rhetoric, caught the attention of newspaper publisher William Randolph Hearst, who instructed his editors to "puff Graham." The results, says Noll, were spectacular: "The rallies extended for another nine weeks, crowds jammed the 6,000-seat 'Canvas Cathedral,' and a new star had arisen on the nation's religious horizon."[49]

Graham put that star status to good use. He organized the Billy

Graham Evangelistic Association to plan and finance his preaching ministry, which soon would go international with radio and television broadcasts, movies, books, and a syndicated newspaper column. "He came to prominence at a moment when there was an emergence of media technologies, and he jumped on them and exploited them brilliantly," observes Balmer of Columbia University.[50]

An important transition both for Graham and for the evangelical movement came in 1957 when Graham rejected an overture from New York City fundamentalists and instead enlisted the city's mainline churches to help organize what was to have been a six-week crusade in Madison Square Garden. Fundamentalist leaders were furious that Graham had chosen to work with liberals, but Graham insisted that he was "willing to work with all who were willing to work with us."[51] The breach between the new evangelicals and the separatist fundamentalists was complete, as Graham made "practical ecumenism" a hallmark of his ministry and a defining characteristic of the new evangelicalism. Meanwhile, the New York crusade ran for nearly four months, resulted in thousands of "decisions for Christ," and drew national newspaper and network radio and TV coverage.

Graham's national stature grew even further as he struck up a friendship with President Eisenhower, setting what would become a career pattern as a confidant of presidents and potentates. His close friendship with Richard Nixon, however, would nearly prove disastrous. In his 1997 autobiography Graham relates how he became a fixture at the Nixon White House and allowed himself to be drawn too tightly into Nixon's inner circle, sometimes participating in partisan deliberations. Sobered and chastened by the Watergate scandal and Nixon's resignation, Graham became decidedly more circumspect in his dealings with public figures. Yet he would continue to become closely acquainted with every American president from that time forward.

Seeing Graham at the White House became a source of

tremendous pride for evangelicals, as did his annual appearance on the Gallup Poll's Ten Most Respected Men in the World list. What kept Graham in such a position of high esteem, according to Noll and others, was the simplicity of his message (he avoided potentially divisive doctrinal discourses), the integrity of his ministry (he received a flat salary and never handled ministry finances), and his ability to resist the seductions that brought down other religious luminaries, especially during the televangelist scandals of the 1980s. Graham became, in Noll's estimation, "the most attractive public face that evangelical Protestantism has offered to the wider world" in the second half of the twentieth century.[52]

While Graham's popular image was a key factor in rallying evangelicals and defining them in the public mind, it was the election of Jimmy Carter, a Southern Baptist, to the White House in 1976 that produced their great cultural coming out. Through media coverage of Carter's religious behavior—he taught Sunday school and prayed and read his Bible daily—the nonevangelical world was introduced to what until then had been to many an all but invisible subculture of born-again Christians.

The 1980s saw many conservative evangelicals venturing as a group into the political arena, first under the banner of the Moral Majority, founded by fundamentalist Baptist preacher Jerry Falwell, and later under the Christian Coalition, which grew out of TV broadcaster Pat Robertson's unsuccessful 1988 presidential campaign. The attempts at harnessing and brokering the evangelical vote produced mixed results, however, as evangelicals proved not to be the monolith that some had expected. But the efforts succeeded in energizing a conservative bloc of voters who previously had put little stock in electoral politics or political solutions. By the 1990s the religious right had become a key constituency of the Republican Party, and it played an important role in helping to elect George W. Bush twice to the presidency. With the White House and other high offices occupied by some of their own, American evangelicals were no longer cultural outsiders.

Another seismic event on the evangelical landscape occurred late in the century, with the rancorous struggle between conservatives and moderates for control of the Southern Baptist Convention. The conflict, which broke out in the late 1970s, in many ways echoed the fundamentalist-modernist controversies decades earlier, focusing on such issues as the inerrancy of scripture and just how literally the Bible should be interpreted. The conflict resulted in a conservative resurgence—moderates called it a "fundamentalist takeover"—in the nation's largest Protestant denomination. Through the 1980s conservatives consolidated their control by purging moderates from positions of influence in the denomination's administrative machinery and seminaries, and by imposing a strict doctrinal uniformity within the denomination. Some moderates went off to form rival Baptist groups. In the aftermath the Southern Baptist Convention would become a major contingent of the religious right.[53]

Today the evangelical mosaic remains, in many ways, a confusing picture. Despite many efforts over the years to unite and mobilize them around assorted religious and political causes, they continue to be a diverse lot who defy easy labels. The neo-evangelicals—the Billy Graham wing if you will, represented by the NAE, *Christianity Today*, Fuller Theological Seminary, and the like—continue to flourish. But so does a large, contentious, boundary-setting faction represented by Southern Baptists and others who see themselves as passionate defenders of the faith. None but the most separatist fundamentalists any longer advocate returning to the cultural isolationism of a previous era. Yet there is little consensus on what engaging the culture should look like or how it should proceed.

The four basic characteristics summarized by the British historian David Bebbington—the need for conversion, the authority of the Bible, the importance of proselytizing, and the centrality of the cross—still aptly describe the core beliefs and overarching aims of most American evangelicals. Yet the difficult challenge, as it has been throughout their history, is in applying those beliefs while navigating the shoals of a constantly changing world. That is where the disagreements arise. And that is where evangelicals will find their future as they sort out what it means to be gospel people in a modern age.

# THREE

# God's Country

## Colorado Springs, Colorado

The first white settlers to arrive in this rugged, rolling region in the shadow of Pikes Peak in the early 1800s were mostly fur traders and prospectors drawn to the western frontier by the majestic mountain scenery and the promise of riches. With the end of the Civil War and the arrival of the railroad, they were followed by wave after wave of hardy homesteaders who were eager to seek their fortunes or eke out a living as ranchers, farmers, miners, and merchants. The Cripple Creek gold rush late in the century brought a new influx of immigrants, along with tourists and health seekers enticed by the region's mineral springs and tonic mountain air. After the gold ran out early in the twentieth century the town became a magnet for the military—the Army and, later, the Air Force built major installations nearby—and for manufacturers, educators, and, more recently, for high-tech entrepreneurs.

The latest newcomers to this historic Rocky Mountain city are entrepreneurs of a different sort. Since the late 1980s evangelical Christians have flocked here by the thousands, drawn by the region's natural beauty, low taxes, and growing reputation as a nerve center of evangelical ministry. Within a radius of a few miles are the headquarters of more than one hundred national and international evangelical organizations, from James Dobson's influential multimedia ministry Focus on the Family to small entrepreneurial groups such as Jesus and Me, a healing ministry for the emotionally troubled. It is also home to the Navigators, a worldwide network of one-on-one evangelists and Bible teachers, CBA International (formerly the Christian Booksellers Association), a trade group for the $4.2-billion-a-year Christian retail industry, and the current head of the National Association of Evangelicals, megachurch pastor Ted Haggard.

With such a large concentration of Christian organizations and ministry workers, the town has been dubbed the "evangelical Vatican." Some consider it a microcosm of the nation in its encounter with a resurgent evangelicalism, and suggest that it may offer a glimpse of what lies in store as conservative Christians become an increasingly visible and vocal presence in the culture at large. To me it seemed a perfect place to get acquainted with some of the movers and shakers and ordinary believers who make up this growing religious movement, and to learn something of the vision and the strategies that drive them.

## FOCUS

Driving into Colorado Springs from the north on Interstate 25, past the glistening spires of the Air Force Academy and a constellation of new shopping centers, office parks, and franchise restaurants along the city's growing northern edge, one encounters an official green-and-white highway sign signaling the exit for Focus on the Family. The sign's presence on the interstate is a good indication of the ministry's status as a popular regional tourist attraction. It also is a fitting symbol of the national notoriety of its founder. Arguably no one has done more to put modern American evangelicalism on the map than Dr. James Clayton Dobson.

Although I had never met Dobson, I had interviewed him by telephone on a couple of occasions for *U.S. News & World Report* during the 1990s. By then his reputation as a rising star of the religious right was well established and, as far as most of the nation's media were concerned, pretty much defined what he and his ministry were all about. But my familiarity with the man and his work went back many years earlier, to a time when, as clueless young parents, my wife and I stumbled onto a helpful child-rearing guidebook entitled *Dare to Discipline*, written by a friendly faced California child psychologist who happened to be a Nazarene, as we were at the time.

When Dobson wrote the book in 1970 he was on the pediatrics faculty at the University of Southern California School of Medicine and the attending staff at Children's Hospital in Los Angeles. Invoking biblical and psychological principles along with lessons learned from his own upbringing as the son of a Nazarene minister, Dobson challenged the reigning wisdom of the day by encouraging, among other things, the judicious use of corporal punishment to "shape the will without breaking the spirit" of defiant children. Spankings, Dobson cautioned, should be restrained and never administered in anger. "It is not necessary to beat the child into submission," he wrote. "A little bit of pain goes a long way for a young child."[1] The real purpose of spanking, according to Dobson, was not so much to punish as it was to affirm the parents' authority over a rebellious and disobedient child. "You, Mom and Dad, are the boss.... When you are defiantly challenged, win decisively."[2]

The book made sense to evangelicals who tended to be theologically inclined toward the "spare the rod spoil the child" school of child rearing anyway.[3] Dobson's tough-love philosophy stood in sharp contrast to the more permissive approach advocated by Dr. Benjamin Spock, a New York pediatrician whose popular writings had so powerfully influenced the previous generation. When *Dare to Discipline* appeared many evangelicals—my wife and I included—welcomed it as a timely and articulate reaffirmation of biblical principles of parenting.

The concerns that drove Dobson to write *Dare to Discipline* would continue to weigh upon him. His years at USC and at the hospital in Los Angeles during the decade following America's sexual revolution, he would later recall, "confirmed what I had long suspected: the family—the very foundation of our society—was crumbling as a result of internal and external pressures on parents and their children. Marriages were disintegrating rapidly and youth problems were multiplying just as fast. I became convinced that only a full-fledged return to the Judeo-Christian concepts of morality, fidelity, and parental leadership would halt the erosion of the family unit."[4]

With his book a runaway bestseller, Dobson quickly became inundated with speaking invitations. He began traveling the country offering biblically based parenting advice and his own prescriptions for saving the American family. Soon the invitations were coming faster than he could handle. Hoping to reach a larger audience without sacrificing time with his own young family, Dobson quit his university and hospital positions in 1977 and launched a radio ministry he called Focus on the Family.

Operating out of a rented two-room office in Arcadia, California, and with the help of one full-time assistant, Dobson produced and hosted a weekly broadcast that initially aired on thirty-four stations. Within seven years he had four hundred employees and was broadcasting daily on more than four hundred stations, and was distributing books and program tapes to a rapidly growing mailing list. In 1988 Dobson and his expanding staff moved into a new headquarters in Pomona, California, but quickly outgrew it. In 1991, with more than two million listeners and eight hundred employees, Focus on the Family packed up its operations and moved to Colorado Springs, where the growth would continue.

Today Dobson's broadcasts are said to reach more than twelve million U.S. listeners and an international audience estimated at over two hundred million. He has now written upward of two dozen books. His multimedia ministry includes television, film and video, an assortment of magazines, and the Internet. His mailing list exceeds four million, and his ministry receives so much mail—more than thirty-six thousand letters a week—that it has its own zip code. It is sometimes said that Dobson commands the largest regular following of any evangelical figure. That may be true, although the extent to which he actually commands and his listeners actually follow is open to question. Nonetheless, it is probably accurate to say, based on audience size alone, that Dobson's influence in the evangelical world is unsurpassed.

It would be easy to mistake Focus on the Family's eighty-one-acre campus for a corporate office park. Four modern redbrick buildings of various sizes separated by manicured lawns and sprawling asphalt parking lots blend in comfortably with the functional architecture of an adjacent shopping center and other nearby office buildings. Aside from the ministry's oval insignia on a small brick sign along the main entry road, there are no visual indicators of the religious nature of much of the business conducted here.

But step inside the visitors' Welcome Center and it immediately becomes apparent that this is both a shrine to the traditional American family and the command center of Dobson's Christian crusade to save it. Inscribed in the building's rotunda are the ministry's five guiding principles: the permanence of marriage, the value of children, the preeminence of evangelism, the sanctity of human life, and the relationship of church, family, and government. On a typical summer day upward of two thousand visitors, many of them families with children, wander through the $4 million structure. The main floor is dominated by a sprawling bookstore, where Dobson's books, videos, and CDs are featured prominently, and by multimedia displays explaining Focus on the Family's various enterprises. There is also an art gallery, a coffee shop, and a theater that shows a twenty-minute film about Dobson and his ministry twice each hour. While parents tour the nearby administration building and Dobson's broadcast studio, kids are invited to the Welcome Center's lower level, a veritable children's paradise with an ice cream parlor, a puppet stage, a climb-aboard replica of a B-17 bomber, and assorted other amusements—all based on themes from Focus on the Family's children's books and videos.

Adjacent to the Welcome Center is the operations building, where hundreds of workers in cubicles handle the thousands of letters, phone calls, and e-mails that arrive daily. It also houses a modern seventy-five-thousand-square-foot warehouse equipped with a computer-guided conveyor system to rush Dobson's books, tapes, CDs, and other materials to callers requesting help on problems ranging from alcoholism to pornography addiction. Crisis calls are immediately routed to a counseling center, where fifteen state-licensed therapists and social workers and two chaplains are on standby, ready to offer psychological and spiritual counseling and referrals.

On the day of my visit the counseling center on the third floor of the administration building was buzzing with activity. About a dozen counselors sat in brightly lit cubicles, jotting notes or tapping computer keyboards as they spoke in hushed voices into telephone headsets. In a typical day more than 250 distress calls from around the United States and Canada reach the center, and this day apparently would be no exception. I wondered what kind of advice a suicidal caller or a victim of domestic violence might receive from a Focus counselor. So I sat down with the center's two top supervisors for a brief chat.

Wilford Wooten and Phillip Swihart are both in their sixties and have worked at Focus since the early 1990s. Together they have more than eighty-two years of experience as professional therapists—Wooten as a licensed social worker and counselor in the Army for many years, Swihart as a clinical psychologist at community mental health centers and in private practice. Most of the issues they deal with at Focus, they told me, are the same as those they faced earlier in their careers as secular counselors—

depression, divorce, substance abuse, family discord, and so on. And while they apply many of the same standard techniques and psychological principles that they always have used in working with troubled clients, at Focus, they said, they bring a distinctly spiritual element into the therapeutic mix.

"We are a Christian ministry, and people calling here know that," said Wooten, the counseling center's senior director. "So we try to use a holistic approach that recognizes that oftentimes problems and their solutions have a spiritual dimension. We don't just thump them over the head with the Bible, but we do try to integrate biblical principles whenever it's helpful and appropriate to do so. Mostly we listen. And we end each session with prayer. That's not something we would have done in a secular setting."

Swihart, who supervises the counseling staff, offered an example. "This morning I took a call from a woman who said her husband was verbally abusive and was addicted to pornography. She described herself as a Christian. Her husband is an atheist. Her friends were telling her to get out of the marriage. What should she do? Well, some counselors might simply have told her, 'He's a jerk. Get rid of him.' But we try to see if there's room for healing and reconciliation, as long as it doesn't jeopardize her safety. I told her that if her husband were to undergo extensive counseling for anger management and possibly for sexual addiction problems, maybe the marriage could be saved. If he refuses, I told her she may need to leave for her own safety. Spiritually they live in two different worlds. That's always tough in a marriage."

Swihart's conversation with the woman ended the way that most Focus counseling sessions do. He referred her to a Christian counselor in her town, one of about twenty-two hundred licensed therapists on a list of Focus-approved counselors. "As clinicians," Swihart explained, "we often find the issues are deeper than we can deal with in a thirty-minute telephone call. And with the volume of calls we receive, we can't do an extended regime of therapy. So we try to offer people a little bit of comfort, and then point

them in the right direction to find help in their local community."
There is no charge for the service.

Along with Dobson's daily radio broadcasts, the counseling operation is considered a central feature of the Focus ministry. "When Dr. Dobson started out in 1977," Wooten recalled, "he personally answered all of the calls and letters. But it quickly grew to the point that that was no longer possible. So now we are Jim's embodiment. We help him do that. People have a tremendous amount of confidence in him and in this ministry, and that gives us a window of opportunity to provide some help and hope."

Near the end of Focus on the Family's first decade, the ministry began to undergo a seismic shift that would profoundly alter both Dobson's public persona and his ministry's agenda. By the mid 1980s Dobson had become increasingly preoccupied with public policy issues. He was convinced that government decisions on matters such as abortion, pornography, parental rights, and homosexuality were antithetical to families, and that the secular media and other powerful cultural forces were leading America into a moral quagmire. Dobson was no longer content merely dispensing advice to married couples on how to communicate better or how to raise their children successfully. He was about to become a leading voice in the culture wars.

In 1987 Focus on the Family launched *Citizen*, a monthly magazine intended to motivate evangelicals to become more politically active. A year later Dobson created the Family Research Council to act as a voice on family issues in Washington, D.C., and he helped establish a network of autonomous state-level councils. Dobson's radio broadcasts, meanwhile, took on an increasingly political tone as he encouraged listeners to pressure their elected representatives on hot-button issues affecting families. Over the next decade he would become widely known as a potent voice of the religious right and as a Republican Party powerbroker.

That reputation seemed to reach a zenith in 1998, when Dobson testily confronted Republican congressional leaders for neglecting the religious right's legislative agenda while benefiting from the support of conservative Christian voters. At a private meeting on Capitol Hill that March, Dobson threatened to bolt the party unless GOP lawmakers made abortion restrictions and other conservative social issues a higher priority. "And if I go," he vowed, "I will do everything I can to take as many people with me as possible."[5] Relatively little changed, however, and although Dobson didn't leave the party, many conservative Christian voters sat out that fall's elections, and Republicans lost ground in Congress.

Meanwhile, Dobson's growing political entanglements raised a chorus of protests from church-state watchdog groups that suggested that he was violating IRS rules against electioneering by tax-exempt nonprofit organizations. But rather than back away from politics, Dobson resigned as Focus on the Family's president in 2003 (he remained its chairman and chief on-air personality) and a few months later created Focus on the Family Action—a separate legal entity without tax-exempt status—to concentrate squarely on partisan politics. His hands no longer tied by IRS regulations, Dobson, in 2004, publicly endorsed a presidential candidate for the first time (George W. Bush) and barnstormed the country on behalf of conservative Republican Senate candidates. His efforts to mobilize Christian voters were widely credited for helping Republicans retain the White House and widen their control of Congress.

Dobson's dramatic metamorphosis from an amiable radio host and family adviser to an intensely partisan culture warrior dominated our conversation when we met in his office on an overcast spring afternoon.

The first thing one notices upon entering Dobson's spacious office, aside from a striking view of the mountains through an arched window beyond his desk, is a large portrait of Winston Churchill and photographs of Dobson's late father prominently displayed on the bright wood-trimmed walls. Both men, as Dobson is happy to explain, were profound influences in his life. The Reverend James C. Dobson, Sr., who died of a heart attack in 1977, just a few months after Focus on the Family began, had been a model of fatherhood and of the Christian faith to his only child. "And frankly," Dobson said, pausing to straighten a framed photograph, "it was as a result of his prayers that this ministry came into being."

Churchill also had been an important role model, exemplifying persistence and fortitude against insurmountable odds during the early dark days of World War II—traits, Dobson said, that evangelical Americans would do well to emulate as they struggle to defend the family. "I love what Churchill said during Britain's darkest hour, when it looked like there was no hope against the Nazis. He said, 'We will never, never, never give up.' And neither will we."

Defending against enemies, refusing to surrender—militaristic imagery I would not have expected from the genial author I had come to know thirty years earlier. But this was Dobson as the world now knew him. And as we took our seats, facing each other across a small coffee table, this was the Dobson I was determined to learn more about.

At age sixty-eight Dobson still had the warm smile and kindly manner I remembered from his book jackets and videos, although his reddish brown hair was much grayer and thinner than before. With his simple rimless glasses and brown tweed sports coat and slacks, he still looked the part of the California college professor.

I threw out a softball question to get things rolling—what did he consider to be the greatest threat to American families?—expecting that it would probably elicit a tirade against a list of political and cultural adversaries.

He answered without hesitation. "It's the pace of living." I looked at him quizzically. "Yes. It's absolutely destroying families. We talked about this on the radio today. Kids come home to empty houses. Parents are exhausted when they get home. They don't have time to teach their children values or to discipline or train them. Husbands and wives are too exhausted to communicate with each other, to go for walks together, to have sex together. It's just the pace at which we run that is creating havoc for families. From that, then, comes everything else: adolescent rebellion, infidelity, alcoholism, other things."

If it's mainly a matter of fast-paced living, I asked, what realistically can anyone do about it? Specifically, what does a Christian ministry like Focus on the Family have to offer families who face that challenge?

Dobson's response, as it tends to be on a variety of subjects, was to look to his own past for guidance. "Fifty to seventy years ago," he said, "there was a basic understanding of how families were supposed to work. It was passed down from generation to generation. A good part of what I wrote in my first books came from my mother, who got it from her mother. When a baby was born in those days, aunts and grandmothers and neighbors and friends came and taught that new mother how to discipline, how to train, how to feed, how to clothe, how to take care of a family.

"Now the families are fractured. If you've got a sister, she lives in Oregon or New York or something. And so we're cut off from that traditional understanding of family life, and especially child rearing, that used to be part of the culture."

It occurred to me that the lost ideal that Dobson had described was a lot like the traditional village it takes to raise a child that another contemporary writer had observed a few years earlier. That writer, as I recalled, had not exactly won the accolades of evangelicals, or of Dobson in particular. I thought it better to keep that thought to myself for the moment. Dobson was on a roll.

"Most of those principles I talk about are rooted in scripture," he continued. "What I have attempted to do is simply put it in a new package. It's not all that new. And I find that parents are just like sponges to capture that, to pick that up—not only in this country but around the world. The cultures may be different, but the problems and solutions are the same."

I politely pointed out that he still hadn't addressed specifically how a Christian perspective, as he had suggested, is more helpful to struggling families than any professional counsel that the secular world may provide.

"The world tends to look at things through a different set of eyes," he said, leaning forward and clasping his hands. His voice and his demeanor were noticeably more intense. "The Christian understanding of the family involves fidelity and loyalty, and sexual restraint in terms of pornography and the way sexuality is expressed. And church experiences—teaching children from a very early age that they are not the products of evolution, of a mindless universe that has no meaning, that they are known and loved by name by God—it gives them a sense of identity and purpose." He leaned back in his chair. "The Christian worldview is just very very different from the secular worldview. And that's what we try to offer."

Yet Dobson's ministry obviously had waded deeply into the political sphere, which suggests that he sees a legitimate role for government in all of this. Was it really the government's business, I asked, to apply a Christian perspective in addressing family issues and other national problems?

"Government can't *solve* all the problems," he said, "but it can *create* a lot of them. And that's why we've gotten involved." Dobson was fully engaged now and growing more animated. I obviously had found his point of passion. "Right now the courts are determined to redesign the family. There's no doubt in my mind but that the Supreme Court and most federal judges want to expand the definition of marriage to include homosexuals. And the moment they cross that Rubicon," he sliced the air with his hand, "there's no place to stop, because if two women can say they're entitled to the rights of married couples, there isn't any reason why some judge won't say three can do the same thing—or five and two, or six and one. From there the family becomes just about anything anybody says it is.

"And that's just the courts. Congress has made it difficult for families to survive. Tell me why a man and woman who have committed themselves to one another in marriage, who bore a child or two or three and are taking care of those children, are packing lunches for them and binding up their wounds and praying with them at night, and doing what they can to raise healthy kids—why should they pay higher taxes than people who are cohabiting and maybe don't even have children? There's no rationale for that, except that Congress couldn't care less. The family has not had an effective lobbying voice. The possum growers of America have a lobbying voice, and everybody else who is trying to promote something, but the family is just ignored. Well, we're not going to let that continue."

As much as he faults Congress and the courts, it became clear as we talked that Dobson places a surprising amount of responsibility for the modern family's plight on evangelicals themselves. "They've been sitting on the sidelines, and that's why most of the things they care about are being lost," he said, shaking his head. "Too many Christians have a mind-set that comes out of an era fifty years ago, when we didn't have to worry about what was going on in Washington, because most of the representatives came out of the Judeo-Christian system of values. They weren't all Christians, but they understood that value system. Well, that's gone now. And if Christians don't watch what's happening, they'll lose their shirts."

This, of course, was the line of reasoning that Dobson and others have used often in trying to motivate evangelicals to become more politically engaged, apparently with some success: The encroachments of modern secular society have made it impossible for conservative Christians to stay sequestered in the comfort and safety of their own insular subculture, as they had through much of the twentieth century. With the spiritual and moral well-being of their families at stake, they could no longer afford to cede the public square to others.

It also became apparent that Dobson blames no one more than himself for not getting involved sooner—which may help explain his present unrelenting zeal. He recalled that in the late 1970s, when Focus was just getting started, "parents lost the right to know when their minor daughters had an abortion. Now it's one thing to say a girl has a right to have an abortion—I don't agree with it, but that's one thing. It's another thing to say to a parent, 'You don't even have the right to know about it.'" He shook his head in disbelief. "For the entire history of this country parents have held the total responsibility for the medical care of their children. Well, that changed one day. Why did it change? It changed because Christians were thinking about something else. I was one of them. And when I finally realized what was happening, I said, 'I'm one voice, but from here on I'm going to do whatever I can to affect that.'"

And the rest, as they say, is history. Dobson jumped into the political fray with both arms swinging and, like Winston Churchill, he was not about to give up. Forget gentle Jesus meek and mild. Forget turning the other cheek. Dobson was not about to let himself be sucker punched.

Nor was he the least apologetic about bringing his religious fervor into the public square. "I resent the fact that some people imply that because we're Christians we're somehow violating the separation of church and state if we get involved. That's just nonsense. In a democracy we all have a right to try to influence the government. And if people feel threatened by our views then let them go work for their own."

Fair enough. But what was Dobson's ultimate objective in the political realm? People do worry about that, I told him. Do non-evangelicals have reason to be concerned about where he and those who agree with him would steer the country if given their way? In a democracy does anyone have a right to impose their personal religious values on others?

"Look," he was visibly irritated and shifted in his seat, "some people say, 'Oh, you want to turn this into a theocracy.' Well, no one I know is calling for that. We know that doesn't work. There is an evangelical in the White House right now, and I don't see any evidence that he's trying to set up a theocracy. That's a sham. That's a red herring.

"If anyone is trying to shove their views down people's throats, it's the other side. Look at the court decisions on homosexuality. They're trying to force that on a majority of Americans who don't want to change the definition of marriage. We're trying to prevent that from happening. As Christians, we're working within the democratic process to promote our values on issues we feel strongly about. As Americans, that's our right. I would say it is also our obligation. We invite others to do the same."

Dobson had grown tired of the political focus of our conversation. He noted with more than a hint of irritation that whenever national journalists come calling "it's all they want to talk about. Nobody wants to report about the correspondence department, where over a hundred people spend their days reaching out to those who have written or called. It doesn't make good copy." It was important, he said, that I understand that Focus on the Family's political involvement "is just a tiny part of what we do." (An aide later would provide figures showing that Focus's political arm raised and spent about $10 million in the 2004 election, while the main ministry's budget that year was $147 million.)[6] "We're here to help parents raise their kids and to help couples stay married and deal with the stresses of living. That's who we are, who we have always been, and most people know that."

I asked about his legacy, but Dobson said he is too busy to spend much time thinking about that, even though his own mortality is never far from his thoughts. Dobson suffered a heart attack in 1990 and a mild stroke in 1998, but is in good health now, he said, for a man in his late sixties. And while he has begun to share the microphone with others, he insisted that there is no designated successor and no plan for retirement. "I'll stay on as long as I think God wants me to," he said, "and when I'm gone, the ministry will move on without me. I'm confident of that."

Even in this brief encounter it became clear that behind Dobson's personal confidence and strong sense of moral certitude was an unshakable conviction that he is doing God's work. He reiterated that belief as I rose to leave his office.

"Apart from God's blessing," he made a sweeping gesture and glanced around the room, "there is nothing here that would have succeeded. I'm absolutely convinced of that. It cannot be explained by anything I have done. It hasn't been my education, or intelligence, or commitment, or anything else. It is simply that God had a plan, and I have tried to carry it out. I haven't always understood it. I still don't fully understand it. I just try not to do something stupid to mess it up."

On my way out of the administration building I found myself walking with a group that had just finished a guided tour of the Focus campus. I struck up a conversation with Elsie and Clayton Groff, a retired couple from Lancaster, Pennsylvania, as they headed toward their motor home, which was parked near the Welcome Center. The Groffs, both in their mid sixties, had just begun a two-week vacation in the Mountain West. "We just had to stop at Focus on the Family," Elsie explained. "We think the world of Dr. Dobson."

The Groffs described themselves as having been regular listeners to Dobson's weekly program during the 1970s and early 1980s, when they were raising their children. "We got a lot of help from his books, too," Elsie said. What they liked most about him was that "he seemed to know so much about the issues families have to face every day. He made a lot of sense." Now that their children are grown, "we don't tune in quite as often. I've noticed that he's gotten a lot more political."

The Groffs aren't sure that's such a good thing. They are active members of a Brethren in Christ congregation in Lancaster, and both sing in the choir. They oppose abortion and same-sex marriage, although they are not sure they would support a constitutional amendment banning them. Their pastor, they said, seldom talks about politics, "except to encourage us to vote. He never tries to tell us who to vote for, though," Clayton said. "We have our own ideas on that."

"When a preacher or some other Christian leader I admire really gets going on the political aspects," Elsie added, "they cross a line, and it really turns me off, because I'm not interested in hearing that. What I want to hear, whether it's at church or on Christian radio, is something that will help me at this stage of my life. I certainly don't need a preacher to tell me how to vote." They weren't sure whether Dobson had crossed that line, Elsie said, "but we did like it better when he focused more on the family."

While the Groffs may not be typical of Dobson's audience, they probably are not altogether unusual. Visiting with them I was reminded that one could not simply assume that the millions of evangelicals who tune in to Dobson's broadcasts necessarily share his political passion. Not every conservative Christian who hears his political call to arms is eager to enlist. Dobson's influence in the evangelical world, though considerable, does have limits.

Still, he and those around him have demonstrated an unquestionable knack for mobilizing people who normally would never write or phone an elected official to speak up when he says the fate of families is at stake, and to register and vote when moral issues are considered paramount. It is that ability to motivate the grassroots, as it is perceived in Washington, which has won Dobson the ear of a Republican White House and a Republican Congress—even if it has not always translated into public policy success.

For all of his influence Dobson has never shown much interest in mastering the skills of a Washington insider. He has little patience for navigating the intricate twists and turns of the legislative process, with all of its requisite trade-offs and compromises. The role Dobson seems to relish most and has proven adept at is more akin to that of an Old Testament prophet—a voice in the wilderness crying out to those in power: "Thus saith the Lord!" Let the politicians who hear his impassioned jeremiads sweat the details of getting the job done, and let them face the consequences of falling short. It is an approach that may win grudging respect and occasional battles, but few lasting friends.

Not that winning friends in Washington is of great concern to Dobson. The world he inhabits, after all, is one of absolutes, where truth and life are plainly discerned in black and white in the pages of Scripture and the images of a sonogram. In Dobson's world ambiguity is error and compromise is defeat. There are no hazy horizons in God's country—only stark snow-tipped mountains and azure skies that clearly define the boundaries of heaven and earth.

## HOOPS

The list of evangelical ministries that make their home in Colorado Springs includes many I recognized from my years covering the religion beat. Along with Focus on the Family are Compassion International, a worldwide child advocacy ministry; Youth with a Mission, a group that organizes short-term missionary projects for young people; the International Bible Society, an organization that translates and disseminates the scriptures around the world; and other ministries with wide national or international reach and reputations.

Some on the list were less familiar but had names that I found helpfully descriptive, such as Bibles for the World and the Parenting Solo Network. A few, however, had monikers that were downright puzzling. Smoldering Wick Ministries, for example, I discovered offers counseling and other help to burned-out pastors, and the Window International Network, I would learn, is a prayer ministry that has absolutely nothing to do with Microsoft's ubiquitous operating system.

One organization that immediately caught my eye was Hoops of Hope, a ministry to young athletes. Even catchier than its winsome name was its somewhat ambitious-sounding slogan: "Impacting Eternity through Basketball." This was one I knew I had to visit.

If there is anything Brent Fuqua enjoys as much as playing basketball (and that's a big "if") it's *talking* about basketball—that, and talking about his faith in Jesus. And as I learned when I met the thirty-seven-year-old Hoops of Hope founder and director one morning at a local restaurant, he does all three with nearly equal intensity. "Before I met the Lord, basketball was my god," the six-foot-two former high school standout confided, leaning over a steaming plate of eggs and sausage. "I lived it and breathed it and pursued it with everything I had. Then, when I gave my heart to the Lord," which happened when he was nineteen years old and in college in his native North Carolina, "I thought I'd have to give up the game in order to serve Him. But God laid this ministry upon my heart and—wow!—I found out I could do both!"

For Fuqua (pronounced FEW-kway), merging his Christian faith with his passion for basketball was like a marriage made, well, in heaven. He launched Hoops of Hope in 1996 after having worked briefly on the Colorado Springs staff of Athletes in Action, a sports ministry connected with the international evangelism organization Campus Crusade for Christ. With help from a part-time assistant and a corps of Hoops volunteers, Fuqua now travels around the country, and occasionally overseas, conducting basketball clinics and camps for young people, staging exhibition games at prisons, and performing in a one-man razzle-dazzle ball-handling show for church groups and at private-school assemblies. At each event, in addition to the rudiments of the game, he talks about his

Christian faith and presents an evangelistic message tailored to young athletes. "Sharing with them how they can have a personal relationship with Christ—that's the real focus of what we do," he said.

As central as faith sharing is to his ministry, Fuqua guesses that most of the young people who come to his camps and clinics already are Christians. "Parents like to send their kids because they know they'll be in a wholesome environment and, at some point in the day, they'll be getting the Bible. But they're also getting good training in basketball skills. We've done this long enough now that we see some kids who have graduated and are getting basketball scholarships or playing college ball, and we think, 'Wow, we had these kids when they were in the third grade!' That's a lot of fun."

While Fuqua seems to have carved out a comfortable niche, the idea of using athletics as a platform to spread the gospel is certainly nothing new. Athletes in Action, Fuqua's former employer now based in Xenia, Ohio, was started in 1966, and the Fellowship of Christian Athletes, probably the nation's largest sports ministry, headquartered in Kansas City, Missouri, has been around since 1954—roughly the same period that gave birth to many of the signature institutions of the neo-evangelical movement. Both groups focus on winning new converts to Christ by reaching out to professional and amateur athletes and, indirectly, to the millions of fans who watch them. David Hannah, the former multisport amateur athlete who founded Athletes in Action, once explained that his desire was that a "society looking up to athletes as heroes must find heroes looking up to God."[7]

Consequently, both organizations have expended considerable amounts of time and energy promoting the evangelical faith of high-visibility sports figures—from former NBA star David Robinson of the San Antonio Spurs to Brent Jones, a former San Francisco 49ers All-Pro tight end who went on to become a CBS Sports analyst. Tom Landry, the late legendary coach of the Dallas Cowboys, served for many years as a national spokesman for the Fellowship of Christian Athletes. Judging by what one sees on national television these days, such efforts seem to have paid off rather handily. Whether it's an NFL running back kneeling in the end zone after scoring a touchdown, a basketball champion thanking God in a postgame TV interview, or a college coach leading his team in a locker-room prayer, public displays of faith have become a familiar presence in the world of sports.

But the symbiotic relationship between sport and spirit goes back even further, predating the two major ministry groups and even the formation of modern professional athletics. It finds its roots in muscular Christianity—a nineteenth-century ideal born in Victorian England that sought to promote rugged manliness and athleticism in a church some felt had become overly feminized. Its proponents argued that not only was there an imbalance of women to men in the pews but, as one writer puts it, "women's influence in church had led to an overabundance of sentimental hymns, effeminate clergymen and sickly-sweet images of Jesus. These things were repellant to 'real men' and boys."[8] Muscular Christianity emphasized sports, especially team sports, as a way of building manly character and both spiritual and physical health. Rather than viewing athletics as an evangelistic tool, it found Christian virtue in the sport itself. Closely associated with the muscular Christianity movement was the birth in 1844 of the Young Men's Christian Association, an organization that also came to link morality and athleticism. In 1891 James Naismith, a YMCA gym teacher from Springfield, Massachusetts, invented the game that would give Brent Fuqua his life's calling.

I had a chance to see Fuqua in action a few days after we had met for breakfast. It was the opening day of a local basketball camp conducted on the asphalt parking lot of Rocky Mountain Calvary, a three-thousand-member undenominational church that Fuqua attends. When I arrived at midmorning about fifty boys and girls ranging in age from about six to sixteen were clustered into groups according to size, and were running ball-handling and -passing drills in front of four portable goals. Fuqua, wearing droopy red-and-white shorts and a white T-shirt emblazoned with "Hoops of Hope" and a cartoon likeness of himself, was walking around with a clipboard, occasionally calling out instructions. "Feet apart, that's it ... Step forward as you release ... Now follow through. Good." Off to one side several women were setting out cups of water and fruit juice on a table set up on a grassy area under a shade tree. A few of the smaller children had already given up on the drills and had wandered over and were helping themselves to the drinks.

At about 10:30 Fuqua blew his whistle and waved the rest of the kids over to the shade. After each found a drink and settled onto the grass, Fuqua turned on a portable sound system and tapped the microphone. It was time for the Bible lesson.

"OK, kids. Can I have your attention please?" Handing the microphone to an assistant, Fuqua picked up a ball and set it spinning on his index finger. "Now my question for you today is, have you ever felt your life spinning out of control?" He raised the ball higher and swung it around. "Has anyone ever felt that?" A little blond boy sitting on the curb, who looked to be about seven, called out "Yeah!" Fuqua continued. "Well, when your life is spinning out of control, I just want you to remember—" he stopped the ball and revealed a smiley face painted on one side "—to put on a happy face." Some of the smaller children giggled.

Next he picked up two more balls and began to juggle them. "Have you ever felt like you're juggling things in your life? Whether it's school, sports, those kinds of things?" He continued to juggle, and the kids began to applaud. "Well, I'm here to tell you that if things are ever spinning out of control, or if you ever feel like you're juggling things in life, remember that we can have security in Jesus Christ. We can have security in him if we know him and have a relationship with him." He stopped juggling and opened a booklet. "Listen to this verse in First John chapter five. It says, 'I write these things to you who believe in the name of the Son of God, so that you may know that you have eternal life.' Did you get that? John is saying if you believe in Christ then you can know that you have eternal life. Isn't that good news?" Several small boys sitting in the front nodded. Near the back two teenage girls were busy whispering. "And it goes on to say that we can have confidence that if we ask anything according to his will, he hears us, and whatever we ask he will give us. Isn't that another great promise?

"You know, God is not someone who is way far off and unknowable. The Bible says we can have a relationship with Christ. And we can go to him with our requests. We can ask him to help us with things like loneliness or problems at school—all kinds of things. It's just as if you were talking with your parents. What's it called when we talk to God? Prayer, right. So let's pray about that right now, that we would seek God in all that we do, and that if we don't have a relationship with Him that we will start that relationship, even today."

He bowed his head. "Jesus, thanks so much for your word. Thanks that even in that simple picture with the basketballs, we know that when life is spinning out of control and we're juggling things, we can turn to you. And we just thank you that you love us and died for us, and that by believing in you we can have eternal life. In Jesus' name, amen."

With that, and after a few announcements, it was back to the hoops. In all the break and the message had taken about fifteen minutes. The rest of the three-hour morning session would be devoted to basketball.

Later, over a cup of coffee, I asked Fuqua to tell me more about his decision to leave an established national sports ministry and set off on his own. He had suggested earlier that God had somehow instructed him to do so—"God laid this ministry upon my heart"—and I wanted him to explain exactly what he meant by that.

Over the years I had heard other evangelicals make similar statements, claiming to have received some specific insight into the divine will, usually in regards to some personal problem or decision. More often than not these personal epiphanies were reported with little sense of drama. They were dropped almost matter-of-factly into everyday conversations with other evangelicals: "The Lord was telling me" to go here or there, or "the Lord showed me" what to do in an otherwise puzzling situation, or, as in the case of Pat Robertson, "I've been hearing from the Lord lately" that such and such would happen. The typical reaction of other believers to these surprisingly casual accounts of personal communication from God was often a simple knowing nod. What were these people seeing and hearing that the rest of us were not?

Evangelicals, of course, are not the only type of Christians—nor is Christianity the only faith—to embrace the notion of divine guidance and divine call. Discerning the divine will is one of the big issues that confront people of virtually every theistic religion. Christians have wrestled with it since apostolic times. But for evangelicals, who consider a personal relationship with God to be so foundational to their understanding of Christianity, knowing and doing God's will seems to be a constant obsession—a validating test, as it were, of the intimacy and authenticity of their relationship.

"For me, it wasn't like a physical presence," Fuqua ventured somewhat tentatively, looking into his empty coffee cup. "I didn't hear a voice, and I didn't see writing on the wall, or anything like that. It was just—just a drawing on the heart, a feeling I had as I prayed and sought after the Lord, that it was the right way to go." While he had been convinced for some time that God wanted him involved in basketball ministry, he said he felt a strong desire to be an exhibition player and performer as well as a Bible teacher and coach. "Athletes in Action wanted me to choose one thing and do just that," he explained. "But I believe God gave me the desire to do all of it. That's how I believe it works: God gives you a desire, and then he pulls you in one direction or another through circumstances, opening some doors and closing others. It also helps to seek the counsel of other Christians."

The rather subjective process Fuqua described, I would learn, approximates what apparently is a general consensus among modern evangelical theologians and writers of popular how-to books on knowing God's will: In the important decisions of life—marriage, career, finances—an individual may discern the right path through a combination of meditative prayer, Bible reading, and proper reflection upon relevant circumstances. Consulting with clergy or other mature believers also is recommended, although some writers hasten to add that skepticism is probably in order if a would-be adviser asserts flat out, "This is what God told me you should do." Charismatic and Pentecostal Christians, on the other hand, believe in prophecy as a spiritual gift, and tend to be much more open to receiving third-party messages from God. But even they do not accept every prophecy as legitimate.

None of this struck me as anything close to a foolproof system. Obviously there was plenty of room for misapprehension and flights of fancy. Discovering God's will, I was left to conclude, is never quite as easy as some would have us believe.

But apparently it had worked for Fuqua. "Looking back now over the past eight years with Hoops of Hope," he said, "I can honestly say, yeah, it's proven to be God's will. This is exactly where God wants me to be."

## NAVIGATORS

It was Bat Day at Sky Sox Stadium, and young triple-A baseball fans and their parents streamed through the chain-link gate, eager for a sunny Sunday afternoon at the ballpark and delighted to receive a souvenir Louisville Slugger handed out by volunteers from the Navigators, a locally based evangelical ministry.

A few yards inside the gate on a crowded walkway Shireen

Barrett, a Navigators employee, and a group of her coworkers were giving away more free stuff—a contemporary language version of the New Testament, a Navigators magazine, and other Christian literature—but with relatively few takers. About one in three passersby accepted the items and walked on, another third gave quizzical looks and politely declined, and the rest just quietly brushed by. To each Barrett and her coworkers offered the same cheerful greeting: "Enjoy the game!"

Even though she is not a huge baseball fan, volunteering at Bat Day has become a tradition for Barrett. In her eight years working at the Navigators headquarters she has missed the annual event only once. "I just enjoy being out here and seeing kids and families having a good time," the thirty-seven-year-old auburn-haired mother of two explained as she handed a New Testament to a young father rushing past with two freckle-faced daughters in tow. "And I think it helps people in the community become a little bit more aware of the Navigators and what we're about." She offered a book to a tanned middle-aged couple in matching Hawaiian shirts, but they shook their heads and hurried toward the concession stand. "Most people don't know who we are," she continued. "But we're not here to try to convert people or to be pushy. We're just trying to be neighborly. It's all just very low-key."

Low-key is probably an apt way to describe the Navigators. An evangelistic ministry that began as an outreach to sailors in Southern California in the 1930s, it is now a worldwide network of missionaries and volunteers who spread the gospel through one-on-one contact and in small-group Bible studies. Unlike some Christian organizations that depend on publicity and spectacle to get their message across to mass audiences, the Navigators tend to shun the limelight, preferring instead to work quietly behind the scenes— which makes even a modest public event like Bat Day seem a bit out of character. But as Barrett explained, the Navigators' presence at the ballpark had not really been intended as a missionary sortie but more as a friendly gesture to the community by one of the largest evangelical organizations in town.

The type of ministry performed by the Navigators has a name in the evangelical world. It is called "personal evangelism"—a process of converting people one by one through personal influence and persuasion, as opposed to the "mass evangelism" that goes on, for example, at a Billy Graham crusade. In theory it is something that every evangelical—by virtue of *being* an evangelical—is involved in out of obedience to Christ's Great Commission to his disciples to "go into all the world and preach the Gospel to every creature." In the Baptist church I attended in the 1960s we called it "soul winning." But unlike the Navigators, we were anything but low-key in the way we went about it.

Effective soul winning, to our way of thinking, required witnessing to people, sometimes aggressively, about their need for salvation and how they could find it. Witnessing, we were taught, was every Christian's duty, and every person who crossed our paths was considered a potential convert. We were given scripts and were drilled on how to present the plan of salvation in under three minutes—less time than it would take a gas-station attendant to fill the tank and check the oil. There was no excuse for letting anyone slip away unevangelized. Needless to say, we didn't close many deals. As much as we may have believed in its importance, few of us actually did much consistent soul winning. Whenever I could muster the courage, I was more inclined to invite my unsaved friends to a Sunday night church service, where I knew they would hear a powerful salvation message from the pastor. I figured I had done my part just getting them there. It was better to leave the heavy lifting to the pros.

By reputation I knew that the Navigators took personal evangelism seriously. And judging by their success, I suspected that their approach was different from the one I remembered. So I arranged a visit to the Navigators' headquarters to learn what I could about their methods and how they managed to motivate and maintain a modern army of soul winners around the world.

The Navigators' international headquarters sits in a rolling wooded canyon just northwest of town on the edge of a magnificent 1,140-acre estate built in the late 1800s by Colorado Springs's founder, railroad magnate, and Civil War general William Jackson Palmer. Abutting the estate to the south is the Garden of the Gods, a towering natural cathedral of jagged red sandstone outcroppings and lush green foliage at the foot of Pikes Peak. In a region known for majestic vistas it stands out as one of the most scenic spots along the Front Range. Palmer obviously thought so when he chose the site for his estate, which he called Glen Eyrie, "Valley of the Eagle's Nest."

After Palmer died in 1909 the estate passed through several hands. The Navigators bought it in 1953 for about three hundred thousand dollars and relocated its headquarters there from Los Angeles the following year. Administrative offices initially were set up in what had been a coal-fired power plant. The Palmer mansion, a sixty-seven-room Tudor-style castle at the center of the estate, was turned into a retreat and conference center. Two modern office buildings were added later on the northeast end of the property. The larger of the structures houses the Navigators' U.S. ministry offices and NavPress, the organization's publishing arm. The smaller is the Navigators' international headquarters. That is where I met with Jerry White, a retired Air Force general and the Navigators' president and chief executive officer.[9]

Even though I knew little about White before our meeting, based on outward appearances alone it would have been easy to peg the sixty-six-year-old Navigators' leader as a military man. His trim physique, short-cropped silver hair, and carefully controlled demeanor suggested someone who had spent a lifetime attuned to the physical rigors and martial disciplines of military life—traits that no doubt served him well at the helm of an organization devoted to a disciplined study of Scripture and sharing of the Christian faith.

When I arrived at White's office shortly before 8:00 A.M., he was just finishing up a Bible study session with a casually dressed young man with a crew cut—a recent graduate of the Air Force Academy and a recent convert, White would tell me later, who he had begun to mentor in the Christian faith. After making introductions and bidding the young man good-bye White invited me in and took a seat behind a large wooden desk with books and file folders stacked neatly on either end. I briefly explained my project and told him of my interest in learning about the Navigators' approach to personal evangelism and whether it reflected a broader trend among evangelicals in general. He pulled a pamphlet out of a stack of papers in front of him and leaned back in his upholstered chair.

"What we in the Navigators are about," he began, "is helping people, as our motto says, 'to know Christ and to make Him known' around the world." He held up the open pamphlet and displayed the slogan. "And we do that not by grabbing people by the collar or hitting them over the head with the Bible, but by encouraging them to search the scriptures for themselves, using the Word of God to navigate the course of their lives."

He briefly recounted the history of the Navigators, how in the 1920s a hard-drinking lumberyard worker named Dawson Trotman was saved after he began memorizing Bible verses at a small church in Southern California, how he began teaching a Bible class at the church, and went on to start a Bible-study ministry among Navy seamen in Los Angeles in 1933, calling it the Navigators. By the outbreak of World War II there were Navigator study groups on nearly one thousand ships and bases, and by 1944 they were in all branches of the military. After the war the ministry spread beyond the military to high school and college campuses, to business and professional settings, to neighborhoods and workplaces throughout the country, and eventually overseas.

Trotman's emphasis from the beginning, White said, was on "one-on-one discipleship and investigative study of the scriptures." Consequently, he said, "you'll seldom see a Navigator preaching to a crowd. We think it is not enough just to give people a set of facts or spiritual formulas. Our fundamental belief is that the truth will become apparent to someone who is earnestly seeking."

Nor, he said, would anyone accuse the Navigators of being hit-and-run evangelists. "Our focus is not just on helping someone come into a relationship with Christ, but to think of it as a lifetime pursuit—of growing strong in God's Word, learning to apply it to every aspect of life, and then mentoring others in the faith and encouraging them to do likewise." He noted that Billy Graham was so impressed with the Navigators' program in the early 1950s that he enlisted their help in designing a follow-up strategy for his crusades that is still used today. "What we're talking about, really, is spiritual multiplication. We tell our people your job isn't finished until you see at least three generations of believers come into the faith as a result of one conversion."

With a worldwide staff of more than 4,000 full-time lay ministers working in 112 countries, and with an annual budget of nearly $100 million (about 75 percent comes from contributions and about 20 percent from publishing revenues), one could easily imagine the spiritual multiplication to be exponential. White insisted, however, that the organization does not keep track of numbers of converts. "We used to, but we found it isn't very meaningful. As they say in engineering, when you measure something you disturb it, and we feel the same way." Still, he estimated that "way over one hundred thousand" are involved in Navigator Bible studies or are under the tutelage of a Navigator mentor at any given time. "And as a result of that, we know that lives are being changed and people are becoming mature followers of Christ, and are learning to live out their faith in the workplace or wherever they may be."

I asked White what he meant by that—living out one's faith in the workplace. I suggested that many employers and coworkers of evangelical Christians would have good reason to object to overt proselytizing on the job, and that many companies have policies against such practices. Was that what his organization was promoting?

"Not at all," he said. "To us, living out one's faith at work means doing your job well and living with integrity. It doesn't mean they go around preaching or leaving gospel tracts on people's desks. They are just there, being who they are—followers of Jesus Christ. And when others see that they are quality people they might think to ask, 'Why are you like this? What makes you tick?' And then they can say, 'It's because of my relationship with Jesus Christ, and if you'd like to know more, I'd love to help you figure it out for yourself.'"

It all sounded rather passive compared to the "don't take no for an answer" approach to witnessing that I remembered from forty years earlier. I told White about my experience as a teenager, and how I was never sure at the time who was made more uncomfortable by our witnessing, the witnessees or the witnessers.

He laughed. "Well, things have changed dramatically since then. The approach in those days was very confrontational. You confronted people with the gospel. Today it is much more relational. As Navigators, at least, we see ourselves walking alongside people, investing in their lives, becoming part of the fabric of the community, and through those relationships we get to know people and they get to know us, and hopefully they will see Christ in us and want to learn from us."

Part of the reason evangelism tactics had changed, White explained, was because American culture had changed. "We've become a far less churched society. Most people don't know much about the Bible. They don't know Moses from Abraham. The confrontational approach was based on the assumption that people knew what the gospel was—they just hadn't committed to it. But today you tell someone, 'You need to pray and receive Jesus,' and they say, 'Who is Jesus? What is sin?' So you've got to start with the basics and help them understand what the gospel really is, and that may take years rather than minutes."

I asked White if he thought most evangelicals took personal evangelism as seriously as they should, as seriously as the Navigators apparently do.

"I do think that most evangelicals take evangelism *very* seriously. The problem is that they don't do it. They would rather give money and let someone else do it. And I think part of the reason they don't do it themselves is that they don't know *how* to do it. They don't know how to share their faith or to study the scriptures, and they don't know how to help someone else to learn.

"There is a tendency today for people to come to faith and then to go somewhere and sit and listen to someone preach, maybe get involved in a small-group fellowship, although the majority do not, and then say, 'This is what Christianity is.' Well, that's *not* what Christianity is. Christianity is a person living out his or her faith in the world and helping to disciple others, and those things don't happen naturally. A person comes to faith and they really don't know what end is up. And so our task is to help them learn to make this work in their lives."

The Navigators' approach to evangelism certainly seemed far less confrontational than the old ways, and apparently it was more effective from their standpoint. But part of it struck me as employing a subtle bit of subterfuge. Sending missionaries into a community to befriend people in order to convert them, it seemed to me, was more than a little deceptive—if that, in fact, was what they were doing. I posed the question to White.

"The test is whether you remain their friend when they reject you totally," he said. "Our commitment is to remain friends no matter what. We've had a lot of discussion about this, because it can become an ethical issue. Do we want people to come to faith in Jesus Christ? Yes. Is that the only reason we befriend them? No. Is it part of the reason? Yes. So you see, it's complicated. I do believe that if you go in with an agenda, if all you care about is whether they buy in, then you delegitimize your message. And that's not what we're doing. We're going to continue to relate to them because we're friends, because we're community, whether or not they buy in. For one thing, it's not our responsibility to convince them. The Holy Spirit does the convincing, I believe."

A few months after my visit complaints about the religious climate at the Air Force Academy began making the national news. Some current and former cadets had reported being pressured by peers and superiors who were evangelical Christians to participate in religious activities at the academy, a situation that was characterized as religious intolerance and discrimination. Over the next several months the controversy would lead to a Pentagon investigation, congressional hearings, a civil lawsuit, and new Air Force guidelines on religious expression. The official inquiries found no overt discrimination but did locate instances of insensitive or overzealous behavior. Guideline changes mainly involved clarifying behavioral boundaries and cautioning senior officers against attempting to influence subordinates on religious matters.

As the saga unfolded a story appeared in the *Washington Post* in November 2005 singling out the activities of two Navigators missionaries at the academy as an example of what the newspaper apparently saw as the kind of unseemly behavior reflected in the initial complaints. Under the headline "Group Trains Air Force Cadets to Proselytize," the story reported that "a private missionary group has assigned a pair of full-time Christian ministers to the U.S. Air Force Academy, where they are training cadets to evangelize among their peers."[10]

There was no indication in the story that the voluntary activity violated Air Force policy, which it did not. Nor did it go beyond hinting that the Navigators had somehow received special treatment from the academy by gaining access to an unused classroom for meetings with cadets. In fact, it was later reported that eighteen other organizations had been offered the same accommodation as part of the academy's Special Programs in Religious Education (SPIRE).[11] The real point of the story, and apparently what the *Post* considered most shocking, was that members of an evangelical organization were training and encouraging cadets to share their faith with other cadets. The Navigators, in other words, were being "outed" for abetting the act of evangelism at the academy.

I called White to get his take on the story. His first inclination was to call it "a tempest in a teapot," and he insisted that the Navigators had "received no special privileges" and were continuing to abide by the rules. "Our people at the academy are there to help cadets who request their help, and that's something we will continue to do. It's what the Navigators have always done."

But the more he thought about it, he said he was afraid it reflected "an ongoing effort to get anything religious out of our society. I think that's what the whole controversy at the academy has really been about. And I'm afraid we're just going to see more of it as time goes on. That just seems to be the direction we're headed as a country."

Ultimately, he said, "it just shows that as Navigators we've got our work cut out for us. We've got to continue to teach and reach people with the gospel, and try to stay in the background and out of the spotlight as best we can."

Keeping it all just very low-key, as always.

## COWBOYS

Heading east out of Colorado Springs, past the municipal airport and the irrigated lawns and terra-cotta roofs of the last outlying subdivisions, one abruptly encounters the seemingly endless and nearly empty horizon of the bleak Colorado plains, which descend gradually from the foothills of the ragged Front Range to the flat and fertile wheat fields of Kansas some 150 miles away. Until the mid 1800s this was buffalo country, where vast wild herds grazed on prairie grasses and provided sustenance to the Arapaho, Comanche, and other hunting tribes of the Great Plains. By the end of the century both the buffalo and the tribes were gone, and much of the land had been given over to longhorn cattle and to the roughneck cowboys who tended them. In relatively short order the cowboy culture—with its emphasis on hard riding, hard living, and rugged self-sufficiency—took firm root in the Colorado territory.

As the region's population grew and diversified corn and wheat farming and sheep herding came to rival the cattle industry as mainstays of the local agricultural economy. Yet the cowboy way of life—at least the romanticized version of it—never fully disappeared. Today modern cowboys up and down the Front Range keep the heritage alive, honing their riding and roping skills at rodeos and other competitive events. Even though relatively few make a living on the rodeo circuit—many are weekend cowboys with construction jobs, or part-time ranchers or farmers who spend a few months on the road each year—the cowboy culture is as vibrant as ever.

It also has become an important focus of evangelical ministry. In the past few decades national groups like Cowboys for Christ and the Cowboy Church of the American West, both based in Texas, and the Colorado Springs–based Fellowship of Christian Cowboys have sprung into action to bring the gospel message to the lonesome prairies and crowded rodeo stadiums where modern cowboys gather.

I was anxious to see what happens when the Sermon on the Mount meets the Marlboro Man. And so, on a brilliantly sunny Saturday morning, I headed east out of town on a gently winding ribbon of blacktop highway to link up with Jerry Wyatt, a former rodeo rider who runs the national headquarters of the Fellowship of Christian Cowboys.

When I called Wyatt earlier in the week I had hoped to arrange an interview at the group's offices, which were tucked under the bleachers of the Norris-Penrose rodeo stadium in the southwestern part of the city. Wyatt had a much better idea. "We're having an event this weekend at a cattle ranch just outside of town, and you're welcome to join us." Perfect, I thought, imagining a calf-roping or steer-wrestling contest, or maybe some bronco busting. I couldn't believe my luck. "You can come out and see for yourself what we're about," he said. "Are you a golfer?"

By pure happenstance I had timed my visit to coincide with the first annual Fellowship of Christian Cowboys Golf Tournament. It wasn't exactly the slice of Wild West Americana I had anticipated, and I felt a little tinge of disappointment. But Wyatt assured me this would be no ordinary golf outing. There would be no fancy clubhouse, no golf carts, no manicured greens. In fact, no golf course. "We're burying a bunch of five-gallon buckets in a cow pasture," he explained. "It should be a real challenge. We're just gonna hit some balls around, and then have a barbecue and a little preaching service. I think you'll enjoy it. You'll meet some good people."

Following Wyatt's directions I drove about ten miles, until I came to a red and white banner bearing the Fellowship's logo that was planted alongside the highway, marking the entrance to a narrow dirt road. I pulled in and passed through a tall metal gate under a faded sign that read "Norris Cattle Company." The road wound back about a half mile along a dusty ridge, past empty pastures covered in brown brush and thickets of bind weed, a noxious flowering plant that thrives on little water. It had been an exceptionally dry winter and spring, the beginning of a sixth year of drought that had stunted agricultural production throughout the region. With natural vegetation in short supply, cattle ranchers especially were hard hit. No cattle were in sight on this ranch.

Up ahead a small grove of aspen and silver maple trees surrounded a brown doublewide house trailer that was flanked by a barn and a handful of smaller outbuildings with peeling white paint. I pulled into a gravel parking lot near the barn and walked toward a cluster of men standing next to a red pickup truck.

"Excuse me, gentlemen," I said, interrupting their conversation. "I'm looking for Jerry Wyatt."

They stopped talking and briefly sized me up. "I'm afraid you're too late," one said rather somberly. "He skipped town. Are you with the FBI?"

The others burst into laughter, and a man in a white cowboy hat and a red western shirt stepped forward and extended his hand. "I'm Jerry," he said. "Welcome to the Fellowship of Christian Cowboys."

Things were about to get under way, and Wyatt was rounding up the golfers and herding them toward a picnic area next to the house trailer, where about thirty men and a few women were milling about. I had never actually been to a rodeo, but this was not what I had imagined an assemblage of rodeo riders would look like. There were only two or three cowboy hats in the crowd. Most of the men wore baseball caps—some with NASCAR or seed-company logos—along with colorful polo shirts or T-shirts, blue jeans, and sneakers. They looked more like the Saturday morning crowd at Home Depot than a bunch of cowpokes. Besides Wyatt, only one man on the edge of the crowd really looked the part. He was a lanky fellow with a walrus moustache and a black wide-brimmed Stetson tipped forward to shade his eyes. He wore a crisp white western shirt, denim jeans with a big golden belt buckle, brown leather chaps, and fancy carved leather boots. Leaning back on his elbows against a split-rail fence, he reminded me of Robert Duvall in *Lonesome Dove*. I learned later that he was our speaker.

Wyatt gathered the men around to explain the rules and describe the layout of the course. There were eighteen holes, and each hole—or bucket—was marked with an orange flag. "It's kind of rough out there, so watch where you're stepping," he said. "There's lots of gopher holes and some pretty steep banks where the creek bed runs through. And watch out for rattlesnakes. If your ball goes down a gopher hole, it's probably best to just let 'er go."

As it turns out I'm not much of a golfer, nor was Wyatt. So we spent most of the morning walking the makeshift course, talking, and watching golfers in groups of four flail their way through the rough terrain.

The fellowship, Wyatt explained, was started in 1973 in Florence, Colorado, about forty-five miles southwest of Colorado Springs, by two veterans of the rodeo circuit: Mark Schricker, a national rodeo repeat finalist, and Wilbur Plaugher, a famous rodeo clown. Both were born-again Christians who knew firsthand the temptations and tribulations of life on the circuit—of long stretches of time away from family, friends, and church, and the physical and emotional wear of rodeo competition. As evangelicals they also felt a duty to share their Christian faith with others. But many of the cowboys they knew tended to fit the old stereotype: hard living, hard drinking, rough around the edges, and fiercely independent—not exactly your average Sunday-go-to-meeting types. It wouldn't be enough merely to invite them along to church and expect them to listen to some preacher they didn't know sermonize on how to get their lives in order. A ministry directed at cowboys, Schricker and Plaugher believed, had to be conducted by cowboys.

So they started out rather modestly, holding Sunday morning services in an empty hay mow or in the shade of a cottonwood tree usually, in the beginning, for just a handful of cowboys who were able and willing to rouse themselves early after a night of revelry. Someone might play guitar or the harmonica, and either Plaugher or Schricker would preach. And gradually people responded, one or two at a time, to the inevitable invitation to receive Jesus Christ. Over time the fellowship grew and expanded its outreach to include Bible studies, rodeo Bible camps for young people, and locally sponsored riding and roping competitions with preaching services tacked on. Today the fellowship has seventy-two chapters and more than four thousand "partners" in twenty-four states, a nationally syndicated TV show, a board of directors, and a national staff of five. In 1990 it moved its headquarters to Colorado Springs.

Wyatt, who was in his mid fifties, had been with the fellowship since the early 1980s, first as the head of a local chapter in southwestern South Dakota, where he owns a small farm, and then in Colorado Springs, where he was invited to come and lead the national staff in 2000. "Financially it wasn't a great career move," he confessed, as he opened a barbed-wire gate leading to a stretch of open pasture. At the far end of the field four men were walking around aimlessly with their heads down—presumably searching for golf balls. We headed in their direction. "I'm still trying to absorb the cost of moving here. But it was an opportunity to serve God full-time. And I owe a lot to the fellowship. I got saved at one of their meetings."

It was 1976, he recalled, during a cowboy service at a rodeo in Cheyenne, Wyoming. The preacher that day was Wilbur Plaugher. "It was the bicentennial, and Wilbur was dressed like Uncle Sam. I remember he preached a strong salvation message. I had never heard it like that before. My wife asked me once, before we got married, if I was a Christian, and I told her I was. I knew I wasn't Jewish or a Buddhist, so I figured I was a Christian by default. But I didn't know the Lord. Anyway, Wilbur didn't give an invitation that day to come forward, but sitting right there in the grandstands, I said, 'God, take the bridle reins of my life. Come into my heart, and forgive me.' Later that day I bought two Bibles and a Jesus bumper sticker for my truck. The Lord's been with me ever since."

We caught up to the four golfers, who by then had found the lost ball in a thicket of dry weeds. One man in a blue T-shirt and a blue baseball cap was standing in a dry creek bed, getting ready to take a swing. The others stood nearby, watching.

"How's it goin' out here?" Wyatt called out.

"Old Charlie there is having the game of his life," said a spectator in a plaid shirt, nodding toward the man in blue. "How many balls have you lost now, Charlie? Six?"

"Five, but who's counting?" Charlie muttered. "You'd think, with the ground as dry and hard as it is, you'd get a good roll out here. But no way. Too many obstacles," he said, kicking a dry cow chip the size of a pizza. The others laughed. "Between them and the gopher holes, you don't get much bounce." He took aim at an orange flag about 150 yards straight ahead and let go with his five iron. The ball sailed off to the right and disappeared behind a clump of brush.

"Good one, Charlie," the man in plaid deadpanned. "I've got some more balls in my bag if you need 'em."

About midway through the course we came upon what looked like an accident scene. A lone faded-blue pickup truck was stopped in the middle of a field, and next to it were what looked like two ambulance gurneys with men lying on them facedown. Two young women appeared to be working feverishly over the victims while two other men stood nearby looking on. "They're getting a massage," Wyatt explained. "Those young ladies are from a therapeutics school in town, and they volunteered to come out here today. It's good practice for 'em, I guess." One of the gurneys opened up, and a masseuse-in-training coaxed Wyatt to take a turn. Reluctantly, he took off his hat and climbed up on the table. For about fifteen minutes the young woman vigorously rubbed and pounded on his back and stretched and pulled his arms and legs. When his time was up Wyatt put on his hat and handed her a five-dollar tip. "I don't know what people see in them deals," he said quietly, arching his back as we walked away. "That hurt like crazy."

We began to head back toward the grove where the barbecue and preaching service would begin soon. As we walked Wyatt described what he called the fellowship's "soft approach" to evangelism. "There's no hard sell involved," he said. "We just invite people to our events, and when they come they hear the gospel. We try not to put people on the spot, and we never get into politics. We just try to disciple people as best we can." The most popular events, he said, were the calf-roping competitions. "We don't charge an entry fee, and we give away a horse trailer as the prize, but they have to stay for the service," each of which usually ends with an invitation to accept Christ. "We've had guys tell us, 'If you Christians are stupid enough to give me a trailer, I can put up with your church for an hour.' And lo and behold, they get saved. It's a cool deal to watch 'em grow in the Lord."

Compared to the roping contests, Wyatt said, the golf tournament had been a fairly modest event. The grand prize that day would be a golden rodeo-style belt buckle. "But the preaching service is the real reason we're here. There are men here today who I know aren't saved, and we need to take advantage of this opportunity to give them the word of God. They're cowboys, and most of them will appreciate the guy who's gonna speak, because he's one of them."

As we crossed the parking lot near the grove Wyatt described his frequent travels for the fellowship and his behind-the-scenes work helping to organize programs at rodeos and at youth Bible camps all over the country. "It's a pretty neat deal to be around kids and cowboys," he said. "I sure do enjoy it. I know there must be a lot of people more qualified than I am to do this job, but they weren't available. So I'm just here, trying to serve God as best as I know how. I just hope I'm having an impact. Sometimes I'm not so sure."

He fell silent for a moment, and we stopped walking. Looking off toward the mountains, he lifted his hat and brushed a hand through his hair. "Some guys, they'll say 'I've just got a real burden, a real burning inside to talk to people about the Lord.' And I don't know if there's something wrong with me—I've even prayed about it—but I don't have that, where you get up every morning just looking for someone to share your faith with. I just don't. I probably should be stronger. But that's where I'm at, and I'm trying to figure out if it's something I'm not doing, or if I'm just not gifted that way. Maybe it's my personality. Anyway," he put on his hat and we resumed walking, "that's something I struggle with all the time."

Listening to Wyatt wrestle with his conscience, I couldn't help but think of Pastor Smith in Michigan many years earlier, sternly admonishing his flock to be constantly looking for opportunities to witness to friends and neighbors about Jesus and telling us that we may be all that stood between them and eternity in hell. I remembered the pangs of guilt I, like Wyatt, sometimes felt as a teenager that maybe I was falling short, never doing enough. Wyatt had described it as a burden, and it was definitely that. Believing that you have the only true answer—that you know the only certain route to eternal life, and that the fate of those around you rests on your shoulders—could be an oppressively heavy burden to bear.

By the time the last of the sun-baked golfers had finished the course and made their way back to the shady grove, it was past one o'clock, and they were plenty hungry. They gathered around makeshift tables (sheets of plywood set up on hay bales) and helped themselves to ample portions of barbecued beef, baked beans, rolls, and potato salad that had arrived moments earlier on a pickup truck, and washed it all down with iced tea and sodas. While they ate a local RV salesman and his teenage son played a guitar and a fiddle and sang a couple of cowboy songs from a low wooden deck attached to the house trailer. They ended their set with a twangy bluegrass rendition of "Oh Taste and See That the Lord Is Good." Then Wyatt made a few announcements, awarded the prize buckle to the top golfer, and introduced the Robert Duvall look-alike as the day's speaker. His name was Gail Allen, a cattle rancher and occasional competitive roper from Model, Colorado. He also was chairman of the fellowship's board and, according to Wyatt, a frequent and popular speaker at cowboy events.

Allen leaped up onto the stage and held a big brown leather-bound Bible tucked under his arm as he adjusted the microphone. After cracking a couple of golf jokes he launched into the earnest business of delivering the message he said God had laid on his heart. "You know, history is an amazing thing," he said with a slight twang. "We read about it. We analyze it. We even make movies. But you know, we fail to heed its warnings. We just don't heed the warnings of history. Why? Because we don't think it applies to us. We just don't think it will ever happen again."

The particular unheeded warning that was on Allen's mind that day was found in the Old Testament book of Isaiah. The ancient Israelites, despite being "blessed beyond measure" as God's people, Allen said, "turned their backs on God and disobeyed God," with disastrous results: Their kingdom fell, and they were conquered by their Assyrian enemies. "Are there lessons we in America should learn from this? Does history repeat itself?"

For the next thirty minutes, while the cowboys sipped their sodas and some stretched out on the grass, Allen drew upon the Bible, history, and his own homespun observations on modern American culture to paint a decidedly bleak picture of the consequences of defying God. "Now some of you may be thinking, 'That would never happen to us. We would never turn our back on God.' But the Israelites didn't just wake up one day and say, 'We're gonna go against God.' No, it happened gradually. They grew complacent. They took things for granted. They probably even took the rain for granted. Do you remember back when we just assumed it would rain?" A gray-haired man sitting across from me nodded. "We took the rain for granted, didn't we? Now it seems like a lifetime that it just won't rain.

"Well, the Israelites took things for granted, and they took their eyes off of God. And what did God do? First he tried to get them to come back. He sent them prophets. But they wouldn't listen, and so he spanked them. He allowed Israel's enemies to overtake them. Some folks say God doesn't cause bad things to happen, but they're wrong. You bet he does."

I wasn't sure where Allen was going with this. He seemed to be treading perilously close to the intemperate remarks of Moral Majority founder Jerry Falwell and *The 700 Club* host Pat Robertson that the 9/11 terrorist attacks had occurred because, in Robertson's words, "God Almighty is lifting his protection" from the United States for tolerating abortion, homosexuality, and other national sins. Even worse tragedies could be in store, Falwell added during an interview on Robertson's show, "if in fact ... God continues to lift the curtain and allow the enemies of America to give us probably what we deserve." The comments were widely repudiated within the evangelical movement, and both Robertson and Falwell later backtracked.[12] I wondered if that was the kind of "spanking" Allen had in mind.

Moving on, he called attention to historian Arnold Toynbee's mid-twentieth-century analysis of the rise and fall of civilizations—a favorite among revival-meeting preachers, who cite it with regularity—which concluded that the collapse of every great civilization was preceded by a period of moral decline. "That's exactly what's happening in this country today, isn't it? Just look around: lack of truth, lack of respect for authority and for parents, sexual sins, *ho-mo-sexual marriages*—" he stretched out the syllables for emphasis, and several in the crowd laughed "—I mean, come on. Give me a break! My dad, he's in heaven now, but he wouldn't let you tell him such a thing as homosexuality even existed. What would he do today if he read the newspapers? It's disgusting, isn't it? How much lower can we get?"

I supposed that Allen felt that he had his audience pretty well pegged—that they were rugged hombres like himself who found the whole idea of gay sex a dirty joke—so he didn't have to mince words or add the obligatory "hate the sin but love the sinner" qualifier that many conservative Christians carefully add when-ever they denounce homosexuality. If this had been an ordinary mix of evangelicals he might have been more circumspect. Or so I thought, giving him the benefit of the doubt. Evangelicals, after all, I knew were not of one mind on the matter. Yes, polls had consis-tently shown them to be overwhelmingly opposed to same-sex marriage and to believe, in nearly as large numbers, that the Bible teaches that homosexual behavior is a sin. But surveys also had found many evangelicals conflicted over some of the more com-plex questions regarding the nature of homosexuality—whether it is purely a behavioral choice, for example, or perhaps an intrinsic trait. Many evangelicals would find plenty of room for nuance in discussing the issue. But there had been nothing nuanced about Allen's remarks. Maybe it had just been an ill-advised part of his cowboy shtick—playing to a perceived stereotype. Still, I was at a loss to understand why he chose to include a graceless rant against homosexuality in a message intended to win nonbelievers to Christ.

Allen wasn't quite ready to leave the subject. "I know one thing," he continued. "We need to be praying for President Bush today. That guy is going through the ringer trying to stand up for what's right. He's fighting homosexual marriage. He's fighting to preserve the lives of unborn kids. We need to stand up for that guy." Several around the tables nodded, and someone said, "Amen." It was just a few months before the 2004 election. So much for the fellowship's no politics rule, I thought. I glanced over at Wyatt, who was sitting near the front. He was looking up at Al-len and nodding.

"I don't think we deserve the blessings we have as a nation, to be honest," Allen said, closing his Bible, signaling that he was wrapping up. "Maybe we deserve to be spanked. But I know one thing: God loves us enough to intervene when we're making big mistakes. It's not how we start out that's important. It's not those areas of life where we fail. No, it's how we finish—how we react after we fall down." He raised his closed Bible over his head. "The Bible says to confess with your mouth that Jesus is Lord, and believe in your heart that God raised him from the dead, and you will be saved.

"I want every head bowed." Several of the men shifted in their seats and leaned over the table, bowing their heads and closing their eyes. "What about you today? Are you strong enough to go through life without the savior? Just shake your head. Are you? No. None of us are. Why would Christ go to the cross if we can do it on our own? We all need a savior, don't we? And if you've never invited Jesus into your life, you can do it right now. Just ask him.

"Father God," he slipped his hat off and bowed his head, "I thank you for your word. I thank you for Isaiah. I thank you for the Assyrians. Father, I've got some Assyrians not too far from my backyard, and it looks like they're winning, and we need to pray for our enemies. Father, I thank you for this group of men. If anyone is here who doesn't know you, may they invite you into their lives today. And Father, we continue to pray for rain. You know how badly we need it. You know all our needs. We ask all of this in Jesus' name. Amen."

Allen put his hat on, looked up, and flashed a big smile. "If you received Jesus today, thank God! Let one of us know. Or if you have questions, get a hold of me or Jerry or someone else and talk to 'em. Don't take this time for granted. It may be the last chance you'll ever get."

The service ended, and the cowboys returned to their clusters of conversation. Some began to gather up their things and head for their cars and pickup trucks. Since Allen hadn't asked for raised hands or invited seekers to come forward, there was no way to know if anyone had been saved that day. Wyatt would tell me later that since no one pulled him aside afterward or telephoned him to ask follow-up questions, he assumed that there had been no takers. "But at least the seed was planted," he said. "Maybe it will bear fruit later on."

As I went to my car a cool westerly breeze swept across the parking lot, sending a cloud of dust swirling into the empty fields. The afternoon sky had turned a hazy gray, and the air was noticeably more humid. A thick bank of dark scalloped clouds suddenly appeared over the mountains, and as I turned onto the highway, arcs of lightning exploded above the foothills and a soaking spring rain rolled out over the parched Colorado prairie. At least part of the cowboys' prayers had been answered.

# FOUR

# Saddleback Seekers

Lake Forest, California

B y Southern California standards the traffic jam at Portola Parkway and El Toro Road in suburban Orange County was nothing unusual. A dozen or so cars were stopped in the left-turn lane ahead of me, waiting to merge into a longer line of traffic creeping northward toward Saddleback Parkway just a few hundred yards away. On a normal weekday morning a moderate backup would have been expected on any one of the major commuter arteries in this sprawling residential area. But early on a Sunday, with nearby shopping malls still an hour away from opening, the mini-rush hour caught me by surprise. As I made the turn and edged my way into the congested right-hand lane I realized that all of us were headed to the same destination.

It was fifteen minutes before the start of the 9:00 A.M. service at Saddleback Community Church, and the scramble was on to get in, parked, and settled on time. Over the course of the weekend nearly 25,000 worshipers would make their way to the church's 120-acre campus to take in one of 22 separate services and to hear the man *Time* magazine has called "America's pastor"— Saddleback's founder and bestselling author of *The Purpose-Driven Life*, Rick Warren.

In the twenty-five years since Warren launched it as "a church for people who hate church" Saddleback had become one of the nation's largest and most influential evangelical congregations. Along with Willow Creek Community Church in suburban Chicago, it was at the forefront of a movement of "seeker-oriented" megachurches whose contemporary worship style and savvy marketing techniques aimed at attracting the "unchurched" had transformed the way many evangelical congregations operate. I had come to observe the Saddleback phenomenon and to meet with its purpose-driven pastor in hopes of discovering what it was about his message and methods that so many had found so attractive.

I fell in line behind a gold Lexus with a Christian fish symbol on its bumper, and followed the stream of traffic along a winding road to a massive parking lot that already was three-quarters full. I had barely gotten out of my car, and was headed for a pedestrian walkway, when a casually dressed elderly man wearing an official-looking name tag stepped forward and shook my hand.

"Welcome to Saddleback," he said. "Where are you from?"

Apparently, the fact that I was overdressed in a blazer and tie was a clear indication that I wasn't a Southern Californian, or at least that I hadn't been to Saddleback before. Virginia, I told him.

"Really? I lived in Norfolk when I was in the Navy. I loved it. That was a long time ago. So, do you know where you're going?"

I wasn't sure if he was inquiring about my soul or offering directions.

"I mean, do you know which service you want to attend this morning?" He explained that there were nine separate worship venues at Saddleback, each with its own style of music, from hard rock to adult contemporary, and Polynesian to black gospel. Four of the venues were open for the 9:00 A.M. service. This had been a stroke of genius on Warren's part. While differences in musical tastes had embroiled many evangelical congregations in divisive bickering during the previous couple of decades, Saddleback had avoided the so-called worship wars by accommodating a variety of preferences. Recently they even had added a Traditions venue that featured old-fashioned hymns accompanied by an organ and piano.

If it made any difference, I said, I wanted to hear Rick Warren preach.

"Well, you'll hear him at all the venues. He speaks in the Worship Center up there at the top of the hill. That's our adult-contemporary service. But his message is piped in to the other services on video screens." He pointed out two tent-shaped buildings near the parking lot that housed the hard-rock and gospel services. A Spanish service was conducted in another building near the center of campus.

I told him I'd probably opt for the adult-contemporary service. I thanked him for his help and set out for the Worship Center. "You have a great morning," he called out as he turned to greet a middle-aged couple who had just climbed out of a gray BMW.

Although it is something of a work in progress, Saddleback's parklike campus has the inviting appeal of a southern Mediterranean oasis. The central promenade from the parking area is meticulously landscaped, with red and yellow flowering plants, lush patches of lawn, and clusters of pine and towering palm trees. A cascading waterfall splits a wide stairway ascending to the Worship Center. Off to the left three modern mission-style buildings house a children's ministry center, a nursery, young adult meeting rooms, and a rooftop café that serves gourmet coffee and a view of the main worship service over closed-circuit TV. To the right an assemblage of boxy portables provides additional classroom space and serves as a reminder that construction at the site is not yet complete. There are plans for more classroom buildings and an eight-hundred-seat chapel.

While the campus has more the appearance of a village than a traditional church, it is not entirely without religious adornments. A sleek modern cross sits atop a tower high above the Worship Center. And in front of the children's center is a life-size replica of

Golgotha, the hill where Jesus was crucified, complete with three wooden crosses and a tomb below that opens and closes with the push of a button.

Except for the cross, Saddleback's Worship Center could easily be mistaken from the outside for a modern commercial building, or perhaps an airport terminal—which would be no coincidence, since its architect also designed Orange County's John Wayne International Airport. It is a three-story rectangular structure with a glass facade that looks out onto a broad pedestrian plaza lined with canvas-covered booths. Between services the outdoor area turns into a veritable bazaar, where worshipers may shop for books, CDs, and assorted religious bric-a-brac, or sign up for classes and projects.

Inside, the thirty-two-hundred-seat auditorium is not impressively large by megachurch standards. It has the look of a college gymnasium—a high ceiling with exposed girders and air ducts, a flat carpeted floor with movable interlocking chairs, and a sloping bleacher section in the rear. Across the front a wide elevated stage is flanked by two giant video screens, with a smaller screen directly overhead. A lone wooden cross is suspended midway between the floor and ceiling just to the left of the stage.

By the time the service began nearly every seat was filled, and worshipers spilled out onto an adjoining patio, some sitting under umbrellas or just basking in the morning sun. It was a homogeneous-looking crowd, almost entirely white, with a smattering of Asians. Most appeared to be in the forty-to-sixty age bracket, and all were casually dressed, some in Bermuda shorts and flip-flops. It was the kind of crowd you'd expect to see at a James Taylor concert.

On stage eight singers and an ensemble of guitars, drums, assorted wind instruments, and an electric keyboard cranked out the opening bars of an upbeat praise song, and the crowd came to its feet and joined in as the words flashed across the bottom of the screens. ("I just want to say / It's a beautiful day / I just want to say

/ Lord you're worthy of my praise.") The lead singer, a fiftyish-looking man with a shaved head and wire-rimmed glasses, danced about the stage under pulsating lights while a video cameraman scurried around the edges, shooting the musicians from various angles. It was a high-energy performance, and it made good TV—so good that most of the audience, even those sitting close to the front, chose to watch the giant screens rather than the live performance. This was church for the TV generation.

After one more song Rick Warren loped onto the stage from somewhere near the rear, looking thoroughly relaxed in a blue-and-white Hawaiian shirt, khakis, and brown deck shoes. He is a large man with a goatee and spikey brown hair that shows surprisingly little gray for someone fifty-two years of age. His smiling face filled the giant screens as he took his place behind a polished wooden pulpit at the center of the stage.

"Good morning, everybody. Good to see you, and welcome to Saddleback." He turned and looked directly into a camera perched on a platform in the center of the auditorium. "I want to welcome those of you who are in the Overdrive venue, and those of you who are in the Praise venue, and those of you who are at El Encuentro, or who are up there in the Terrace Café, or wherever you are—we're glad you're here. And now if you'll take out your message notes, we're going to talk about making a difference with your life."

It is Warren's style to get down to business quickly. Alan Wolfe, a noted Boston College political scientist who has written often and incisively about American evangelicals, once described Warren as "not only the best preacher, but simply the best public speaker I have ever heard."[1] No doubt a big part of what impressed Wolfe and others is Warren's uncanny knack for simplifying and clarifying complex subjects. Both in the pulpit and in his books he prefers storytelling to scholarly exegesis, and is fond of using lists and easy-to-remember alliterations to communicate a point. The purpose of life, for example, as he famously explains in his bestseller, may be easily summed up in five bullet points. ("You were planned for God's pleasure. You were formed for God's family. You were created to become like Christ. You were shaped for serving God. You were made for a mission.") So, too, the secrets of building a strong and vibrant church. Midway through this morning's message Warren would reassure his flock that there was nothing to fear about engaging in missionary work. "It's not about location; it's about dedication. It's not about where you are; it's about who you serve. It's not about crossing the sea; it's about seeing the cross." It was classic Warren-speak.

"God designed you to make a difference," he gently admonished his listeners at the outset of his message. "He didn't put you on this planet just to take up space. You're not here just to use resources, breathe, and die. God intends for you to make an impact with your life. He wants you to leave the world a better place than you found it. And the only way you do that is by serving other people. No one has ever left the world a better place by being selfish or living for themselves. Jesus said, 'You want to be great? Learn to be a servant of all.' "

On this weekend Warren was unveiling his latest and undoubtedly his most ambitious project to date: a worldwide Saddleback-led campaign to battle the "global giants" of poverty, disease, ignorance, egocentric leadership, and spiritual emptiness. He called it the PEACE Plan—an acronym based on five strategies he said were drawn from the teachings of Christ: Planting churches, Equipping servant-leaders, Assisting the poor, Caring for the sick, and Educating the next generation. For the next forty days Saddleback members would study the strategies and begin applying them, first locally, and then globally. This was to be the "beta version" of the PEACE Plan, and after a year of testing and adjusting, it would be rolled out as an international campaign involving thousands of churches and millions of Christians around the world. Warren called it "a revolution that will ignite a second Reformation."

It was an unabashedly grandiose undertaking to say the least, and as such, it was vintage Warren. In his twenty-five years in the ministry no one had ever accused him of thinking small. Shortly after he arrived in Southern California with his young family in 1979, fresh out of seminary, Warren audaciously announced to a handful of worshipers that the church they were starting from scratch would one day number twenty thousand and would occupy a fifty-acre campus. Early in 2005 they surpassed that goal and held a celebration service at Angel Stadium in Anaheim. Saddleback was now one of the three largest churches in the nation, with a paid staff of over three hundred and an annual operating budget of more than $30 million.

Warren spoke for about thirty minutes and then stepped away from the pulpit while a troupe of actors performed a humorous skit to illustrate one of his sermon points. When he came back he addressed the "fear factor"—the reluctance that he said some people may feel about participating in the PEACE Plan. "You may be sitting there saying, 'But it just seems so big and so overwhelming. Why us?' I would say to you the same thing Jesus Christ said in Matthew 19:26: 'Humanly speaking it is impossible. But with God everything is possible.' I would rather attempt something great and fail than attempt to do nothing and succeed. Throughout the history of the world, in God's timing there are always three phases: impossible, possible, and done. Everything is considered impossible until somebody does it. And God wants to use you."

Warren repeated the same message at each of the weekend services, and after each service members queued up in long lines on the outdoor plaza to pick up information kits and study materials for the 40 Days of PEACE campaign. The revolution was under way.

Peter Drucker, the late legendary management consultant and a longtime Warren mentor, once pronounced evangelical megachurches like Saddleback "the most important social phenomenon in American society" in the second half of the twentieth century.[2] While traditional Protestant denominations were in a steady decline, Drucker observed in 1998, the megachurches had exploded. Indeed, according to a study in 2005 by the Institute for Religion Research at Hartford Seminary, the number of congregations with weekly attendance greater than 2,000 had doubled in the previous five years, to more than 1,210.[3] The overwhelming majority of them were evangelical.

The reason for the amazing growth, according to Drucker, was that the megachurch leaders had dared to ask a basic marketing question: What does the consumer want? And the answers they received and responded to, he said, looked nothing like what traditional churches were offering. Most had adopted a seeker-oriented approach, designing their programs to attract nonchurchgoers and bring them to a personal faith in Christ. Many conducted their services in facilities scrubbed clean of traditional church trappings: theater seats replaced pews; soft-rock ensembles replaced organs and pianos; overhead projection screens replaced hymnals; and few religious symbols were in sight. The sermons—they usually were called teachings or messages—tended to be more therapeutic than theological, and often seemed geared more toward helping people find happiness and fulfillment than a heavenly reward.

The growing popularity of the seeker approach was largely the result of deliberate efforts by churches like Saddleback and Willow Creek to package and promote their methods to other congregations. Some 10,500 congregations are members of the Willow Creek Association, a loose network of churches in 90 denominations that follow the seeker-friendly church-growth model pioneered in the late 1970s by Willow Creek's founding pastor, Bill Hybels. Each year more than one hundred thousand congregational leaders attend Willow Creek's leadership conferences in hopes of replicating its success.

At Saddleback Warren's *The Purpose-Driven Church,* a book

for pastors that has sold more than a million copies since 1995, has been used as a training manual for some four hundred thousand church leaders in 160 countries. While Saddleback does not keep a membership roster as Willow Creek does, it estimates that more than one hundred thousand congregations are following the purpose-driven principles—which Warren describes as a "biblically-based approach to establishing, transforming, and maintaining a balanced, growing congregation that seeks to fulfill the God-given purposes of worship, fellowship, discipleship, ministry, and missions." A separate department at Saddleback's headquarters writes curriculum and oversees training conferences for congregational leaders. Warren also provides sermons and other resources for pastors over the Internet.

As popular as the giant seeker churches have become in the evangelical world, fewer than 15 percent of all evangelical church-goers attend them. More than half belong to congregations with fewer than three hundred members.[4] But even many of those smaller churches have been affected by the megachurch movement. While not all have eagerly embraced the seeker-church paradigm, it is becoming increasingly rare to find an evangelical congregation that has not adopted at least some of its user-friendly features. Such is the influence of men like Hybels and Warren and the appeal of their vision for ministry.


Warren is a gregarious man who laughs easily and often, with a loud and hearty Robert De Niro kind of laugh: head tilted back, chin jutted out, the corners of his mouth tipped slightly downward. He's also a hugger, embracing even the most casual of acquaintances—journalists included—as though they were family. When we met for dinner at a sushi restaurant not far from his church after an evening service, he seemed eager to talk about the genesis of Saddleback and his vision for ministry.

"I really didn't set out to be a church pastor," Warren volunteered as we settled into a small booth after placing our orders. As a student at Southwestern Baptist Theological Seminary in Fort Worth, Texas, in the late 1970s he had dreamed of becoming a missionary to China. But by the time he graduated, he said, "I felt God was telling us—I've never heard God speak, but it was an impression—that we were supposed to stay in the United States. That was a big disappointment for Kay and me, because we wanted to go overseas. But God said no."

So they packed their belongings in a U-Haul trailer and arrived in southern Orange County late in December 1979. "I knew there were plenty of great churches in Southern California, and that anyone who was the least interested in church already had a place to go. So we chose to go after people who had no interest."

For the first twelve weeks he conducted market research. "I went door-to-door with a notebook and I'd say, 'My name is Rick Warren and I'm taking a survey. I'm not here to sell you anything. I'm not here to convert you.' And I'd ask, 'Are you an active attender of any religious house of worship?' If they said yes, I'd say, 'Thank you, congratulations,' and I'd go to the next house, because I wasn't interested in the opinion of churchgoers. But when I found someone who said, 'No, I don't go anywhere,' I'd say, 'Great! You're just the person I want to talk to. Let me ask you a couple questions: Why do you think most people don't go to church?' And I listened and wrote it all down. And then I'd say, 'If you were thinking of going to church, I know you're not, but if you were, what kinds of things would you look for?' And I discovered rather quickly that what most churches offered was not what most people wanted."

The four biggest complaints, he said, were that "sermons are boring and don't relate to my life; members aren't friendly, it's more like a clique; churches are more interested in your money than in you; and they worried about the quality of children's care. So the hang-ups were not theological. They were sociological. People said, 'I don't have anything against God. I just don't see it relating to my life.'

"And so I went back and wrote an open letter to the community, and I said, 'At last, a new church for people who have given up on traditional church services.' We were going after people who don't like church but would like to know God."

The first service was Easter Sunday, and 205 people showed up at the rented high school auditorium. "That was more than I expected, and it included only about five church people. So I said, 'Let's open our Bibles,' and nobody had a Bible. And I said, 'Let's sing a song.' Nobody knew the songs. I said, 'Let's pray.' They went, 'Ommmm.'" He threw his head back and laughed. "So, that's how it started. We really were starting from scratch."

A year into it attendance had leveled off at about 150. He was working eighteen-hour days, and it was wearing him down. "I felt like I was the director of a spiritual orphanage—taking care of all the needs of these people who had no previous religious background at all." One Sunday he collapsed behind the pulpit. "I needed to take some time off. So I took my family to Arizona and went into the desert for a few weeks. I guess you'd say that was my period of doubt and depression. And out of it came a conviction. I felt like God was saying, 'Now whose church is this, Rick?' And I said, 'Well, it's yours.' He said, 'Then you focus on building people, and I'll build the church.' And I said, 'God, you've got a deal.' And that's where I came up with the paradigm of the purpose-driven church. It came out of that year of depression, in 1981, when my whole goal was not, 'God, build a great church,' but 'God, get me through Sunday.' When you know what your purposes are, you stay focused. You're less stressed because you know where you're headed."

Over the next thirteen years, he said, "I wanted to prove you didn't need a building to build a church. So we used seventy-nine different facilities. Every time we'd outgrow a warehouse, a bank building, a school, a tent, a stadium, we'd move somewhere else. Then finally, in 1992, we bought the land and put up a big tent to seat a couple thousand, and eventually we put up a building.

"So in twenty-five years the purposes have never changed. Our methods have changed. One of the purposes of the church is worship. We've changed our style of worship three times in twenty-five years. The style changes but the purpose doesn't."

As one might expect Saddleback's seeker-oriented approach to ministry has plenty of vocal critics. Some describe it as offering a pale version of the Christian faith—a sort of "Christianity lite" that is focused more on meeting felt needs for comfort and support than on promoting the more demanding doctrines of traditional Christianity. A writer for the *New York Times Magazine* summed up some of the common complaints of some conservative pastors: "Should churches really be chasing popular culture? Isn't preaching only positive messages a reductive, if not distorted, approach to the Gospels? Shouldn't true believers be in natural conflict with the secular world? 'There's a healthy reaction here against a legalistic religion of dos and don'ts,' says Eddie Gibbs, professor of church growth at Fuller Theological Seminary, referring to the Purpose-Driven approach. 'The danger, though, is that you end up with a Gospel that endeavors to meet your needs without challenging your priorities.'"[5]

Warren rejects such criticism out of hand. "The problem is, when most people come to Saddleback all they see is the service. They go, 'Hmm. Big church. Must be shallow.' But the service is just the tip of the iceberg. It's like two percent of the church. What goes on the rest of the week, beneath the surface, is much more revealing of who we are. It's two hundred different ministries. It's more than three thousand small groups. It's six thousand hours of counseling a month. It's all sorts of things that people don't readily see on a Sunday morning."

Far from propagating an undemanding Christianity lite, says Warren, Saddleback "is built on a system where we're constantly turning up the heat, helping people grow in their commitment and knowledge. You meet people where they are, but you don't leave them there. They may be down here," he said, gesturing, "but you're going to take them here. To join the church you have to make certain commitments, like tithing and participating in ministry. So most people who casually drop in to observe us would never see this."

One of Saddleback's key principles, Warren said, is that "the church must grow larger and smaller at the same time. Larger through the Sunday services, smaller through the proliferation of small groups. If you get sick in our church, you will be visited almost every day you are sick. Why? Because it's organized through the small groups that meet every week in eighty-three cities, from Santa Monica to Escondido." More than simple Bible-study groups or prayer cells, which are common among evangelicals, he said, Saddleback's small groups are at the core of the church's ministry.

"Unless you've seen our small groups in action, you really haven't seen what Saddleback is about."

At seven o'clock on a Monday night, just as they do every week, five Saddleback couples in their middle to late forties gathered for Bible study at Tom and Jane Crick's comfortable mission-style house in Mission Viejo, a tidy residential community about five miles from the church. Tom, a former technology worker who now is on Saddleback's ministry staff, and Jane, who works part-time in a women's mentoring ministry, were the group's leaders and had hosted the weekly gatherings since the mid-1990s.

Tom explained before the meeting that while the mix of couples had changed during that time, with some moving away and newcomers being added, the group had grown close over the years. Besides the weekly Bible studies they often socialized as families and worked together on local ministry projects. On one recent weekend they had gone to a homeless shelter, prepared a meal for its residents, and then conducted a worship service. They were making plans for a short-term mission trip to Malaysia. "We do life together," he said. "It's really a family bond."

On the evening I visited the group was nearing the end of a

thirteen-week study of a book entitled *Sacred Marriage*, by Gary Thomas, a popular evangelical speaker and writer.[6] As luck would have it, the topic of discussion that night was sex. More precisely, it was the role of sex in a Christian marriage and how it can enhance—or potentially weaken—a person's spirituality and Christian character.

It was not exactly the kind of conversation one would expect people to feel comfortable having with fellow church members, even if they were "family." And as the couples took their seats around the perimeter of the Cricks' crimson-colored living room, I sensed that they were a little nervous. The fact that a journalist was present with a notebook and recorder probably didn't help matters. Jeff, one of the younger members of the group and the designated discussion leader for the evening, offered an opening prayer asking God to "take control of our conversation, and put a protective hedge around each one of us. The subject we are discussing tonight, we know the enemy could easily use it the wrong way. So just help us to focus on your will for sex in our marriages, and to be comfortable to share the things we need to share in order to draw closer to you."

For the next ninety minutes or so the couples skimmed through the assigned reading, a chapter entitled "Sexual Saints," singling out statements that they had found helpful or thought provoking, and then discussing them. Jeff's wife, Jeanine, jotted the statements on a flip chart.

Jim, a tall man with salt-and-pepper hair, started out. "The first one I underlined was that most of us are introduced to sex in shameful ways."

"Ditto," Tom said, and several others around the room agreed. "When we were kids, sneaking a look at a dirty magazine, and our parents not wanting us to think or talk about sex—it's the whole guilt thing that kind of skews our attitudes." The author apparently argues that it is important to get beyond those feelings and to recognize that sexual pleasure in marriage is God's gift.

"And yet," Jim's wife, Darlene, chimed in, "he also says if we stray outside of God's perfect will, we *should* feel guilty. So there is that tension right from the beginning."

Jane spoke up next. "I like this statement that we should 'redefine sex as it was in the Garden of Eden, when Adam knew Eve, and then think of how God can reveal himself to you within your marriage through the gift of sexual pleasure.' I like that because it goes back to what sexual desire was designed to be—a mirror of our desire and passion for God."

That led to a brief discussion of how church teachings on sex had changed over the centuries. The second-century church father Clement of Alexandria, according to the author, had begrudgingly allowed that sex for procreation purposes was acceptable as long as it was done in the dark of night. In the fourth century St. Augustine taught that sexual intercourse transmitted original sin, and St. Ambrose concluded that while marriage was "honorable," a life of chastity was even "more honorable." By the Middle Ages a detailed set of church rules forbade sexual relations on or around holy days and at various points in a woman's menstrual cycle— some 252 days of the year in all.[7] Marital sex, it seemed, was a necessary evil to be tolerated but carefully circumscribed. "It's like they were commanded not to enjoy it," Jeff noted, and the others laughed. "It's humorous now, but it's kind of scary to think that's what they believed."

Fortunately there were more enlightened moments in church history. Some medieval priests, for example, according to the author, were known to bless newlyweds in their marital bed. And the seventeenth-century English Puritan leader Richard Baxter obviously was at ease with sexual pleasure when he urged his flock to "keep up your conjugal love in a constant heat and vigor."[8]

But what the Saddleback couples found more fascinating and instructive were ancient Jewish teachings that viewed marital sex as a mystical experience. "When a man unites with his wife in holiness," they read from a saying of the medieval rabbinical scholar

Nahmanides, "the *shekinah*"—the glory of the physical presence of God—"is between them in the mystery of man and woman."[9] It was the same presence, the author explained, that Moses experienced when he met God face-to-face on Mount Sinai.

"That's amazing to think about," Jane remarked. "When Moses came down from the mountain it was like he was on fire. He was changed because he had been with the Holy One. That's what *shekinah* glory is. And Gary Thomas is trying to tell us that our marital bed can be *shekinah* glory in honor of God. Think of that the next time you have relations with your spouse, that it's *shekinah* glory just like Moses had!"

"Kind of gives you something to look forward to, doesn't it?" Tom interjected with a grin, putting an arm around his wife. "Hey—it's *shekinah* time!" Everyone laughed, and Jane playfully pushed him away.

Jeff steered the discussion back on track. "It makes sense, though, because as Christians we believe God is present in us through the Holy Spirit. So when a husband and wife are united in the sexual act, God is present in that. It becomes a spiritual as well as a physical act."

"Sure is different from the way the world views sex, isn't it?" Tom said.

The subject shifted to prayer. If marital sex was a spiritual experience, as the author suggested it was, should Christian couples talk to God before or even during the act? I was waiting for someone to deliver another punch line—the delicatessen scene from *When Harry Met Sally* came to mind—but everyone seemed quite serious.

"The book says we shouldn't turn our eyes from God when we share intimate moments with our spouse," Jim noted.

"Thinking about God during the actual act?" Jeanine looked quizzically at Jeff. "I don't think we've ever thought about that, although sometimes we've prayed before sex, when we were trying to have kids."

"I know it seems kind of awkward," Jeff admitted, "but I think his point is that if you think of sex in God's terms—as only within the sanctity of marriage—then you can really begin to focus on God and on preparation and prayer beforehand. It starts to make a lot of sense when you think about it, although it doesn't come naturally, that's for sure."

I had to ask. Was the author actually suggesting that couples should pray before having sex? Wouldn't it kind of—I don't know—break the mood?

"I don't know that he's suggesting that you go into the bedroom and pray right before sex," Tom offered. "But if you have a consistent prayer life then it becomes part of your thanksgiving. You thank God for the gift of sex."

Inevitably the discussion turned to lust and marital infidelity. The author described illicit sex as "spiritual junk food—immediately sweet, but something that will poison our spiritual appetite until we crave that which will destroy us." And he cautioned men especially against allowing pornography to dictate their sexual appetites.

"With this group," Tom said, "I think it's not so much an issue of sex outside of marriage. It's probably more of a lust issue, at least for us guys. It's the role of the eye in sexuality. Satan takes our natural propensity and uses it to tempt us."

"When we first got married," Jane confessed, "I bought Tom a subscription to *Playboy*. I figured if he was going to look at it, I was going to look with him. That's how warped my thinking was."

"Some people think in a marriage anything goes," Tom continued. "But I don't think so. Any time you bring a third party into it—and that can be a pornographic magazine or a video—I believe it's wrong because you're objectifying the sex act and you're placing unrealistic expectations upon your spouse. You're making her compete with an airbrushed image that is not real. Sight is important to us men. We're wired that way. But like the book says, as Christian husbands we can mature in what we long to see."

The final few minutes of the discussion focused on setting boundaries and avoiding temptation. It was suggested that seemingly innocuous things like going to lunch with or sending personal e-mails to members of the opposite sex could lead to trouble and should be avoided. "These are the kinds of things couples should talk about, to lay down some ground rules," Jeff said. "Sex is such a powerful thing. We can never be too careful."

Tom suggested that the group members should make themselves accountable to one another. "It helps to have other men or other women who you can talk to on a regular basis about these things, and who can help you avoid compromising situations," he said. "Hopefully, that's what we can be as a group. As men we need to be there for each other. As women you need to be there for each other. That's why we're here."

When time ran out the couples had completed about two thirds of the chapter. They agreed to continue the following week, discussing how to have a healthy body image, the importance of cultivating passion, and how to use the sex drive to groom Christian character.

"Are there any more comments or questions?" Tom asked. "No? ... Well then, I guess everybody's anxious to get started on their homework." The group shared a laugh and a closing prayer, and headed for home.


Although you won't find it mentioned on its signage or in any of the literature distributed to weekend worshipers, Saddleback is a Southern Baptist church. It holds membership in both the denomination's state and national conventions and contributes financially to its missionary endeavors and some other projects. But consistent with a long Baptist tradition Saddleback relishes its independence as a congregation, and while it embraces the classic Baptist doctrines, it goes its own way on matters of ministry.

Like most Baptist churches and many other evangelical congregations, Saddleback practices what is known as "believer's baptism." According to Baptist belief only those who have accepted Jesus as savior may undergo the ancient Christian initiation rite. Baptism, in their view, is a public testimony of one's personal faith and, as such, may not be administered to infants. From my own experience I knew that Baptists encouraged new converts to be baptized as soon as possible as a way of reinforcing their decision to follow Christ, and that immersion, not sprinkling, was the only acceptable mode. Consequently, it is rare to find a Baptist church that doesn't have a baptismal tank, or baptistry, as a prominent architectural feature.

The baptistry at Saddleback is a decorative flagstone pool with a narrow waterfall in the corner of a beautifully landscaped plaza just outside the Worship Center, and on any given Sunday it gets a heavy workout. In just over twenty-five years Saddleback has baptized more than twenty thousand people—an average of more than fifteen per week.

After the 11:15 A.M. service on the weekend of my visit about a hundred people crowded around the pool to witness the baptism of a dozen adults and teenagers. In keeping with Saddleback's laid-back style, rather than the traditional white baptismal robes, each of the baptism "candidates" wore a blue Saddleback T-shirt issued by the Baptism Ministry Team, along with Bermuda shorts or cut-offs. One of the church's associate pastors, a spike-haired young man who bore a striking resemblance to former *Saturday Night Live* cast member Rob Schneider, was officiating.

"There is nothing magical about these waters," the pastor explained, as he stepped into the waist-deep pool. "Baptism for us is not a means of salvation. It is a symbol and a testimony. As we go down into the water it symbolizes Christ going into the grave, and as we come up out of the water it symbolizes his rising from the dead. In doing this we are identifying publicly with Christ. We are saying, 'I am a Christian, and from this day forward I am going to live for him as best I know how.' "

He beckoned an auburn-haired teenager into the pool; a name tag was pasted to her sleeve. "Jennifer, have you accepted Jesus Christ as your Lord and Savior?" She nodded, and said yes. "I baptize you in the name of the Father, and the Son, and the Holy Spirit." He put his hand over her nose and leaned her backward into the water—"We are buried with Christ in baptism"—and lifted her out again—"We rise with him to new life." The spectators cheered and applauded as a team member helped the drenched teenager out of the pool and handed her a towel.

The ritual was repeated for each of the remaining candidates— three more teenagers, a single elderly man, two young married couples, and a couple and their teenage daughter. Presumably all were recent converts and relatively new to the church. I thought it might be a good opportunity to hear some personal stories of what attracted seekers to Saddleback and to its evangelical brand of Christianity. But as soon as they came out of the pool most of them hurried off to a changing room and disappeared into the crowd.

I managed to catch up with the father who was waiting for his wife and daughter outside the changing room. His name was Mike, and he was a technology director for a local school district. He and his family had been coming to Saddleback for about a year, after having attended another church near their home in Trabuco Canyon. They were introduced to Saddleback through a small group that met in their neighborhood. "What we liked most about it, and kept us coming back," he said, "was its focus on helping others. They're not just sitting in the pew. They're actually out there doing something. That to me is what church should be about."

As we finished our brief conversation I noticed one of the other couples still in their wet clothes lingering near the pool, and I went over and introduced myself.

Beverly and Clayton had a bohemian look about them. She

wore shoulder-length brown hair, silver wire-rimmed glasses, and a stylized cross on a long silver chain around her neck. He was mostly bald, with a laurel wreath of wispy brown hair around his ears. Both looked to be in their early forties. They, too, had been attending the church for about a year, and had made their first contact through a neighborhood small group. For two years prior to coming to Saddleback, they said, they had practiced witchcraft.

"We toyed with Wicca. We were exploring it," Clayton said, using the popular name for what its practitioners sometimes simply refer to as "the Craft." While the name conjures up images of black hats and broomsticks, and is sometimes confused with Satanism, Wicca consists of a constellation of neopagan religions and forms of goddess worship, some of which are loosely based on ancient Celtic and Norse pagan practices that were cobbled together by devotees in Great Britain and the United States in the second half of the twentieth century. I had reported on it once or twice for U.S. News. "But then," he continued, "we got involved in the small group, and we realized that Wicca wasn't really working for us. So we decided to come here, and found that this was the church home we'd been looking for."

I asked how they had made the huge theological leap from Wicca to evangelical Christianity. Wiccans, to my understanding, worshiped a pantheon of deities, believed in reincarnation, rejected notions of heaven and hell, and embraced a decidedly permissive moral code ("If it harm none, do what you will.").[10] Plus, they went around casting spells. Could two belief systems be any more different?

Beverly explained that someone in their Saddleback group had recommended C. S. Lewis's classic apologetic Mere Christianity. Reading it, she said, "I was impressed by his argument that there is a universal law, that there are notions of goodness and fairness that all people more or less hold in common. And it grew from there."

This exposure to conservative Christianity, she explained, had not been her first. "What drove me from the church twelve years ago was the fundamentalist belief that people who are not Christians were going to hell. But C. S. Lewis says we do not know that. And that's what helped to bring me back. One of the main tenets of this church is that you believe in Christ, but it's not exclusionary to that extreme. So I found a church I could finally belong to."

I didn't want to put a damper on her baptism celebration by saying something that might make her think differently of her church. But my guess was that if Rick Warren had been listening he would have winced at her characterization of Saddleback's teachings regarding the fate of nonbelievers. One needed only to visit the church's Web site to learn that Saddleback believes, as most evangelical churches do, that "only by trusting in Jesus Christ as God's offer of forgiveness can man be saved from sin's penalty," and that penalty was "to be eternally separated from God [in] Hell."[11] Perhaps she had not yet taken the membership course where this was made clear. Or if she was aware of it, maybe the fact that one seldom heard eternal damnation addressed in the Saddleback pulpit constituted, in her mind, a less than extreme position on the issue. In any case, I opted to let the subject slide. I asked what she thought of Wicca now.

"I look upon it the way I think C. S. Lewis would look upon it—that there are some people in Wicca who are closer to the tenets of Christianity than there are in some churches, in the way they live their lives. When we were into Wicca we did spell craft"—the casting of spells—"and worshiped a goddess. We dealt with spirits and different things, and I think that softened Clayton up a bit in his scientific approach." She looked at him. "He's a physicist, and I think seeing that spell craft actually works made him more accepting of spiritual things, enough to bring him to the church. Being in Wicca helped bring us to this place in our lives. The goddess actually brought us closer to Christ."

Later in the week, during my dinner conversation with Warren, I would think of Beverly and Clayton when he described how

Saddleback accepts people "where they are, but we don't leave them there." As a seeker-sensitive congregation they endeavor to make it easy for people to come to church—too easy, according to some critics—by removing unnecessary obstacles, and by being welcoming and attentive to people's felt needs. Once inside the task is to help them come to an authentic faith, and then, gradually, to grow in their understanding of scripture and its demands on their lives. Christian conversion, as Saddleback and other evangelicals practiced it, is an instantaneous transaction, but maturing in the faith is a lifelong process.

In the case of the former Wiccan couple it appeared that the Saddleback system—if it may be called that—had worked the way it was supposed to, at least up to this point. Apparently they had been warmly and unconditionally welcomed into their small group, and gently counseled on the more inclusive aspects of the Christian faith. As evangelicals like to say, they were being fed "the milk of the Word"—fit food for newborn believers. Only when they were more mature would they be ready to receive the "meat." Had they been hit up front with some of the more exclusivist doctrines of classic Christianity, it is doubtful that they would have begun the journey of faith. I wondered if they would feel deceived when they learned the rest of the story.

I had a chance later to visit with another recent convert, who had followed a more conventional path to faith, but whose life, I would discover, had undergone no less radical a change.

When I first met Ali he was sitting on a bench near the church administration building reading a pocket-size Bible. "Whenever I get a few extra minutes I take it out and read," he explained. "I can't get enough."

Raised in a nonreligious but nominally Muslim home, the thirty-eight-year-old soccer coach had been a Christian for a little over a year, and it was easy to see that he was thoroughly enraptured by his newfound faith. He had just come from morning worship, and was wearing a navy blue T-shirt with THE NARROW ROAD emblazoned across the front. A coarse iron nail, a symbol of the Crucifixion, dangled from a silver chain around his neck. And as he spoke in rapid-fire bursts about his faith in Jesus, his eyes flashed, and he could barely sit still. "It's full," he said, pointing to his heart. "That's the only way I can explain it."

Ali described how he had been introduced to the faith fourteen months earlier by the father of one of his soccer players, who also happened to be one of Saddleback's pastors. "We got into this dialogue about God. I had all these questions, and we would e-mail back and forth. Ever since I was a child I had this fascination about God. I didn't know what it was then, but I had this void, this emptiness inside that only God could fill."

The pastor gave him a Bible and a copy of Warren's *The Purpose-Driven Life*, "and as I read, everything clicked. Everything fell into place—the reason why I'm here, my purpose in life. Everything started making sense. So one day I'm reading, and I put the book down, and I'm like, 'Okay, this is it'—I get goose bumps just thinking about it—and I closed my eyes, and I prayed the prayer, and I gave my life to Christ."

Right away he started attending a Bible study on Thursday mornings at the church, and before long had joined two small groups, in addition to attending weekend services. He also recently had begun helping out with Saddleback's high school ministry.

"So now I'm here at the church four mornings a week, and every day I wake up to the Word, I go to sleep to the Word. I keep the Word in my back pocket wherever I go. That's a lot, I know," he laughed. "It's hard to explain to people. But you know how it feels when you fall in love for the first time? And you have this tightness in your chest, and you just want to be with her constantly? It's that same feeling, only multiplied. I want this relationship to be as strong as possible. I know God's love for me is perfect. But my love for him, I just want it to grow. I love this feeling."

Ali's weekly schedule was not all that had changed dramatically. "My friends noticed a difference in me. They said, 'What's wrong with you? You're happy.' They noticed that I stopped swearing. I used to drop the F-bomb like about every third word. Not any more. So I explained to them what was going on in my life. And so far, four of them have come to know the Lord, and I have a dialogue going with some of the others. They keep asking me questions.

"But we still go out, and I might have a couple of beers. And then I go home. No more getting drunk and hanging out at the bars until three or four in the morning. I feel like I want to stay pure now—physically, socially, sexually. Sometimes people will say, 'You're nuts! You're not going to have sex until you're married?' And I say, 'Why should I? It says here, don't do it.'" He tapped on his Bible.

"I explain to them that when I invited Christ into my life, he came inside me. Jesus is *inside* me. He sees through my eyes, he touches through my hands, he speaks through my mouth, he feels through my heart. So every time I go out, if I'm going to grab that third beer, I'm getting him drunk, too, you know? If I'm going to open a magazine and look at a suggestive picture, I'm making him look at the same thing. How can I subject him to that? How can I do that to him when he took the nails for me?

"My relationship with the Lord is the most important thing in my life. It's not my car, it's not my job, it's not my girlfriend, it's not money. And no one can take that from me. Wherever I go, whatever I do, I know he's always going to be with me."

As I sat listening to Ali speak so passionately about his relationship with God I recalled a sermon I had heard many years before at a Nazarene revival meeting. The preacher that night had taken it upon himself to chastise his listeners, who apparently had lost their zeal and grown lax in their commitment to God. It wasn't that they had backslid into sin, or neglected the work of the church, or even fallen behind in their tithes. The fire simply had gone out.

"You have forsaken your first love!" he thundered, quoting from the book of Revelation. "Remember the height from which you have fallen. Repent and do the things you did at first." Faithful service and personal discipline were good, but they were not enough, the preacher insisted. He wanted his people to rekindle the passion that had moved them when they first met the Lord.

The Nazarene preacher would have been pleased to know Ali. A year into his Christian journey, it was clear that he was experiencing the intense emotions of a passionate first love, and the fervor showed no signs of abating. It was easy to imagine that some more seasoned church members might consider what Ali was experiencing to be a type of spiritual infatuation—not uncommon among new believers—that could not, and perhaps should not, be sustained. With time, after all, youthful exuberance inevitably must subside, giving way to a more mature and reasoned faith and a steadier more routine form of practice. Yet I doubted anyone could convince Ali of that.

Hearing Ali's testimony reminded me of my own first year as a Christian. Even though I was much younger than he at the time—I was fourteen years old—I recalled feeling some of the same emotions. Like Ali, I wanted to read my Bible nonstop. I devoured every piece of Christian literature I could get my hands on, hoping to learn everything I could about my adopted faith. Had it been possible I would have lived at the church, I was that much in love—or infatuated. Whatever the feeling was, it didn't last. And when it faded I mourned the loss. Regardless of how hard I tried, I never got it back.

Most of Saddleback's growth and its success as a model for other evangelical congregations preceded Warren's personal rise to national prominence. In fact, writing a runaway bestseller created a unique set of challenges for Warren and his family: how to handle the instant fame and fortune.

Since its debut in 2002 *The Purpose-Driven Life* has sold more than twenty-five million copies and has become the bestselling hardcover of all time. "It brought in a ton of money—I mean a *ton* of money," Warren said. "The first thing we decided was that we wouldn't let it change our lifestyle one bit." So they live in the same house and drive the same Ford SUV as before. No yachts. No vacation homes. No expensive wardrobes. "Next, I stopped taking a salary from the church. Then I added up all the church had paid me in the previous twenty-five years and I gave it back, because I didn't want anybody thinking that I did this for money." He and his wife, Kay, began to "reverse tithe"—they now give away 90 percent of their income and live on 10 percent. Finally, they formed three charitable foundations: one to train pastors, another to help fund the PEACE Plan, and a third to help AIDS victims and orphans in Africa.

Dealing with the financial windfall, he said, was the easy part. "The hard part was, what are we going to do with the fame?" For years Warren had carefully avoided the national limelight, refusing to allow his weekly services to be broadcast so as not to compete with other pastors. Suddenly he found himself deluged with speaking invitations from heads of industry, academia, and government, and unending requests for media interviews.

He said he turned to the Bible for guidance, and found a passage in Psalms where King Solomon prays for greater influence. "When you read it," Warren said, "it sounds like a very self-centered prayer. Solomon already is the wisest and wealthiest man in the world, and here he prays for more power and influence. But then you read the rest of it, and he says, '[S]o that the king may support the widow and orphans, care for the oppressed, defend the defenseless, speak up for the prisoner, help the immigrant.' He basically talks about all the marginalized of society."

That marked a turning point in his life. "I realized that the purpose of influence is to speak up for those who have no influence. And in religious terms I had to say, 'God, I repent, because I can't think of the last time I thought of widows and orphans.' There are two thousand verses in the Bible that talk about the poor. How did I miss that? I went to Bible college and two different seminaries and got a doctorate. How did I miss two thousand verses on the poor?"

He insists that he has no interest in trying to leverage his influence in the political realm—"God called me to be a pastor, not a politician"—and refuses to be drawn into public policy debates. Instead, he says, he plans to continue ministering to his Saddleback flock, helping the poor and marginalized through the PEACE Plan, and providing resources and training to other pastors.

His resolve to maintain that course, he said, was strengthened during a trip to South Africa in 2003. After leading a weeklong training seminar for pastors he asked his hosts to take him to a village to see a local church. They took him to Tembisa, a poor township just outside Johannesburg, where a congregation of about seventy-five worshiped in a tent that also housed about twenty-five AIDS orphans.

When he arrived, Warren said, "a young African pastor walked up to me and said, 'I know who you are. You're Pastor Rick!' I said, 'How in the world do you know who I am?' And he said, 'I get your sermons over the Internet.'" The pastor explained that he walks an hour and a half every week to a post office, downloads Warren's sermons, and preaches them on Sunday. "He said, 'You are the only training I have ever had.' I burst into tears, and I thought, 'I will give the rest of my life for guys like that.'"

# FIVE

# Wheaton Thunder

Wheaton, Illinois

Even a casual visitor to this picturesque campus west of Chicago can't help but notice that something sets Wheaton College apart from other highly regarded liberal arts schools. Etched into a concrete and limestone sign prominently displayed on the southwest edge of campus, just across from the redbrick colonial Billy Graham Center (named for the school's most famous graduate), is Wheaton's founding motto: "For Christ and His Kingdom." More than just a historic slogan, it is a guiding principle that permeates the culture and curriculum of an unabashedly evangelical institution that has been called "the Harvard of Christian colleges" because of its reputation for academic rigor. Wheaton is a school where scholastic achievement and Christian discipleship get equal billing, and where a vigorous life of the mind is deemed inseparable from a fervent walk of faith. It is a school where only serious Christians, as opposed to nominal ones, need apply.[1]

It is also the flagship of a burgeoning network of evangelical colleges and universities in the United States—102 institutions in all—that has seen enrollment skyrocket an amazing 71 percent since 1990. That's more than five times the growth rate of public institutions, and nearly three times that of all private schools combined.[2] Part of the increase, says Robert Andringa, president of the Council for Christian Colleges and Universities, is due to the growth of the evangelical movement. "But we've also seen a dramatic increase in the quality of these schools," he says. "They're attracting more Ph.D.s who want to teach from a Christian worldview." And, he says, the schools are "doing a better job marketing themselves" to Christian young people and their parents "as an alternative to the big public universities." Together they are turning out graduates in record numbers who are eager to take their evangelical faith into the workplace and into the culture.

No school has been more zealous or successful at that task than Wheaton. It is one of the most selective schools in the country, with 30 National Merit scholars in its most recent freshman class of 578 and SAT scores exceeding the national average by more than 300 points.[3] Over the years, it has produced senators, congressmen, and diplomats; leaders in business, science, education, the arts, and the media; and legions of ministers and missionaries. And that is a point of personal pride for Duane Litfin, Wheaton's president since 1993 and a former church pastor in Memphis, Tennessee.

"Our goal," Litfin told me during my visit to the Wheaton campus, "is to send out wave upon wave of graduates who will make a difference in the world for Christ." Litfin recalled watching President Bush's nationally televised speech before a joint session of Congress a week after the 9/11 terrorist attacks. In words crafted by presidential speechwriter and Wheaton alumnus Michael Gerson, Bush paid tribute to Todd Beamer, the "Let's roll!" hero of United Flight 93, and to his wife, Lisa, both Wheaton grads. Sitting behind Bush was House Speaker Dennis Hastert, also a Wheaton alumnus. "That one frame on national television," Litfin said, "captured so well what this college is about: serving and having an impact."

My visit to Wheaton was a journey to the epicenter of evangelical higher education and its mission of confronting and transforming culture. Here I could expect to find some of the best and brightest of the next evangelical generation. I was eager to witness the much vaunted interplay of faith and learning in Wheaton's classrooms to discover if—as some critics have suggested—the spirit of academic freedom and scholastic achievement invariably is squelched by a closely circumscribed religious agenda. I also wanted to learn how Wheaton's reputation as an incubator of neo-evangelical social conscience—the kind of spiritually motivated altruism that dominated American Protestantism in the nineteenth century—was holding up against a resurgence of otherworldly pietism and narrowly focused political partisanship within the broader evangelical movement.

And so I flew into O'Hare International Airport and drove twenty-five miles over the busy interstates and commercial thoroughfares of Chicago's western suburbs to spend a few days on the idyllic Wheaton campus, observing the processes at work in shaping the minds of a rising generation of evangelical leaders.

In the decades just before the outbreak of the Civil War the small farm towns of DuPage County were way stations for runaway slaves making their way across the Mississippi River and the gently rolling Illinois prairie to safe haven in Chicago and points beyond. Abolitionist sentiments ran strong in this part of Illinois, much more so than in the downstate counties that bordered the slaveholding states of Missouri and Kentucky. And even though Chicago was only thirty miles to the east, getting there from the villages of Naperville, Turner Junction, Prospect Park, and Wheaton could take two or three days by foot or by wagon over rutted dirt roads through dense woods and shoulder-high prairie grass, along routes worn by the native Sauk and Potawatomi. And so the fugitive slaves would find food and shelter at places like Israel Blodgett's blacksmith shop in Downers Grove, Frederick Graue's grist mill in Oak Brook, and in the upstairs of a three-story limestone building on the outskirts of Wheaton that housed the Illinois Institute, a common school run by teetotaling Wesleyan Methodists.

In 1859 the Illinois Institute was in deep financial trouble. Hoping to find a way out, its board recruited a new president, Jonathan Blanchard, a fiery Congregationalist preacher and staunch abolitionist who had recently left the presidency of Knox College in the Mississippi River town of Galesburg, Illinois. At Knox Blanchard had proven himself a strong administrator and fundraiser, but his outspoken views on slavery had gotten him into trouble with some of the town's leaders and college trustees. He gladly accepted the job in Wheaton. The Illinois Institute's board offered its new president carte blanche to do what he deemed necessary to turn the school around, so long as he maintained its historic stands against slavery and Freemasonry, and for temperance. Blanchard happily agreed. Within a year he had returned the school to fiscal solvency, added secondary and postsecondary classes to its curriculum, obtained a state charter for the new advanced programs, and accepted a gift to the school of forty acres from town founder Warren Wheaton. Out of gratitude Blanchard renamed the school Wheaton College.

In many respects Wheaton's first president was a classic nineteenth-century evangelical. His social activism was shaped by the theological perspective known as postmillennialism—the belief that Christians were duty-bound to work for the betterment of society in order to make the world fit for Christ's second coming. Ironically, Blanchard's spiritual heirs in the twentieth-century evangelical movement would embrace quite the opposite view—called premillennialism—which holds that the world's troubles are beyond human repair, must inevitably deteriorate, and will only be remedied when Christ returns to establish his kingdom.

Blanchard was convinced that the nation's Christian educational institutions were in a unique position to influence the culture. Years earlier he had called for a "martyr-age of colleges and seminaries" where invigorated faculty would "lead their students, both by precept and example ... into a zeal for reformation." His thoughts on the subject were published in pamphlet form and reprinted widely in newspapers and tracts. Ultimately, Blanchard believed that "society is perfect where what is right in theory exists in fact; where practice coincides with principle, and the law of God is the law of the land."

One of the greatest barriers to a perfect society was slavery, which he saw as exhibiting "all the worst principles of European despotism and Asiatic caste." It was insufficient, Blanchard believed, merely to pass judgment against slavery and other social ills. It was a Christian's duty to work for change, and change ultimately could be accomplished only through transformed hearts. "An enlightened intellect with a corrupt heart," Blanchard wrote, "is but a cold gas-light over a sepulcher—revealing, but not warming, the dead."[4] And so it was Blanchard's desire that Wheaton College devote itself to a combination of vigorous intellectual growth and zealous Christian faith—a double-edged sword that he believed would roust the twin evils of sin and ignorance from an embattled social order, and help to establish the kingdom of God on earth.

Blanchard's vision of a culturally engaged institution would wane during the middle years of Wheaton's history. Blanchard's son, Charles, succeeded him as president in 1882, and held the post until his death in 1925. During the younger Blanchard's tenure both he and much of the evangelical movement came to embrace the bleak premillennial and separatist outlook of an emerging Christian fundamentalism. From roughly the turn of the century to the end of World War II the college would shift its emphasis to revivalism, proselytism, and personal piety. By the mid 1960s the pendulum would begin to shift again, and Wheaton's mission returned to its founder's vision of engaging and redeeming the culture through academic rigor and fervent faith.

✝

Ask almost anyone on campus what makes a Wheaton education distinctive and you're likely to get a close variation of the same answer: "the integration of faith and learning." But just how the oft-repeated mantra of Wheaton's educational mission works out in the classrooms and in campus life has not always been clearly understood or appreciated beyond the borders of religious academia. Like other evangelical Christian colleges, Wheaton places a strong emphasis on Christian values and conduct. Chapel attendance three times a week is mandatory. And many students participate voluntarily in prayer groups and Bible studies in their dorms. Students also are encouraged to find and be active in a local church, and to donate time to community service projects. All of that, of course, is in addition to carrying a full course load.

Like most evangelical colleges Wheaton requires its faculty to sign a statement of faith, pledging personal allegiance to a set of core evangelical doctrines. In Wheaton's case that means acknowledging belief in a triune God, salvation through the death and resurrection of Jesus, the inerrancy of Scripture "in the original writing," the existence of "Satan, sin, and evil powers" in the world, and the divine creation of the universe and of "Adam and Eve as the historical parents of the entire human race."

Though common in evangelical circles, in the broader academic community requiring professors to sign such statements is controversial to say the least. Wheaton's leaders insist that the statement is necessary to help preserve the school's evangelical character and to define the biblical perspective that informs a Wheaton education. "We are teaching here from a Christian worldview," Litfin explained unapologetically. "We are not just teaching *about* the Christian worldview. We are looking for people who themselves embody it. So our faculty will be people who have committed their lives to Jesus Christ."

But critics argue that doctrinal loyalty oaths like Wheaton's are hostile to academic freedom, hamper serious academic inquiry, and invite mediocrity by excluding talented faculty who happen to be of other faiths. One of the most vociferous of those critics is political scientist Alan Wolfe, director of the Boisi Center for Religion and American Public Life at Boston College. Writing in the *Atlantic* in October 2000, Wolfe declared that "of all America's religious traditions, evangelical Protestantism, at least in its twentieth-century conservative forms, ranks dead last in intellectual stature."[5] Most of the Ivy League universities, he noted, have roots in mainline Protestantism; top-notch universities like Georgetown, Notre Dame, and Boston College were founded by Roman Catholic clergy; and Brandeis and Yeshiva universities are among the nation's highly regarded institutions of Jewish origin. Evangelicalism, Wolfe wrote, has "no comparable legacy." It has not produced a single major research institution.

Yet far from intending it as a malicious slam, Wolfe, in an article entitled "The Opening of the Evangelical Mind," went on to observe that many of the liberal stereotypes about evangelicals as anti-intellectuals steeped in creationism and biblical literalism were wildly out of date—that Wheaton and a handful of other Christian colleges, in fact, were at the forefront of "a determined effort by evangelical-Christian institutions to create a life of the mind."[6] He warned, however, that "as long as evangelical scholars insist on drawing up statements of faith that shut them off from genuine intellectual exchange, they will find it difficult to become the kind of intellectually exciting institutions they hope to be."[7]

Questioning the quality of evangelical scholarship has not come entirely from outside the movement. Perhaps the most stinging indictment, in fact, came from one of Wheaton's own faculty stars, history professor Mark A. Noll, who wrote famously in 1994 that "the scandal of the evangelical mind is that there is not much of an evangelical mind."[8] For generations, according to Noll, evangelicals had neglected the intellectual life, focusing their educational resources instead on ministry and other religious and utilitarian purposes. "Virtually without exception," Noll wrote, Christian colleges and universities "were not designed to promote thorough Christian reflection on the nature of the world, society, and the arts. It is little wonder they miss so badly that for which they do not aim."[9]

Yet both Noll and Wolfe include Wheaton in a growing number of evangelical colleges and seminaries that have made substantial progress since World War II in promoting scholarship alongside the more general goals of broad learning and basic Christian worldview. Among those other highly regarded institutions are Calvin College, in Grand Rapids, Michigan; Westmont College, in Santa Barbara, California; Gordon College, in Wenham, Massachusetts; Seattle Pacific University in Seattle, Washington; and Fuller Theological Seminary in Pasadena, California. Since the 1960s, says Wolfe, schools like these "with roots in American fundamentalism have indeed created a life of the mind broader and more imaginative than anything previously found in their tradition. The big question is whether they can maintain it."

At Wheaton, faculty and administrators articulate their academic mission as helping students learn to "think Christianly" about all aspects of life. What does that mean exactly, and how does it play out in the classroom? I was curious to discover just what makes a Christian liberal arts education distinctively Christian.

I dropped in on an early morning political philosophy class in a recently renovated wing of Blanchard Hall, the historic limestone structure that once housed the Illinois Institute. Fourteen students sat around a rectangular table—some sipping coffee or colas as they jotted notes on the day's topic: the political and cultural impact of globalization in the modern world. As do all classes at Wheaton, the session began with a student-led prayer. A young man with spiked blond hair bowed his head and read aloud from the Anglican Book of Common Prayer: "Grant, O God, that your holy and life-giving Spirit may so move every human heart that barriers which divide us may crumble, suspicions disappear, and hatreds cease; that our divisions being healed, we may live in justice and peace; through Jesus Christ our Lord. Amen."

A quick shifting of gears, and the class launched into a spirited discussion of the day's reading, a socialist critique of globalization as an extension of western hegemony. The professor, Ashley Woodiwiss, a bearded man who looks to be in his early forties, with a Ph.D. from the University of North Carolina, scribbled on the white board as students outlined and critiqued the author's arguments. He did not lecture, but occasionally summarized a point in the reading, posed a question, or pressed a student to clarify a remark.

One young woman, recently returned from a teaching internship in Kenya, cited the presence of a Coca-Cola bottling plant and American fast-food restaurants near the school where she taught in Nairobi as examples of what the author described as a neocolonialism and a "loss of particularity" that globalization often brings to nonwestern cultures. "I sometimes found myself thinking, you know, this could be anywhere in the United States or Europe. It felt so familiar and, I don't know, homogenized."

Across the table a young man in a gray Wheaton sweatshirt raised his hand and asked to respond. "You're looking at it as a bad progression," he said to the former intern. "But maybe Kenyans like to drink Coke. And I assume the factory employs, what, hundreds of Kenyans? Thousands maybe? That can't be all bad."

Finally, with ten minutes left in the fifty-minute session, the discussion turned to Christian roles and responsibilities. Woodiwiss suggested that "the church, as a global community, preserves diversity in harmony," and is a force against the "fictive unity" of globalization. But a young man sitting to my right disagreed. "Too often, the church plays along with globalization," he said. "My denomination went into Kosovo to do humanitarian work, and they passed out Nikes and set up an Internet café."

It struck me as an insightful comment, but it was carried no further in this discussion. Certainly one could argue that the Christian church had acted as a force for globalization through missions and proselytizing long before Coca-Cola first arrived in Africa. Modern missionaries may have ceased long ago the intentional practice of pressing indigenous people to adopt Western modes of dress and behavior. But that was the legacy.

As the discussion wound down Woodiwiss announced the next session's topic: Christianity as a "sanctified subverter" of globalization. "I want you to be thinking about how, in the situation of globalization, can we further the kingdom of God? What are we as Christians going to do given that we are not going to overcome—that the Christian church is not going to rule the world?"

It was a discussion one would rarely expect to find in a secular setting. Yet if there was a party line at work here, or an agenda to impose conformity of viewpoints, it clearly was not present in this discussion on this particular day. Students had engaged one another vigorously, obviously at ease with the notion of challenging one another and the professor, and of being challenged.

Yet it was also clear that underlying the discourse was a common worldview, a set of shared assumptions centered on the notion that there is a way of "thinking Christianly" about the issues of modern life—political and economic issues in this instance—that, if properly apprehended and applied, was a distinctive and desirable way of understanding the world. It may not always yield pat or jingoistic answers, or even basic agreement on complex issues. Yet it was a trustworthy lens through which to begin to examine life in all of its complexity, and to seek to grasp its elusive truths.

For young Christian students and their academic guides this default assumption no doubt provided a comfortable context for their intellectual explorations: the belief that there is a divinely ordered logic and purpose underlying all of the confounding complications of life. Whether it spurred them on in their academic inquiries to pursue "a clearer understanding of the mind of God," as one Wheaton professor explained it, or whether it simply made young scholars more accepting of paradox and of mystery, was not altogether clear.

Several of the students and professors I spoke with later described a "safe atmosphere" where students are encouraged to think deeply and provocatively and not to merely absorb a particular doctrinal or political point of view.

"We have the freedom here to explore faith issues in ways that I couldn't somewhere else," history professor Paul Robinson told me during a brief visit in his office. Robinson had come to Wheaton five years earlier, after having served on the faculty of St. Lawrence University in New York for twenty years. "All of us, students and faculty, begin at the starting point of the Christian faith. That's a given. But it never dictates where we will come out in our discussions or the conclusions we will draw." Owen Handy, a political science major from Holland, Michigan, explained that rather than trying to teach a particular political or theological line, "the professors push us to think critically. It's not so much what you think, but you are expected to know why and be able to defend it."

Working the faith angle in a history or political philosophy class was one thing. But what about math and science? Can a science program be taken seriously that adheres to a biblical account of creation?

Dorothy Chappell, dean of natural and social sciences, insists it can. Sitting in her small windowless office, she pulls out a folder and extracts a series of statistical tables from the National Science Foundation that lists the nation's top producers of doctoral candidates in science and engineering. One showed Wheaton ranking twenty-first in the nation among four-year liberal arts colleges whose graduates went on to earn doctorates.

"Our students are recognized as among the best," she said. "That must say something about our program. We don't teach Christian science here. We teach science, period. It's the same science as the University of Illinois teaches, or the University of Chicago." What was different, she explains, is the broader context. "We teach science from within a Christian worldview, starting with the assumption that all truth is God's truth. We believe there is biblical truth—what we call special revelation—and there is natural truth, or general revelation. Generally there is no conflict between the two."

Generally, perhaps. But what about the Genesis creation story—God creating the universe out of nothing in six days, Adam formed out of the "dust of the earth," and Eve made from Adam's rib, the talking serpent, Noah and the Flood, and so on? How did Wheaton's science curriculum deal with all of that?

"We do believe that God created the universe, and that Adam and Eve were the first humans," Chappell said. "But we are agnostic as to how God did it." In practical terms, that means the school doesn't push what Chappell called "young earth creationism"—a view drawn from a literal interpretation of Genesis that asserts that God created the universe in six twenty-four-hour days just a few thousand years ago. It is a view that would find little support among the science faculty at Wheaton or at most other evangelical colleges, but that still has a significant following among the evangelical rank-and-file and, if the pollsters are right, in the general population at large. (A 2004 Gallup poll found that a plurality of Americans, about 45 percent, believe God created humans "pretty much in their present form" within the past ten thousand years. Thirty-eight percent said humans evolved over a longer period of time but God had a role in it, and only 13 percent said God had no part in human evolution.)[10]

At the same time, she said, Wheaton's acceptance of evolutionary theory is limited to changes within a species rather than the widely held view that humans evolved from apes. "There is no assent given here to the view that Adam and Eve descended from primitive hominids."

So what happens when the two sources of data—revealed truth and natural truth—seem to be in conflict?

"It means we haven't interpreted the data correctly," Chappell said. "Either we've missed something in our science or we are failing to understand the scriptures correctly. We're not afraid here of exploring truth. That's what scientific research is all about. That's what life is about."

As serious and rigorous as the academics are at Wheaton, campus life is not all hard work and religious solemnity. Like all college students "Wheaties"—as they like to call themselves—find time for fun, most of it of the good clean variety, in keeping with the school's Christian character.

On most weekends and many week nights students choose from a variety of campuswide activities, from talent shows and film nights to late-night skating and bowling parties. There is a full schedule of concerts, plays, and athletic events. An NCAA Division III school, Wheaton fields teams in twenty-two intercollegiate sports, and had won fourteen championships in the preceding five years.

"There's a lot of lightness and laughter on campus," Christina, a petite dark-haired sophomore from Irvine, California, explained to me at the campus coffee shop. "People at Wheaton know how to have fun." With Chicago just fifty-two minutes away by train, she said, "people are always going downtown, to Cubs games, restaurants, shopping. It's great being so close to the city."

What you won't find at Wheaton are the beer busts and casual sex that are often considered rites of passage at many colleges and universities. Wheaton students must agree to abide by a community covenant that spells out biblical principles of behavior and prohibits drinking, smoking, engaging in premarital sex, and any behavior "which may be immodest, sinfully erotic, or harmfully violent."

The college received national attention early in 2003 when its board voted to abandon an older and much sterner list of "thou shalt nots" that also forbade Wheaton students from dancing. Under the new covenant, for the first time since its founding, students were permitted to dance with impunity off campus and at official school-sponsored events, and faculty, staff, and graduate students were permitted to drink and smoke away from campus.

While the changes irked some Wheaton alums and supporters, they stirred few ripples on campus. In a letter to alumni Litfin asserted that "Wheaton's standards are not weakened; they are strengthened" by the change. The old rules were based more on tradition than the Bible, he said. It was a major change of tune from six years earlier, when Litfin had denounced contemporary social dancing as "very sensual ... the kind of thing that doesn't add to the Christian atmosphere on campus."[11] In the mailing Litfin offered a hint of what may have changed his mind. He noted that a 1991 Illinois law forbids discrimination against employees who engage in otherwise legal activities off the job unless those activities violated a "sincerely held religious belief." By keeping the ban in place the college was subject to lawsuits.[12]

Most students welcomed the lifting of the ban on dancing. And according to one student-body leader, most also favored keeping the campus dry. "That way we don't have to deal with the kinds of issues that plague most other campuses."

There are exceptions, to be sure. Each year some eight to ten students are suspended for breaking the conduct code, and who knows how many more violate the code without getting caught. "For the most part," said Edee Schulze, dean of student life, "those are people who don't really care to be here." She said most students prefer the strict rules, and find the wholesome lifestyle at Wheaton a definite plus.

Another change of no less historic import under Litfin's watch occurred in 2000, when the school retired its old mascot, a Crusader mounted on a rearing horse. The decision, Litfin insisted at the time, was "not about 'political correctness.' I am utterly unmoved by such arguments." Rather, it sprang from the realization that the old mascot "conjures up for significant numbers of people, including some within our own community, troubling images of the historical Crusades"—images that included "Christians massacring Muslims; Muslims massacring Christians; Western Christians killing Eastern Christians, and vice versa," all ostensibly in the name of Christ. It was not exactly in keeping with the school's peaceful purposes.

After due deliberation and careful consideration of over thirteen hundred suggestions, a special committee came up with a new Wheaton mascot: thunder. The new logo would be a bolt of lightning descending from an ominous cloud. Litfin called it an excellent choice. Thunder does, after all, appear in the Bible several times, where it usually is associated with God. And the students thought it would lend itself to some awesome cheers. As one freshman put it at the time: "At games, we can make a lot of noise."[13]

Not every Wheaton grad makes it big in Washington, but many find less visible venues of service. More than half of Wheaton's students spend a semester or more working as interns or volunteers in mission projects or humanitarian relief agencies in the United States and abroad. For some the experience leads to careers in ministry or humanitarian work. But for many others it provides firsthand exposure to issues of poverty and justice. "At Wheaton, they're not just shuttling us off to find a job and make a lot of money," said Caroline Crouch, a political science major from Ocala, Florida. "It's more about finding a vocation and God's calling in your life."

It was a view poignantly expressed in a student prayer at the final chapel of spring. "You are the reason we are here," Christy, a junior from Minneapolis, prayed, her face uplifted, as students throughout the Edman Chapel clapped and shouted, "Amen!" "We want to find you in our studies, in our classes, and in our homework.... I'm grateful I came to Wheaton, because this is where God found me."

# SIX

# Mayan Mission

Guatemala City, Guatemala

The Delta Airlines Boeing 757 descended with a bump into a soupy gray layer of low-lying clouds and heaved about for several uncomfortable seconds before it finally broke into the clear, revealing a first glimpse of the scarred landscape of the Guatemala City outskirts. As the plane banked to make its final approach for landing, the patchwork of emerald foliage and rolling muddy fields below gave way to a hazy sea of corrugated metal rooftops and congested rows of drab concrete and cement-block buildings, some painted in faded pastel yellows or pinks or greens.

From an altitude of a few thousand feet there was nothing visually impressive or inviting about this teeming city of three and a half million people—the capital of a country beset by poverty and crime, and by a painful modern history of violence and corruption. And yet, first impressions aside, I knew it to be a land of contrasts. Beyond the urban squalor of its largest city lay a country roughly the size of Tennessee that was rich in natural beauty—a land of majestic volcanoes and azure mountain lakes, of verdant rain forests and pristine beaches. I had heard Guatemala described as a scenic and cultural jewel in the rough and, after a decade of relative peace since the end of its thirty-six-year civil war, an increasingly popular tourist magnet. More than a million visitors now come here annually, many from the United States, to take in the scenic vistas and to visit the rich archaeological treasures of the ancient Mayan culture.

It also has become a popular destination for American evangelicals, who flock here by the thousands each year, but not as tourists. They come in small groups from places like Myrtle Beach, South Carolina, Sault Ste. Marie, Michigan, and Avon, New York, to work as lay missionaries in the barrios and rural mountain villages on short-term assignments of a week or two. Some come to do humanitarian work—building houses, assisting at medical clinics, or distributing food and clothing to the poor. Others seek to spread the gospel by helping out at vacation Bible schools, summer youth camps, or local churches. And many come to do a little of both.

I had come to Guatemala in the company of one such group, a team of nine men from the First Wesleyan Church in Tuscaloosa, Alabama. Their mission was to build a house in a small Mayan village on Lake Atitlán in the country's western highlands, and, if time permitted, to do additional construction work at a church in an impoverished neighborhood in Guatemala City. While they did not expect to do any direct proselytizing, they were accompanied by the Reverend Luis Martinez, a Wesleyan evangelist originally from Guatemala, who planned on doing some gospel preaching in addition to acting as the team's interpreter. They had permitted me to join them as an observer.

As popular as it is Guatemala is just one destination for short-term missionaries from the United States. Over the past three decades evangelical volunteers numbering in the millions have been dispatched all over Latin America, Africa, Eastern Europe, and elsewhere. It is part of a growing trend that is changing the way many American churches go about the business of spreading the gospel around the world—a task that goes to the very heart of what it means to be an evangelical. I hoped to get a firsthand look at how, and how well, it works.

Missionary outreach across cultures has always been an important part of evangelical ministry. Its modern roots lie in the early missionary journeys of German Lutheran pietists to India in the seventeenth century, in Methodism founder John Wesley's work among Native Americans in Georgia in the eighteenth century, and in the nineteenth-century Asian travels of Baptist missionary William Carey, who is widely considered the father of modern Protestant missions.

But the missionary impulse in Christianity goes back to New Testament times, when Jesus commanded his disciples to "go into all the world and preach the gospel to every creature."[1] It is a command that has motivated Christians in every century and in every tradition to carry the gospel to the next village or town or across continents and oceans. And it is a command that American evangelicals continue to take seriously. Todd Johnson, director of the Center for the Study of Global Christianity at Gordon-Conwell Theological Seminary in South Hamilton, Massachusetts, estimates that of about 448,000 full-time Christian missionaries worldwide, roughly a third are evangelicals.[2] One scholar has estimated that evangelicals make up 90 percent of missionaries from the United States.[3]

Through most of Christian history being a missionary has meant a full-time and often a lifelong commitment. Typically it begins with a divine "call"—people sensing that God has chosen them for such work—and is followed by rigorous religious and cultural training, and an assignment by a denomination or missionary agency to a mission field for a period of years. Often missionaries must raise their own financial support before going abroad. Some support themselves by holding down jobs in the host country. It is not an easy life, to say the least.

And yet, as a vocation and a calling, it has grown remarkably. A century ago, according to Johnson, there were some 62,000 full-time Christian missionaries throughout the world, roughly one missionary for every nine thousand Christians. Today, he says, one Christian in every 4,800 is a full-time missionary. And per capita giving for missions, adjusted for inflation, has grown fourfold in that period of time. While some mainline Protestant denominations have cut back on missionary endeavors since the 1960s, says Johnson, among evangelicals the opposite has occurred. "Fundamentally," he explains, "it exemplifies the very definition of the word 'evangelical' as a people who are committed to spreading the good news. They see it as everyone's job, not just the clergy's."[4]

The rising popularity of short-term missions is a natural extension of that commitment. "Churches today want to be more directly involved," says Johnson. "Many aren't satisfied just sending money. With air travel as inexpensive and relatively easy as it is, ordinary laypeople can have a hands-on experience as missionaries. It is no longer the exclusive domain of professionals."

Yet as one might expect, the upsurge of lay involvement in overseas missions has not been without controversy. Some critics have reasserted the classic critique of Christian missionaries as agents of cultural imperialism who seek to impose Western ideals on indigenous peoples in underdeveloped countries. They see the deployment of zealous but untrained churchgoers on short-term forays into foreign lands as culturally arrogant and potentially destructive. What good can they hope to accomplish, the argument goes, when most don't even speak the language? Advocates of short-term missions, on the other hand, including many of the missionaries themselves, say exposing ordinary Americans to unfamiliar cultures helps to broaden their understanding and respect for cultural diversity, and they come home from their missions with a fresh perspective on the economic and political hardships in other countries. Not to mention the fact that they perform work that helps people in need.

The critique against Christian missions as a tool of Western imperialism probably would have carried more weight a century ago, when nearly all Christian missionaries and 90 percent of the world's Christians were North Americans or Europeans. Today, however, according to Johnson and others, nearly half of the world's missionaries are from Africa, Asia, and Latin America, where 75 percent of the Christian population now resides. As world Christianity's center of gravity has moved steadily south and east during the past century, it has ceased being—if it ever really was—a Western religion. As Philip Jenkins observed in his 2002 book, *The Next Christendom:* "Already today, the largest Christian communities on the planet are to be found in Africa and Latin America. If we want to visualize a 'typical' contemporary Christian, we should think of a woman living in a village in Nigeria or in a Brazilian *favela*."[5]

In coming to Guatemala I hoped to see for myself how all of this plays out on the ground. Traveling with the men from Tuscaloosa and working alongside them for the next several days, I hoped to observe from their actions and their attitudes exactly what is accomplished—for good or for ill—when ordinary evangelicals take up the missionary mantle.

I met my traveling companions for the first time at the airport in Atlanta just a few minutes before boarding the flight to Guatemala, and we had little time to get acquainted. They had flown in from Birmingham about an hour earlier, and had been up since about four that morning, but were in high spirits. When I found them they were standing near the departure gate clustered around Martinez, a handsome dark-haired man in his late forties, who was briefing them on what to expect upon arrival in Guatemala.

"The people in the village, they have been praying for your safe travel, and they are happy that you are coming," he said, with a heavy Spanish accent.

Luis was a full-time evangelist for the Wesleyan Church, an evangelical denomination formed in 1968 through the merger of the Wesleyan Methodist and Pilgrim Holiness churches, and which now has about 225,000 members worldwide. Having grown up in Guatemala as the son of an evangelical preacher, Luis started a Bible school for children in Guatemala City in the mid-1980s that grew to become the country's first and largest Wesleyan congregation. Now a U.S. citizen, he lives with his wife and two daughters in Virginia, but returns to Guatemala several times a year, often with mission teams from the United States, to conduct evangelistic crusades and to help train local Wesleyan pastors.

The team's leader was the Reverend John Vaughan, a soft-spoken man in his early sixties with oval wire-rimmed glasses and a neatly trimmed gray mustache. This would be his fifteenth trip to Guatemala and his thirty-fifth missionary outing overall. One of six assistant pastors at the seven-hundred-member Tuscaloosa church, John—like Luis, he insisted upon being addressed by his first name—had become a minister just eight years earlier, after retiring from a career as an electrical engineer. "I just felt God calling me to go to seminary—I had no idea why," he would explain to me one evening about midway through the week. "Then when he opened the door for this position at the church I already was attending, it just kind of blew me away."

One of John's main duties at the church was overseeing its missions program and helping to raise local financial support for Wesleyan missionaries around the world. He described the congregation as "very missions minded," noting that it supports ten full-time missionaries, and has an annual missions budget of more than $200,000—money that is donated by church members "above and beyond their regular tithe." A portion of the budget goes toward defraying some of the expenses of short-term projects like the

Guatemala trip, which John said have become increasingly popular in the congregation. During the preceding year the church had
sent out four teams—a total of about eighty men, women, and
teenagers—on foreign and domestic mission trips. "The Lord
supplies the money and the people and the worthwhile projects,"
he explained. "We're just thankful to be able to participate in his
work."

It would take me a few days to get to know the rest of the team.
They were ordinary laymen who were accustomed to working
with their hands, and who saw the Guatemala mission as a chance
to contribute something of value to the cause of Christ. As I became better acquainted with each of them I would find that while
they had much in common, they had not signed on for the trip for
exactly the same reasons, nor with the same expectations. Each
would derive something personal from the experience.

Our three-and-a-half-hour flight from Atlanta arrived at Guatemala City's La Aurora International Airport around noon, and
even though our luggage included four big footlockers filled with
tools and equipment, we passed through customs relatively quickly.
Once we were cleared John gathered the team around him in the
middle of the crowded terminal.

"Gentlemen, I'll need your passports," he said. "You won't be
needing them until we leave, and I just want to make sure they're
kept in a safe place." Without hesitating, the men around me began handing over their passports.

This did not strike me as a particularly good idea. My passport
was my ticket home, not to mention a lifeline in the event of trouble. In all my international travels I had never given up control of
my passport, and I was not inclined to do so now. I didn't really
know these guys, and I was not part of their team. I was an embed-
ded journalist. And even though I would be living and traveling
with them, I needed to maintain a degree of independence—as well
as some journalistic boundaries.

On the other hand, I realized that their allowing me to join them had been no small thing. Over the next several days I would be observing them closely and prying into their private lives, asking lots of personal questions about their faith and their families, with the declared intention of writing about it. I would be asking them to open up to a complete stranger. Perhaps I needed to exercise a little trust as well.

John turned to me and held out his hand.

"You take good care of this for me now," I said, as I gave up my passport. I smiled and winked as I said it. I just hoped I wasn't making a huge mistake.

Outside the terminal a white Toyota van and a silver Mazda pickup truck were waiting for us in a snarl of honking traffic. Luis was standing at the curb with a young Guatemalan whom he introduced to us as Tony, an elementary school teacher who had spent several years working in the United States, and who spoke nearly perfect English. Tony would be with us for the entire week and, along with Luis, would serve as a translator.

While it was not uncomfortably warm, the air outside was humid and thick with exhaust fumes and the smell of burning trash. I had read that air pollution was a serious problem in Guatemala, that there were no government controls over vehicle emissions, and that most cooking, especially in poor rural areas, was done over wood fires. Not surprisingly, respiratory ailments were said to be the country's most common illness. I was heartened to know we were about to leave the congested city for what surely would be cleaner and fresher air in the less populated western highlands. We quickly loaded our luggage onto the truck and piled into the van, and we set out for Lake Atitlán with Luis in the driver's seat and Tony following along in the truck.

Heading out of town we passed what looked like a gleaming new sports arena with a blue-and-gray-striped dome perched on a hill overlooking the city. Luis informed us that it was an evangelical church, Fraternidad Cristiana de Guatemala ("Christian Brotherhood of Guatemala"), a ten-thousand-member independent

Pentecostal congregation. It was one of about thirty evangelical megachurches in the country, most of them Pentecostal, and each with at least one thousand members. The largest, Lluvias de Gracia ("Showers of Grace"), had more than twenty-five thousand congregants, according to Luis, and worshiped in a massive stadiumlike building in another part of the city. "The Pentecostal churches have done very well here," he said.

That was an understatement. During the preceding three decades Pentecostal and other evangelical churches had attracted millions of followers in this predominantly Roman Catholic country. With more than a third of its people identifying themselves as born-again Christians, Guatemala had become the most Protestant country in the Spanish-speaking world, and other Latin American nations were not far behind. Brazil, Chile, and Mexico all have large concentrations of evangelicals. In all some sixty-five million people, roughly 12 percent of the Latin American population, now call themselves *evangélicos.*

In part it reflected a burst of missionary activity during the 1960s and 1970s by the Assemblies of God and other Pentecostal and charismatic groups from the United States that had succeeded in launching a vibrant evangelistic movement led by indigenous pastors. In Guatemala it coincided with a massive urban migration that saw Guatemala City's population surge from less than six hundred thousand in 1965 to nearly four million in 2005. New arrivals from the countryside often gravitated to the small storefront churches springing up in the barrios, where they found instant support networks and an exciting style of worship that emphasized ecstatic personal experiences, such as speaking in tongues and receiving the "gifts" of healing and prophecy. Many of those small urban congregations grew to become megachurches.

Among the Maya in the outlying villages where we were headed, Luis explained, evangelical inroads had been more modest. Much of the Mayan population practiced native religions or a syncretistic blend of Roman Catholicism and Mayan spirituality. The Wesleyan Church had focused much of its efforts in recent years on starting new churches in the villages around Lake Atitlán. "Many of the people there have never heard the true gospel of salvation," he said, "and they are hungry for God."

The four-hour drive from Guatemala City to the lake area is a gradual ascent through rolling farmland and terraced hills that rise up between Guatemala's southern coastal plain and its rain forests to the north. We were traveling on the Pan American Highway, the country's main east-west artery, which stretches from El Salvador to the southeast, across the central and western highlands, and on northward into Mexico. In another season the fields and foothills we were passing would have been lush with corn, squash, beans, and other crops worked into neat rows by Mayan farmers whose ancestors have cultivated the land for more than three thousand years. But being near the end of the dry season the fields were mostly brown and empty. In some roadside patches farmers with machetes were busy clearing brush and tossing it into smoky bonfires in preparation for planting.

About forty miles outside of Guatemala City we came upon the outskirts of Chimaltenango, a congested strip of rundown storefronts lining the edge of the highway. "This is a rough town," Luis explained as we sped past. "Much drunkenness and prostitution." Even in the middle of the afternoon the littered sidewalks were crowded with men loitering in front of drinking establishments. A sandwich board out front of one seedy-looking shop advertised *masaje* ("massage") and displayed the painted silhouette of a woman. "These are people who need the Lord," Luis concluded.

We continued to wind our way westward, through tiny villages of cement-block houses and past isolated clusters of mud-brick huts with thatched roofs, and with chickens and goats roaming in and out. Several times along the way traffic on the two-lane asphalt highway slowed to a crawl as smoke-belching trucks loaded with livestock or cement blocks or fifty-five-gallon drums of diesel fuel struggled to climb the steep winding grades. Without warning an impatient driver just ahead of us swerved across the centerline and made a hair-raising dash past two or three vehicles before swerving back, barely avoiding a head-on crash. I looked around our van and saw a couple of the men with their eyes closed. Whether they were praying or napping I couldn't tell. In any case I was thankful to be riding with a group of missionaries.

For those of us who were first-timers in Guatemala, Luis proved to be a helpful and informative tour guide. The country's population of over fourteen million, he explained, was almost evenly divided between the Maya and the Ladinos, those of mixed Mayan and Spanish descent. Ladinos lived mainly in and around the major urban areas, and dominated the country's politics and commerce, while the Maya made up 75 percent of the rural and small-village population. A much smaller group, the Garifuna, or Black Caribs, inhabited the Caribbean lowlands, and were of African descent. Although Spanish is the official language in Guatemala, Luis explained, both the Maya and the Garifuna speak their own traditional languages. Nearly two dozen distinct Mayan dialects are spoken in Guatemala.

Every few miles along the highway we noticed the letters FRG stenciled in blue on roadside boulders or buildings. Luis explained that this was political graffiti left over from the 2003 national election. The initials stood for Frente Republicano Guatemalteco— "Guatemalan Republican Front"—which until the election had been the country's ruling political party. "They were very corrupt," Luis said shaking his head. "*Very* corrupt."

Indeed, the FRG was led by former Guatemalan dictator José Efraín Ríos Montt, one of the most controversial figures in the country's violent history—and an evangelical Christian.

A fierce anticommunist, Ríos Montt had come to power in 1982 in a U.S.-backed military coup that had toppled the country's elected government. Once in power he suspended the constitution, declared himself dictator, and began a brutal campaign to root out leftist dissidents. Although he ruled for less than two years he is accused of presiding over some of the worst atrocities of Guatemala's thirty-six-year civil war—a conflict that left hundreds of thousands dead, most of them Mayan villagers suspected by the government of being leftist sympathizers. In 1999, three years after the war ended, a United Nations–supported "truth commission" documented 626 massacres of civilians and the annihilation of entire villages—men, women, and children—by the Guatemalan army during Ríos Montt's regime, acts characterized by the commission's chairman as genocide against the Mayan population.[6]

Ríos Montt was deposed in a bloodless coup in 1983, and constitutional government eventually was restored. In 1989 he formed the FRG with the intent of running for president, but was blocked from doing so by a constitutional provision barring former coup leaders from the presidency. So he ran for Congress instead and won, and the FRG became Guatemala's ruling party. But the government under the FRG was rife with scandal. Former President Alfonso Antonio Portillo, an FRG party member and Ríos Montt protégé, fled to Mexico when he left office in 2004 to avoid prosecution on charges of embezzlement and money laundering. His vice president and ten other former government officials were jailed on various corruption charges. Meanwhile, drug trafficking and gang-related violence in the country ran almost unchecked by police and military forces who were either unable or unwilling to stop it.

Despite the constitutional ban Ríos Montt ran for president in 2003 after Guatemala's highest court suspended the prohibition, but he came in third in an eleven-man race. Óscar Berger, a Roman Catholic and former mayor of Guatemala City, won a two-man runoff election representing a centrist coalition, the Grand National Alliance. The FRG also lost seats in Congress, and Ríos

Montt was put out of office for the first time in years. No longer protected by official immunity, human rights activists say he too could face criminal prosecution.

Luis was understandably reluctant to discuss his own political views or his personal opinion of Ríos Montt. He still had family living in Guatemala City. And as a preacher, he said, he tries to steer clear of partisan politics. But it was clear that he was disappointed by the corruption under the FRG, and by the association of its evangelical leader with atrocities against the Maya—people the Wesleyan Church now was working hard to reach.

"I don't believe it has hurt us," he would tell me later. "I think that people here understand that as evangelical Christians we are preaching the gospel and the power of God to bring healing to the land. At least, that is how I hope they see us."

It was after four o'clock when we pulled off the main highway and onto a narrow winding road to make the final ascent of the hills immediately surrounding Lake Atitlán. The sky was overcast, and as we slowly climbed the steep zigzag route a cool mist enveloped us and dampened the asphalt pavement.

About midway to the top we rounded a hairpin turn and encountered a battered pickup truck barreling toward us with its brakes howling with the shrill sound of metal against metal. Luis swerved to a stop on the narrow dirt shoulder and let the vehicle pass. It was just then that I realized there were no guardrails on this stretch of road, and that in some spots there wasn't much of a shoulder separating the road from a sharp drop-off. I recalled reading a few weeks earlier that twenty-one members of a local evangelical church were killed when their bus tumbled into a ravine after colliding with another vehicle on a mountain road not far from here. Seeing the condition of this road, I was amazed that it didn't happen more often. At least it was reassuring to know that Luis was accustomed to driving this route, and that he was taking precautions. I decided that a little silent prayer probably wouldn't hurt.

After a few more tense minutes of careful climbing we were rewarded with our first glimpse of what the British novelist Aldous Huxley is reputed to have pronounced "the most beautiful lake in the world." Even on a cloudy day the azure waters of Lake Atitlán glistened against the deep-green backdrop of three nearly perfectly shaped volcanoes that rose abruptly from the shoreline and towered over a string of Mayan villages in the distance. The 50-square-mile lake was itself an immense volcanic crater formed by a violent eruption some 84,000 years ago that was flooded by underground aquifers to a depth of more than 1,500 feet. It was Central America's deepest lake, and undoubtedly its most picturesque. One could easily understand why Huxley was so impressed by it.

Our steep descent toward the lake was even more nerve-racking than the climb. But as the road leveled out, we passed quickly through the villages of San Lucas and Santiago, and finally arrived at our destination, San Pedro.

The village of San Pedro sits on the water's edge at the foot of a volcano on the lake's western shore. With a population of about five thousand it is one of the larger of the dozen or so Mayan villages that ring the lake. And while many of its inhabitants labor in nearby coffee and vegetable fields or fish the teeming waters from dugout *cayucos*, the village thrives on the tourist trade. Its scenic waterfront is dominated by hotels, pubs, and restaurants that cater to a North American and European clientele, many of them young backpackers.

In the center of the village a white Spanish colonial-style Catholic church sits in a plaza ringed by souvenir shops and produce stalls. As we wound our way along the narrow cobblestone streets we noticed religious slogans—"Cristo Viene," "Dios Ti Ama," "Jesus La Unica Solucion"—neatly painted on several shops and other buildings that did not appear to be churches. "These are evangelical slogans placed there by local Christians," Luis explained.

"It is a way of expressing their faith. There are many evangelical Christians in San Pedro, and they are spreading the gospel."

We arrived at the Hotel Mansion del Lago and pulled into a neatly landscaped courtyard surrounded by a wrought-iron fence covered in deep red bougainvillea. This would be our home for the next few days. The four-story walk-up hotel was clean, but the accommodations were definitely spartan. Each room had two cot-size twin beds and a small water closet, and a shower with an electric water heater at the showerhead. Noticing the exposed electrical wires connected to the heater, I immediately decided that my showers for the week would be cold and refreshing.

John had assigned each of us roommates. I was paired with Morgan Spiller, a thirty-nine-year-old fireman who was on his first mission trip. We quickly settled into our rooms, and then reassembled downstairs for dinner.

Our meals throughout the week would be prepared by women from the Wesleyan church in Guatemala City, who had been hired to be our cooks. Each meal was a combination of Guatemalan and American dishes and was served in a small open-air dining room on the ground floor.

After a satisfying dinner of hot dogs, corn tortillas, black beans and rice, and sliced pineapple, we lounged around the hotel for the rest of the evening. Most of us turned in early, hoping to be well rested for the next day's work. But that was not to be. At about ten o'clock salsa music began blaring from a bar across the street and continued until well after midnight. Then a pack of barking dogs took over, and they kept up a pretty steady ruckus until their shift ended around four in the morning, when it was the roosters' turn. The wake-up knock on the door came at six.

Each morning of the trip, shortly after sunrise and before breakfast, the men assembled for devotions—a time of Bible reading and prayer together before heading out to work. John explained to me that one of his hopes for the week was that the men would "draw closer to the Lord and to each other." Morning devotions were to be an important component of that effort. Each man had been given a copy of a pocket-size devotional booklet entitled *A Heart Like Jesus,* by Max Lucado, a popular evangelical author and Texas pastor. Several would take a turn during the week leading the devotional time.

On the first morning the men gathered around the dining room table, and Dick Kienitz, a retired shipping executive and a lay leader at the Tuscaloosa church, led a brief discussion on the importance of having "a forgiving heart." The teaching was based on Colossians 3:13. ("Be gentle and ready to forgive; never hold grudges. Remember, the Lord forgave you, so you must forgive others.") Forgiveness, Kienitz said, "doesn't come naturally for us humans. Our ego tends to get in the way." It was "only through the power of Christ and by following his example," he said, that Christians could humble themselves enough "to be able to forgive someone who has wronged us."

After spending a few more minutes summarizing Lucado's thoughts on the subject, Kienitz shifted gears.

"I'd like us to go around the table," he said. "You don't have to make a speech, but in a phrase or two, tell us why you are here. Why did you come on this trip?

"Who wants to go first? OK, Bill."

Bill Sadberry was a man of few words. For the retired postal worker on his third mission in Guatemala, the reason for coming was quite simple. "I just feel like the Lord led us here," he said. Several others nodded in agreement.

Sitting next to Bill was Al Straiton, a plumbing contractor on his fourth mission trip. A stocky man with silver hair, Al shared that he had undergone quintuple bypass surgery a few years earlier, and that the doctors had told him they weren't sure he would survive the operation. "If it wasn't for the Lord, I don't believe I'd be here today," he said. "But I firmly believe he spared my life so as I could do some good in the world, and I think this is good what we're doing here."

Next up was Kurt Kienitz, Dick's son. A marine-terminal supervisor from western Tennessee, he was the only non-Alabaman on the team. This was his second mission trip. "I came here to be with you," he said to his dad, flashing a mischievous smile. "I also wanted to get away from the rest of the world for a week, to just step back and shut it all off and focus on helping others."

Kurt, I would discover, tended to be the most outspoken of the group. Although he was always good-natured about it, he didn't hesitate to express a differing viewpoint during devotions or other discussions. He confided to me later that while he takes his Christian faith seriously, he does not consider himself an evangelical like the rest of the men, and that he has some difficulty with organized religion in general. "People who make up rules or interpret the Bible and say, 'Unless you abide by our rules and interpretations you're not going to heaven,' well, I just don't buy that," he explained. But he appreciated the Tuscaloosa team's commitment to helping others, and that was what had brought him back a second time. "To me that's what being a Christian is really about."

Morgan, my roommate, spoke up next. "I appreciate the support y'all have been giving me," he began somberly. "Yesterday coming up here from the airport, I was really struggling. I was questioning why I came and whether I should even be here with y'all. I dealt with it the whole way. But after I got here I went up to the room and I realized it was spiritual warfare. I was under attack, and I just had to claim the power of Jesus over it. And when I did, it's like it just turned on the light switch, and I got the feeling back that I had before—the spirit of anticipation of seeing these people the way Jesus sees 'em, and just being here to help somebody out. That's the main reason I came here—to help somebody out. But I do appreciate your being there for me yesterday. I feel a whole lot better today."

"That's great," John responded, from across the table.

The next speaker was Larry Miles, a recently retired carpenter with a walrus mustache who, next to John, was the most traveled of the group. This was his seventh trip to Guatemala. "The Lord has given me the gift of being able to work with my hands," he said. "I just thank him for that, and for the opportunity to come here and use those gifts for him." John later would describe Larry as probably the most talented member of the team in terms of construction skills. "The Bible says that when King Solomon built the temple, God provided him with craftsmen," John explained. "Well, Larry is our craftsman. It's amazing what he can do."

Scott Roland, a truck driver, was back for a second time, and had brought along his fifteen-year-old son, Tyler. "When I came here last year to help out, I really felt blessed," he said. "It was overwhelming. I believe it did more for me than for the people we were helping. During the past year, though, I kind of lost touch with what I experienced here, and I just want to regain that. I brought my son this time, and I think it will be a good experience for both of us."

Scott would turn out to be the most tenderhearted of the group. His eyes welled up on a couple of occasions when he spoke about his children, his divorce three years earlier, and how he struggles sometimes to be the kind of Christian he aspires to be. "Last year when I was here," he told me one day, expanding on what he had said that first morning, "I felt like I was closer to the Lord than I've ever been. Since then I feel like I've gotten off the path, and I just need to get back on it." He said he and his ex-wife had begun talking about reconciling, and were thinking of seeing a counselor. "If we're going to make that happen," he said, "I feel like I need to get right spiritually. I also want to have a little bonding time with my son. We're not real close, unfortunately. He didn't want to come, but now that he's here I think he's enjoying it. So hopefully, when we get back I'll be in the right frame of mind, and all these things will come together." He obviously had a lot riding on this one-week trip.

John picked up on Scott's opening comment. "A number of years ago, after I'd been here a few times," he said, "I realized that the real reason I came here was that I needed these people here to help me grow. And then it turned out that I needed each of you to help me grow. It gives me a lot of encouragement just watching y'all and seeing your commitment to serving the Lord."

Breakfast was about to be served, so Dick wrapped up the discussion. "When I look at this group," he said, looking around the table, "I see us as being a lot like Barnabas." He was referring to a figure in the New Testament, a member of the church in Jerusalem who is described as playing a supporting role to the Apostle Paul on his early missionary journeys. "None of us are superstars. We're not going to be out there putting on evangelistic crusades. But we're being obedient. We're doing God's will, and God will bless us as we do that." He said a closing prayer, thanking God for "the privilege to serve," and asking God's protection over the team as it began its work.

It was clear that these men felt good about the job they believed God had sent them to do. As Dick had observed, they did not see themselves as gifted teachers or communicators. They were average workingmen, perhaps a little rough-hewn. Yet in coming here they believed they were responding to the biblical mandate to spread the gospel, not by preaching or proselytizing, but by putting feet to their faith and serving others in the name of Christ as best they knew how.

I was thoroughly familiar with the kind of therapeutic soul-baring I had witnessed around the table, and would continue to see throughout the week. It is common practice in evangelical small-group gatherings to give a public accounting of one's personal standing with the Lord or to report, as Morgan had, on some faith-challenging situation that was confronted and conquered with God's help. The point in telling these stories, generally, is to affirm one another's faith by providing testimonial evidence of God's faithfulness. In some respects it reflects the same dynamic that goes on in any support-group setting where people are encouraged to share openly about their personal struggles and successes. Sometimes it tends to get a bit melodramatic.

Yet in this group the discussions during morning devotions revealed a level of trust that the men appeared to have for one another as fellow believers—that they could ask for and offer prayer or a word of encouragement without fear of being branded a weakling or, even worse, a doubter. For them it was a way of building faith accountability, of drawing closer to God and to one another, just as John had hoped they would.

After a hardy breakfast of eggs, corn pancakes, and fresh fruit the men loaded their tool chests onto the truck and piled into the van and headed for the village of San Pablo about six miles away.

Shortly before eight in the morning the narrow asphalt road that winds above the lake was busy with foot traffic—groups of women in colorful Mayan dress carrying bundles of sticks or baskets of vegetables on their heads, men on their way to the coffee fields with hoes or machetes slung over their shoulders. Occasionally we would pass a battered pickup truck retrofitted with rusty handrails and loaded with passengers heading in the opposite direction. These, Luis told us, were the local buses that shuttle people from the smaller villages to jobs in San Pedro or in nearby Santiago for a fare of about three *quetzales,* or roughly forty cents, each way. It is considered relatively expensive and many people simply choose to walk.

The village of San Pablo sits back from the lake on a broad sloping plain, surrounded on three sides by rugged hills and terraced coffee fields. Like most villages in the area it is a warren of adobe and cement-block houses, simple squat structures with rusty metal roofs lining narrow cobblestone streets. A few commercial buildings made of block or reinforced concrete rise up two or three stories. But there is relatively little commerce here; San Pablo is one of the poorest villages on the lake. Most of its inhabitants are Tz'utujil Maya, one of twenty-one distinct Mayan ethnic groups in Guatemala. Many of the men work on nearby farms, or *fincas*, tending corn and coffee crops for subsistence wages while the women work tiny garden plots, if they are fortunate enough to have them, or spend their days scavenging for firewood, crocheting souvenir craft items to sell to tourists, and caring for small children.

Our van pulled up in front of a row of adobe buildings and parked next to several pallets of fresh cement blocks and sheets of shiny corrugated metal stacked neatly on the edge of the street. In the next two and a half days we would use the material to craft a modest one-room house for a young Mayan family.

The project, as Luis explained it, was part of an ongoing construction program coordinated by local Wesleyan pastors to provide homes for needy families in the villages around the lake. Originally, he said, they were called "widow's houses" because most of the early recipients were women whose husbands had been slain by government death squads during the Guatemalan civil war. The houses each cost about $1,200 to build with volunteer labor, and were given away free and clear. Recipients, he said, were selected by the pastors on the basis of need. The only requirement was that they owned the property on which the house was to be constructed. So far, Luis said, about sixty-five homes had been built and given away with materials and labor donated by American mission teams.

I asked Luis what strings were attached. Surely there had to be some. Were the recipients required to attend one of the Wesleyan churches in the area in order to be selected?

"Most do attend the churches, but it is not necessary," he said. "Anyone may apply." Nor, he insisted, were they under any obligation to the churches afterward.

While that may have been the case officially and legally, I told him it was difficult to imagine someone receiving a free house, compliments of the Wesleyan Church, and not feeling substantially indebted. It seemed unavoidable, even if left unspoken, that people would assume there was a quid pro quo.

"Of course, the people are very grateful," he said. "But that is not why we do this. It is not about evangelism. It is about compassion. It is about caring for people in need, and doing it in the name of Jesus Christ, not just to get them to come to church."

Luis had a point. If evangelism had been the main objective, there certainly were more efficient and less expensive ways to go about making converts. From a strictly financial standpoint the Wesleyan Church would never recoup its investment in a house from whatever meager amounts a poor widow or a subsistence farmer might be expected to drop into the offering plate in a lifetime.

Still, even if the program was not designed primarily to attract loyal church members, my guess was that it had that ancillary effect, and that the Guatemalan pastors knew it and encouraged it. It is not exactly surprising, after all, that people would be attracted by acts of kindness and generosity. And yet even if there was such a calculation—if there was, in fact, an ulterior motive behind their benevolence—it did not strike me as a self-serving one. The Guatemalan pastors and the American missionaries were trying to address needs that otherwise would not be met. That, it seemed to me, was the bottom line.

The tiny plot of ground where we would be working was invisible from the street. To reach it we had to climb a narrow alleyway between two adobe houses to a small dirt courtyard in the rear. There, off to one side, concrete footings already had been poured and a row of cement blocks had been set, forming a twelve-by-thirteen-foot rectangle, the foundation of what would be a very modest house indeed.

A young Mayan man wearing a New York Yankees baseball cap who looked to be in his early twenties was busy in a corner of the yard, mixing a batch of mortar, and he barely looked up as the Americans filed in and inspected the foundation.

"How many people are going to live in this thing?" Kurt asked no one in particular, as he stepped inside the rectangle.

"Three is what I was told," John replied, "a husband and wife and their baby. Compared to where they're living now this will be a palace, believe me."

The team immediately got down to work. Some of us started hauling material from the street, while others broke out trowels and mortar buckets and began the tedious process of building the walls block by block. While none of the men were professional masons, several had done enough of this kind of work on previous trips that they had become quite adept at it. Kurt and Larry took the lead, setting blocks on each corner and using stretched string and plumb lines to make sure the walls lined up straight and true. The young Mayan man—we learned that his name was Diego— also seemed to know what he was doing. After standing back and watching the Americans work for a while, he jumped in and started laying block, occasionally using hand gestures to instruct his co-workers to make sure the rows were properly aligned.

Communicating with the locals posed a bit of a problem through-out the week. None of the Americans except Luis spoke Spanish, and few Guatemalans we encountered spoke English. But as long as either Luis or Tony was around to interpret, usually we were able to get along without too much difficulty. In San Pablo, how-ever, it was a different matter. As in most of the villages around the lake, the people spoke the Tz'utujil language—a guttural-sounding dialect with lots of clicks and glottal stops. Even though Spanish is the country's official tongue, and public schools teach it to Mayan children beginning at age six, few adult villagers use it or seem to understand it, and neither Luis nor Tony spoke Tz'utujil.

Fortunately, starting on the second day, we were joined at the work site by a Mayan pastor from the Wesleyan church in nearby San Marcos. His name was Chepé, and while he mainly spoke

Tz'utujil, he knew enough Spanish to get by. From that point on verbal communication between the Americans and the Maya was able to proceed, albeit circuitously, through both Tony or Luis and Chepé, from English to Spanish to Tz'utujil and back.

We had not been at the site long before an audience began to gather. Small children from neighboring houses peeked furtively into the courtyard through open doorways, and several ventured in and sat in the dirt to watch the workers. Soon they were joined by a group of women, who appeared to be a mother and her three teenage or young-adult daughters. All were dressed in similarly colored long woven skirts and lacey blouses. One carried an infant in blue pajamas. They stood off to the side, carefully scrutinizing the work and whispering to one another in Tz'utujil. Trying to be friendly, one of the Americans called out, "Buenos días, señorita!" But it only elicited a giggle from the younger women.

The work that first morning seemed to progress well, although with nine men working in a confined space, just avoiding bumping into each other sometimes became a challenge. By noon the walls were more than a third complete, and as we broke to head back to the hotel for lunch, Larry predicted that we'd finish the job the following day—a day earlier than planned.

After lunch the work continued apace. By midafternoon the top of the window and two doorway openings were about to be enclosed, and the men were in a jocular mood. Larry, working from a platform inside the house, looked down and noticed that two of the young Mayan women seemed to be paying close attention to fifteen-year-old Tyler, a shy mop-haired lad who was busy pointing mortar joints on the outside walls. "Hey there, Tyler," he called out. "Looks like you got yourself a fan club. Boy, we may just get you married off before we leave here." The men laughed, and Tyler blushed. Everyone was in high spirits. But that was about to change.

About three in the afternoon a Guatemalan man in a short-sleeve white shirt and khaki work pants showed up and began measuring the walls and checking their alignment. He climbed up on one wall, took a quick look down, and called out something in Tz'utujil. His gestures made it clear that he wanted the work to stop.

The men put down their tools and backed away from the house. "What's going on?" Bill asked. Kurt shrugged and leaned back against a post, waiting to see what would happen next. "Must be he's the building inspector," he said.

Neither Luis nor Tony were around at the moment, and even if they had been it was unlikely they could have communicated with the man who still was atop the wall and had begun pulling down blocks and dropping them to the ground. The Americans were not happy. A few rolled their eyes and began to grumble.

John stepped up and faced his teammates. "Men, this isn't about us," he said in a calm voice. The man on the wall was loosening more blocks and resetting them in different positions.

"But we've got to finish this tomorrow," Larry insisted.

"We don't *have* to finish tomorrow. Remember, we're here to serve these people. If it doesn't happen tomorrow, it'll happen the next day."

Just at that moment Tony arrived, and John explained to him what had happened. Tony went over to the man on the wall, and the two began talking in Spanish. He listened and nodded as the man pointed at the top layer of blocks. Then he called John over and the three of them talked for a few more minutes.

John waved the rest of the men over and explained that the man was the *maestro* who had been assigned by the local pastors to supervise the project. The *maestro* had pointed out that in order to make the house earthquake resistant—apparently a requirement for new construction—the layer of blocks lining the top of the window and doors needed to be hollowed out and filled with steel-reinforced concrete, forming a horizontal brace that would connect with vertical reinforced columns inside the corners and at other points in the wall. The men had been filling in those vertical columns as they went along, but apparently had not been aware of the need for the horizontal brace. The blocks the *maestro* had removed were part of the layer that needed to be reinforced.

It made perfect sense, and now that the men understood what was needed they were happy to oblige. The *maestro* took a machete and demonstrated how to hollow out a block by hacking at its inside partitions, turning it into a U shape. He smiled and handed the machete to Larry. "*Muchas gracias,* señor," Larry said, and he laughed as he shook the *maestro*'s hand.

The mood lifted, and the men went back to work. Everyone seemed relieved that a tense moment had passed without anyone losing his religion.


The next day work at the house went smoothly and quickly. Chepé, the pastor from San Marcos, was *maestro* for the day, and he and Diego worked together, checking to make sure the last few layers of blocks were set straight and plumb. By early afternoon the final sections of the metal roof had been fastened into place, and the house was finished.

The men stood back and admired their work. It was solid and very simple—one rectangular room about the size of a child's bedroom in a typical middle-class American house, with two doorway openings and one uncovered window, a dirt floor, a bare electrical lightbulb attached to an exposed wooden rafter, and a slanted metal roof that overhung the lower wall by about three feet. Presumably, that was where the family would do its cooking. It was just a few feet away from a partially enclosed concrete latrine in the corner of the courtyard that apparently served several of the adjoining houses. It certainly didn't look like much. But for a small family that currently was living in a rented mud-brick hovel somewhere on the edge of the village, it probably would be, as John had suggested, a considerable improvement.

Dick Kienitz asked Tony, our interpreter, if we were going to meet the family who would be moving into the house. Tony posed the question in Spanish to Chepé, who smiled and put a hand on Diego's shoulder. Chepé called over one of the young women who had been watching the construction for the past two days and introduced her to Tony.

"The house belongs to Diego," Tony relayed to the Americans, "and to his wife, Rosario." The men applauded, and Rosario, who looked to be about eighteen, blushed and smiled nervously while Diego stood expressionless. Now we understood why Diego had been working on the house so conscientiously—we had assumed he was the *maestro*'s helper—and why the women had been such avid spectators. The older woman was Diego's mother and one of the other younger women was his sister. They lived in one of the adjoining adobe houses. Diego's father, who worked at a nearby coffee farm, had given his son the patch of land.

Through Tony, Chepé explained that Diego and Rosario and their three-year-old son were part of his Wesleyan congregation in San Marcos, the next village over. Diego also worked in the coffee fields, and most of his wages went to pay the monthly rent. Diego spoke to Chepé in Tz'utujil. "He says they are very happy to have this house," Chepé said. "And they are very thankful that you came here."

The men snapped pictures of the young couple, and of themselves posing in front of the house. Then they packed their tools and cleaned up the site, and as they prepared to leave, John called them together.

"Gentlemen," he said, "I also want to thank you for coming. It was a miracle what you accomplished here in two days, and I believe God is going to bless you for it. Before we leave I'd like us to have a word of prayer together." The men took off their hats and bowed their heads.

"Father," John began to pray, "you have said that unless you build a house, then the house is built in vain. Lord, we thank you for what you have done here this week. We ask you to bless this little house as a testimony of your kingdom, that your church in this area will grow, and that more and more people will come to know you because of this little house and others like it. We thank you, Lord, for this family. Bless them, and guard and protect them. Lord, we just thank you for the privilege of being here and for using us in a tiny way to grow your kingdom. We pray all of this in your precious name."

That evening back in San Pedro a slight chill breeze sent wisps of low clouds gliding over the lake and brushing against the tops of the volcanoes, a reminder that the rainy season was fast approaching. It was our last evening at Lake Atitlán. In the morning we would travel by boat to the town of Panajachel, a popular tourist destination with a large outdoor market, before driving back to Guatemala City for a few days of work at the Wesleyan church there.

After dinner at the hotel several of the men retreated to the card table for a final game of spades, while a few others set out on a leisurely stroll of nearby shops in search of ice cream bars and souvenirs. I was headed for my room to pack when I noticed an attractive young blond woman whom I hadn't seen before sitting in a lounge chair on the hotel balcony smoking a cigarette and reading a paperback novel. She appeared to be an American or a European in her late twenties or early thirties, and as I walked past we exchanged greetings, and I stopped and we introduced ourselves.

Her name was Shannon Baines, and she was a Canadian, from the town of Nanaimo on Vancouver Island, British Columbia. She had come to San Pedro for a few days of relaxation before starting a job in Quetzaltenango, Guatemala's second-largest city, about three hours away. She would be working on the staff of Habitat for Humanity, the Georgia-based international charity made famous by former President Carter's frequent work as a Habitat volunteer, building houses for the poor.

I told her about the team from Alabama and the work they had just completed, and remarked that she and they were in the same business. But I was curious to learn how similar her motives and methods and those of the Wesleyan missionaries really were. I asked how she happened to find her way to Habitat.

"I came to Guatemala four years ago on vacation and just fell in love with the place," she explained, "and I decided I wanted to come back and do something to help the people in any way I could." So she had quit her job as a graphic designer, sold her house and most of her belongings, left her parents and friends behind, and moved to Guatemala to look for work with a nonprofit organization. "I had nothing lined up before I arrived," she said. "Once I got here I met a woman who works for Habitat, and she told me they had an opening. So I applied and I got the job."

For a small salary she would be helping to coordinate Habitat volunteers coming into Guatemala from other countries, arranging for their travel and accommodations inside the country, and helping them adjust to the local culture. Like the Wesleyans, she said, Habitat relies on volunteer labor, and many of its workers are from church groups, although some have no religious affiliation. "People want to help others for a variety of reasons," she said, "and Habitat welcomes them all."

Unlike the Wesleyans, she said, Habitat does not give houses away. "We believe in giving a hand up, not a handout," she said. The typical Habitat house in Guatemala, she explained, was made of cement block, and it had four rooms plus a bathroom and a concrete floor, and was sold at cost for about twenty-eight hundred dollars with a six-year no-interest loan. That amounted to payments of less than forty dollars per month—"which is very affordable in Guatemala."

I asked whether her own motivation for coming to work in Guatemala had been religiously inspired.

"I am not really a religious person," she said, "although I am very spiritual. I was raised Catholic, and I do believe in God, but I practice my own sort of faith. But yes, very definitely, that is why I am here. I feel that I have a purpose to fulfill, and I want to be of service. I'm not doing it for the money. I'm doing it for my soul."

She also was planning to be in it for the long haul. "I am here indefinitely," she said, adding that one day she hopes to establish permanent legal residency. In the meantime she would be living in a rented room in a small hotel in Quetzaltenango with a shared bath and kitchen, not exactly the creature comforts she was accustomed to at home. "I'll go back to Nanaimo to visit friends and family every now and then," she said. "But this is where I want to be. This is my home now."

We left the hotel late the next morning, loaded our luggage onto the truck, and boarded a boat for Panajachel, where we spent a couple of hours shopping for souvenirs before heading back to Guatemala City. By the time we arrived it was late afternoon. We checked into a dormitory in an affluent gated neighborhood not far from the University of San Carlos, Guatemala, and drove over to the Wesleyan church for a quick look around.

The Adonai Iglesia Evangelica Wesleyana is a congregation of about 350 people who worship in a spacious white concrete building in a poor neighborhood just south of the city. It sits at the foot of a steep hill that is covered by a sprawling slum of metal and mud-brick shanties that sprang up in the aftermath of Hurricane Mitch in 1998. Many of the families attending the church live in the slum or in modest apartments within a short walking distance.

The church's pastor was the Reverend Carlos Rivas, who also served as the denomination's district superintendent for Guatemala, an administrative and supervisory position comparable to that of a bishop. Pastor Carlos and his wife, Delmi, had been at the church for seven years. This was the congregation that Luis had started as a Bible school for children in the mid-1980s. Through the children he began evangelizing the parents, and soon a Wesleyan congregation was born. It was the first of nine Wesleyan churches in Guatemala—the others all were in the lake area.

The church building consisted of two conjoined structures, a plain rectangular building that might easily have passed for a warehouse and a larger, more ornate building with a high-pitched metal roof and a decorative blue-tiled turret and blue-tinted windows. The men from Tuscaloosa and other American mission teams had done much of the original construction; a year earlier they had installed lighting in the new sanctuary. Starting in the morning they would do a number of odd jobs: painting, installing some interior partitions, and building and painting furniture for the pastor's office.

The work on Saturday went smoothly, with Larry designing and cutting wood panels that others assembled into a desk, two tables, and three bookcases. After taking a break on Sunday they would return on Monday to finish up the furniture and to enclose and paint the pastor's outer office.

The Sunday morning service at Adonai was lively and well attended, with lots of neatly dressed children and young families filling the freshly painted blue wooden pews. A worship band consisting of five young vocalists, an electric guitarist, a drummer, and Tony playing an electric keyboard, led a medley of upbeat hand-clapping choruses. The Americans recognized a couple of the tunes and sang along in English. Except for the language difference, it was identical to the contemporary-praise style of worship that has become standard in evangelical churches in the United States. Luis preached the sermon, and when he gave an altar call at the end of the service about a dozen people went forward and knelt in front of the platform. Pastor Carlos and Luis prayed with each one.

After the service Delmi, the pastor's wife, pulled the Americans aside and spoke to them through Tony. "Today we caught a very big fish," she said in Spanish. She explained that one of the men who had gone forward was a notorious gang leader who had relatives in the church. "We have been praying for him for a very long time."

The man, whose name also was Carlos, had told the pastor that a week earlier a member of his gang and a close friend was shot and killed by police. A few days later two more gang members were killed by a rival gang. "And now," she said, "he believes he will be next. He told the pastor that he wanted to accept Jesus so that when he dies he will go to heaven. And so today this very tough criminal knelt at the altar and accepted Jesus as his savior. We are praising God for this answer to prayer. Please continue to pray for him, that God will truly change his heart."

That afternoon the men went sightseeing in the old capital city of Antigua, a collection of quaint shops and restaurants and Spanish colonial ruins at the foot of the Volcán de Agua just a few miles west of Guatemala City. It is one of the most popular tourist destinations in central Guatemala, and on a sunny Sunday afternoon its streets and market stalls were crowded. At least two other American missionary teams were in town. Both were wearing team T-shirts with their churches' names emblazoned on the front. (I made a mental note to thank John for not requiring uniforms for his team.)

I spoke briefly with the leader of a team from an Assemblies of God church in St. Louis that had been working at a youth camp near the Pacific Coast. "Our guys have been working hard, and they deserve the R & R," he explained, as we stood outside a leather goods stall in the center of the market. "It would be a little disappointing, after all, to come all this way and not see anything outside the camp." As leader, he said, he usually tries to work in at least two days of touring in a weeklong mission. That was approximately what our work-to-play ratio had been. It seemed we all were doing our part to support the local economy.

✝

On Monday the team finished its work at the church and spent a quiet evening packing and preparing for the trip home. The week had gone by quickly, but everyone was ready for it to be over.

On Tuesday morning, before heading to the airport, the men gathered in the dormitory lounge for one last time of devotions. John read a passage from the Gospel of John, the story of Jesus walking on water, and suggested that "miracles still happen when Jesus comes into a situation—when we are willing to invite him into our lives." He ended by recounting a story about King David in the Old Testament book of Second Samuel.

"You know, King David was the king of Israel, and he had most everything he could ever want. One day a man tried to give the king a plot of land so he could build an altar on it—the king needed to make a sacrifice to the Lord—and he told the king, 'You don't have to pay for this. I'll just give it to ya.' Well, King David said, 'I don't ever want to give anything to the Lord that doesn't cost me something.'

"Boy, that was profound right there. 'I don't want to give anything to the Lord that doesn't cost me something.'

"This week has cost y'all and me something. There have been lots of sacrifices made, and we can start naming them: from leaving family, to giving up your vacation time, to living somewhere where you normally wouldn't go—all sorts of things. Giving up your passports," he looked straight at me, "for y'all to give that up and say, 'I'm not worried about it,' I think that's an act of faith right there. I could go on and on.

"I just appreciate y'all's willingness to give to the Lord what cost you something. Not only to give to him but to Diego and his wife. That little wife lives in a culture where women don't say much. I bet if we could have gotten her somewhere where she could have told us what she really felt, she would have had a lot to say about what y'all did. You made a real difference in their lives. So thanks very much, guys.

"And we thank you, Lord," he bowed his head, "for all that you've done this week. You've performed miracles around us, and we are grateful. We thank you for drawing us close to you and to each other. When we get home, help us to depend on you as much as we have this week. In everything we do, may we trust you and lean on you and invite you to continue to work miracles in our lives. Lord, we need you. We can't do anything without you. We ask that you'll continue to bless the people we have met here this week. We pray all of this in your strong name. Amen."

It is perfectly legitimate, I think, to question the worth of short-term mission trips.

A few years back a friend of mine who recently had returned from a ten-day mission in Moldova in the former Soviet Union shared with me how he had come home with serious second thoughts about whether short-term missions made sense. He had been part of a team of Presbyterian laymen doing light construction work and helping with a children's Bible school at an evangelical church in the capital city of Chisinau. He said he had enjoyed the work and had felt at the time that the team was having a positive impact.

But late in the trip, over lunch in the church fellowship hall, a lay leader of the Moldovan congregation made a disturbing comment that he said challenged his thinking. "We do appreciate the work you and the others are doing," the elderly man told him. "But you know, if you were to add up what all of you spent on airfares to come here, if you had just sent us the money we could have accomplished so much more."

The man had intended no malice, "and of course he was right," my friend said. "After all, it wasn't as if people in Moldova don't know how to use a hammer and saw. And how helpful were we really sitting in a Bible school classroom with kids whose language we didn't speak? Maybe it would have made more sense to have sent the money. The same work would have been accomplished and a few unemployed Moldovan carpenters would have had jobs."

A similar thought had occurred to me as I watched the Americans bumping into each other at the work site in San Pablo. Chepé and Diego seemed more adept at laying cement block than most of the rest of us, and probably could have worked more efficiently on their own, or at least with fewer of us around. Why *not* just send money and pay locals to do the work? If the object was to provide low-cost housing for needy families, why not multiply the effort with an additional infusion of cash?

My friend's pondering of the situation hadn't stopped there. "Then I began to think about my teammates," he continued. "Like me, for many of them the trip to Moldova had been a first-time experience. Before the trip most of us hadn't thought all that much about missions, and probably hadn't been particularly enthusiastic or consistent in terms of financial support. But going to Moldova changed that. Suddenly we were sold on missions and probably will remain so for the rest of our lives. I don't think that would have happened had we not gone on a mission trip ourselves. It made believers out of us, and earnest givers."

And that, it seemed to me, was the point. It was not a matter of whether money raised for short-term mission trips could be spent better, but whether it would have been raised at all absent the motivation of a personal missionary experience. Clearly there were more efficient ways of delivering humanitarian services, or of promoting economic development, or of spreading the Christian message than by sending in untrained teams of laymen for a week or two. But whatever good they did accomplish on the ground, it was accompanied by the transformation of millions of lay missionaries into faithful long-term supporters of Christian missions. Whether designed that way or not, the trips turned out to be as much for the benefit of the missionaries as for the people they were sent to help. In the end both gained something from the encounter.

The Americans had every right to go home feeling good about themselves and what they had accomplished in a week's time. They had worked tirelessly and in a spirit of self-sacrifice, believing that by serving others they were serving their God. In the process they had made life a little better for a poor young family they probably would never see again.

As we left for the airport I couldn't help thinking of the young woman from Canada whose work in Guatemala was just beginning. She did not consider herself conventionally religious, and her eclectic brand of spirituality probably would not be accepted by most evangelicals as measuring up to biblical standards. Yet if anyone had sacrificed to serve others it was she. Knowingly or not, she was following almost to the letter the instruction Jesus gave to the rich young ruler in the Gospel of Luke who asked what he must do to inherit eternal life: Sell everything you own, give to the poor, and follow me.

## CHAPTER POSTSCRIPT

During the first week of October 2005, just six months after the trip, Hurricane Stan ripped into the Yucatán Peninsula and lashed Guatemala with torrential rains, unleashing deadly mud slides around Lake Atitlán. Thousands of villagers were buried alive, and many thousands more lost their homes. Hardest hit was the Mayan village of Panabaj, at the foot of the Toliman volcano not far from San Pedro, where an estimated fourteen hundred people were entombed under a twenty-foot-deep apron of sludge that crashed through the village shortly before dawn on October 5. The Guatemalan government declared the town a mass grave and ordered it left undisturbed. The village of San Pablo suffered only minor damage, and the house built by the Wesleyans for Diego and Rosario was unscathed. But in San Juan, through which the missionaries had passed each day on the way to San Pablo, and in nearby San Marcos, where Pastor Chepé's church is located, dozens were killed and hundreds of homes were destroyed. Most of the coffee, corn, and bean crops around the lake were lost, and hundreds of acres of agricultural land was covered over in mud and debris.

About a month after the storm the Wesleyan church in Tuscaloosa sent a team to the lake area to deliver clothing and other relief supplies. John Vaughan led the team and later described the devastation in a phone call: "It looked like the Lord just took his fingernails and scraped hundreds of paths down the mountainside, and it all came together at the bottom and just wiped out entire villages. It was heartbreaking." The following March he went back with another team to help the local churches rebuild homes in San Marcos and San Juan.

A couple of additional updates: A few months after the trip I checked in with team member Scott Roland, who happily reported that he and his ex-wife had begun seeing a counselor, and that the process of reconciliation was moving forward. Scott and his son Tyler were part of the group that returned to Guatemala in November. And finally, Carlos, the gang leader who had accepted Christ at the altar of the Wesleyan church in Guatemala City, was still alive and still involved in his criminal gang, according to church members. He never set foot in the church again.

SEVEN

# Back to the Garden

Mt. Union, Pennsylvania

A n unbroken line of traffic wound north on Route 522 as far as the eye could see. Mammoth motor homes and sleek minivans, pickup trucks pulling pop-up campers, SUVs like mine with roof racks loaded with camping gear snaked slowly along the two-lane blacktop through quaint villages and rolling farmland nestled between the heavily wooded slopes of the Allegheny Mountains. Directly ahead of me a green pickup truck with Maryland tags followed close behind a silver minivan filled with teenagers. Both vehicles sported colorful hand-painted messages on the rear and side windows: "Honk if you love Jesus!" "God Rocks!" "Creation or Bust!"

As the procession meandered through the sleepy boroughs of Shade Gap, Orbisonia, and Shirleysburg, past century-old brick and clapboard houses with American flags draped from whitewashed porches, past hardware stores and gas stations and beauty parlors and redbrick churches with white steeples etched against the hazy summer sky, couples on porch swings waved and elderly men in coveralls glowered at the stream of out-of-towners clogging the usually quiet thoroughfare. In Shirleysburg a yellow-and-black sign out in front of the Homespun Gifts and Crafts shop offered a friendly greeting to the passing multitude: "Welcome Creation."

Our ad hoc caravan was on its way to Creation 2005, an outdoor rock music festival that each summer draws tens of thousands of evangelical young people and their chaperones to the bucolic hills of south central Pennsylvania for what is often described as a Christian version of Woodstock. While it is not the only Christian rock festival in the United States—there are at least a dozen others—it is one of the oldest and is easily the largest. Overnight a tent city of more than 80,000 would sprout on a 285-acre tract of rolling land called Agape Farm—pronounced "uh-GAH-pay," Greek for "divine love"—almost tripling the population of rural Huntingdon County. For four days and nights the normally placid countryside would thunder and shake with the electrified sounds of Christian rock, rap, and pop music punctuated by fervent gospel preaching and performed by some of the biggest names in contemporary Christian music.

Part rock concert and part revival meeting, it is a chance for Christian teenagers to let loose and mosh for Jesus. For me it was a chance to become acquainted with some of the artists and fans of a musical genre that has become a billion-dollar-a-year business and a mainstay of the evangelical subculture.

Just beyond Shirleysburg the traffic on Route 522 suddenly came to a halt. About 150 yards ahead was the turnoff to Agape Farm, still another four miles down a winding country road past the Brumbaugh Lumber Mill and a handful of small farms. The traffic was backed up onto the highway. It was after 1:00 P.M., a little more than four hours before the music was scheduled to begin. People had been arriving since early the day before, and I was caught in the last-minute rush. It would take another two hours in bumper-to-bumper traffic to reach the main gate.

As I finally crossed the last ridge just above the entrance I caught my first glimpse of the outer perimeter of the festival grounds. Vehicles were pouring into a freshly mowed hay field already half filled with colorful tents and campers shimmering in the humid heat of the afternoon sun. Beyond a thin line of trees in the distance were other fields and wooded knolls, all of them seemingly filled to capacity and bustling with activity. The encampment appeared to stretch on endlessly. Agape Farm had, indeed, become a city unto itself.

Once inside the gate I was greeted by two cheerful teenage girls wearing CREATION STAFF T-shirts. They checked my press pass and directed me to the hay field I had seen from the road, and that for the next four days would be my home. The field, I would learn later, was one of two parcels of land that had been rented from neighboring farms to accommodate the overflow crowd. The amenities were rustic, to say the least. There was no electricity. Two two-hundred-gallon water tanks with spigots sat on a hay wagon in the middle of the field. A long row of blue portable toilets flanked the entry road. People were lined up twenty to thirty deep at both facilities. I quickly set up my small tent and set out on foot for the stage area about a quarter mile away.

When it's not hosting the Creation festival Agape Farm is a retreat center used throughout the year mainly by church groups. Most of it lies in a tranquil valley traversed by two small streams and winding dirt roads with names like Hallelujah Highway, Jerusalem Street, and Glory Lane. A dining pavilion, a small dormitory, several shower houses, and a handful of other permanent buildings are scattered around the main campground. This week they were dwarfed by several giant tent tops and other temporary structures assembled just for the festival.

At the center of it all was the main stage area, a natural amphitheater at the foot of a small mountain. The stage itself was a towering structure of gauze-covered scaffolding, multicolored lights, and sound equipment, and it was flanked by two giant video screens. A long white banner with red letters—A TRIBUTE TO OUR CREATOR—formed a proscenium arch overhead.

Directly in front of the stage was the mosh pit, a standing-only section already packed tight with young people, many of them with spiked or spray-colored hair, bouncing to the beat of recorded music blaring from the speaker towers behind them. (Actual moshing, the frenzied dancing and violent colliding that often goes on at rock concerts, was strictly prohibited at the festival. "Up and down is fine," an announcer instructed the crowd a few minutes before the show began. "But no sideways, please. We don't want anyone getting hurt.")

Beyond the sound towers a wide grassy slope ascending several hundred yards to the tree line was covered in a colorful blanket of humanity—tens of thousands of music fans of all ages and sizes sitting on beach chairs or on blue plastic tarps amid coolers and strollers and beach umbrellas. The diverse palette of color, however, didn't extend to skin tones; the Creation audience was almost entirely white, as were the artists on the program.

I found an empty space near the back and set up my folding canvas chair. Just as I settled in the canned music began to fade and a wave of applause rolled across the hillside as the Reverend Dr. Harry L. Thomas, Jr., known to Creation fans as Pastor Harry and cofounder of the twenty-seven-year-old festival, walked to the center of the stage. His smiling, ruddy face and snowy hair and beard filled the giant TV monitors.

"Hello, Creation!" Thomas called out. The audience responded with an exuberant cheer. "What a sight you are to behold," he said, scanning the hillside. "This is the largest opening-day crowd we've ever had at Creation, and people are still coming in." Off in the distance behind the stage a line of vehicles could be seen creeping along a ridge on the campground's western perimeter, edging slowly toward a field to the south.

"Well, you're in for a wonderful week," Pastor Harry continued. He knew that the audience by then was well acquainted with the festival's musical lineup, which included Gospel Music Award winners MercyMe, Michael W. Smith, the Newsboys, and crossover rock sensation Switchfoot as headliners. In all, some forty-four bands and individual artists would play the main amphitheater or perform at the fringe stage, a smaller venue for up-and-coming acts.

"These next few days are going to be filled with great music, great teaching, and great fellowship," Thomas went on. "But I hope none of us will lose sight of the real reason we're here." He pointed to the banner above him. "And that is to pay tribute to our Creator. It's my fervent prayer that each of you will find this to be a real time of worship and of drawing close to him."

Aside from the mass of humanity, the music, and the mud—although at this year's festival, dust was the greater affliction—the similarities between Creation and Woodstock actually were very few. (I can say this with some authority as a member of the Woodstock generation. Not that I actually *attended* the legendary event in upstate New York in the summer of 1969. I did see the movie, however. Twice.) No one could possibly mistake Creation for a sixties-style celebration of sex, drugs, and rock 'n' roll.

For starters, there were the rules, which were printed prominently in the festival program. First on the list: no drugs or alcohol. "Those found under the influence or in possession of such," the program warned, "will be escorted off the property, and/or, turned over to law enforcement officers." The ban on illegal drugs, of course, was a no-brainer. The prohibition against alcohol, however, was not aimed just at underage drinkers. Drinking alcohol is a traditional taboo in most evangelical circles, dating back to the temperance campaigns of the late nineteenth century. Some denominations still require adult members to swear off all forms of alcoholic beverages, although the hardline stand is beginning to soften in some quarters.

Then there was the dress code, which simply called for modesty—"no bathing suits please." Despite the sweltering heat and humidity young men kept their shirts on for the most part, and relatively few halter tops or bare midriffs were evident. The most skin I saw exposed all week, in fact, was that of a paunchy middle-aged man who stripped to his bikini briefs on one particularly hot afternoon and began bathing in a creek just a few yards off a main walking trail. A security patrol with orange vests and crackling walkie-talkies quickly swooped in to rectify the situation.

Public displays of affection, though not directly addressed in the rules, seldom went beyond chaste hugs and hand holding. I suspect the presence of so many parents, youth pastors, and other adults had something to do with that. Most of the festival rules related to more mundane matters—disposing of litter, late-night curfews, campfire safety—the kinds of regulations one would expect to keep such a large gathering safe and contented. While police were always present, as required by law for such events, there were no reports of trouble. This was a decidedly law-abiding crowd.

What distinguished Creation from secular rock festivals more than anything else, of course, was its singular focus on worship and on encouraging young people to commit to Jesus. "When we started this in 1979," Pastor Harry told me one afternoon during a program break, "we just felt a real need to reach young people with the new music that was coming out then. Music can be a powerful, motivating thing. But there's something more than music going on here. We think there's a real strong pull of God in people's hearts."

After Pastor Harry's welcoming remarks and a few more preliminaries, the first band was ready to take the stage. It was a group called BarlowGirl, a trio of fresh-faced sisters from Elgin, Illinois. All brunettes with model-like good looks, modestly dressed in T-shirts and jeans, the Barlow sisters—Becca, twenty-five, Alyssa, twenty-three, and Lauren, nineteen—had made a splash in the Christian music world a year earlier with a debut album extolling the virtues of virtue. As much as for their pop-rock style of music, they had become known for their radical stand against sex before marriage.

"Do you think you guys could help us out with this song? Would that be at all possible?" Lauren, the drummer, yelled to the crowd, her shoulder-length hair flying as she pounded out a driving beat while her sisters backed her up on electric guitar and bass.

The audience roared its assent and jumped to its feet, clapping to the upbeat rhythm.

"I'll sing first and then you," she yelled. "Are you ready?"

*"You got it ... you got it ... you got it all ..."*

The audience echoed the melodic refrain right on cue, and then repeated it twice more.

The mosh pit was hopping as the group cranked up the volume and launched into the opening verse of "Pedestal," a song from their first album. The crowd seemed to know the lyrics by heart. It was an ode to an unnamed teen idol ("You're the coolest person that I have ever seen ... you're a god, I know it") whose disappointing foibles ultimately are revealed in the tabloids ("add you to my fallen list, one more has hit the ground"), prompting the singer to abandon her quest for the perfect guy and to seek instead "the One who's worthy of all worship."

The decidedly introspective theme was revisited with some variation in other BarlowGirl songs: "Clothes," a critical reflection on immodest dress ("Clothes aren't what they used to be ... Flaunting what you've got and more is in"); "Average Girl," a spirited repudiation of teen dating ("Chasing after boys is not my thing ... I'm waiting for a wedding ring"); and "You Led Me," a pensive ballad suggesting that the most satisfying relationship in life is with Jesus ("You found me ... you led me, you set me free").

A few songs into their set Lauren spoke up again, this time to explain how she and her sisters became convinced that God did not want them or their young Christian fans to get caught up in the messiness of boyfriend-girlfriend relationships, let alone in pre-marital sex.

"So we're all mad. We're like, 'Why don't you want us to date, God? What's the deal with that?' " she said, recalling how they had prayed for God's guidance and received what they believe was God's answer. "And he's like, 'Because I have not created my children's hearts to be broken.' "

The audience let out a somewhat subdued cheer. Obviously many in the crowd bought the explanation, although by no means had the verdict been unanimous. In all likelihood many already were familiar with the rationale behind the Barlow sisters' no-dating stance, which is spelled out on the band's Web site: "We believe that God has one perfect man already chosen for us; therefore we have no need to worry ourselves in searching for him. When the time is right we know God will bring us together. In the meantime we are not hiding in a closet avoiding all males. We are still liv-ing our lives, just without the pressure of having to have a boyfriend."[1]

In any event, BarlowGirl's message clearly seemed to resonate with the Creation crowd. As the band finished its last song and the applause faded, a group of girls a few feet behind me let out a boisterous yell—"Woo-*hoo*!" One of them, a short brunette with braces, looked to be about fourteen and wore a black BarlowGirl T-shirt with a message printed on the sleeve: DO NOT CONFORM ... BE TRANSFORMED (ROMANS 12:2).

"You must be a big fan," I remarked.

"They are so *awesome*!" she squealed. "I just *love* their music and what they stand for."

Standing next to her was a taller and slightly older-looking girl with short blond hair peeking out from under a baseball cap. She was wearing an orange T-shirt with a round insignia spelling out the words "True Love Waits." I recognized it as the emblem of a Southern Baptist–initiated campaign to get teenagers to agree to abstain from premarital sex. Since it began in 1994 some three million young people reportedly have signed pledges vowing to remain celibate until they marry.[2]

"It's so cool being here with the bands and all these kids our own age who believe like we do," the blonde said, surveying the crowd. "It's not like at school, where some people think we're weird or something just because we're Christians and we want to keep ourselves pure."

I acknowledged her T-shirt and asked if she had taken the pledge. She raised her left hand and showed me a silver ring inscribed "*TLW.*"

"Absolutely," she beamed. "There was a ceremony at church this spring. Two of my best friends at school did, too. And they don't even go to my church." Several guys she knew also had taken the pledge. "But if you talk to most kids at my high school, they think it's a little strange. Not that they're all having sex or anything. They just think we're a little bit overboard. It doesn't really bother me, though."

The brunette interjected that she knew a girl at her middle school who had gotten pregnant the previous year, and that one of her friends had been sexually active but had recently stopped. "I just think it's creepy that they would do that," she said. "They're too young, and it's just wrong." While she hadn't yet taken the True Love Waits pledge herself, she added, she planned to do so in the fall.

I asked the girls about dating and whether they agreed with the Barlow sisters on that as well. Four years of high school, I reminded them, is a long time. No date for homecoming? No proms? And after that, four years of college? No dating at all?

"Hmm. I'm not sure," the blonde said, wrinkling her nose and tilting her head in thought. "There's a guy in my youth group at church who I kind of like." Her voice suddenly got quieter. "We don't date or anything right now, but I can't say for sure that I never will."

"I can!" the brunette blurted out. "I'm not going to date. Period!

I'm just going to wait for God to send me the right one in his own time, just like BarlowGirl!"

It may simply have been youthful bravado on their part, or it may have reflected something deeper. I was impressed, nonetheless, by the girls' resolve, which I sensed was sincere. Still, I couldn't help wondering—"doubting" probably would be more accurate—whether they and the other BarlowGirl enthusiasts around me would feel as strongly in three or four years, or in three or four months for that matter, as they did standing on this Pennsylvania hillside. Back home, facing the relentless onslaught of a sex-obsessed culture and the pressure of a different group of peers, not to mention their own raging hormones, it surely would take more than a ring and a T-shirt or the lyrics of a rock song to sustain them in their vows.

I was a little amazed, too, that the girls had been willing to speak so openly about such personal matters. I had tried to be careful not to pry too deeply, and intentionally had avoided asking their names. In part, I supposed that their openness reflected the comfort level that evangelicals often experience at gatherings such as this. Being among so many fellow believers, as the young blonde had suggested, afforded a sense of security and affirmation that they seldom get in more secular settings. It was like being at a large family reunion where, even though you may not know the name of every distant cousin, you sense the strong familial bond of a shared history. In this case everyone (it was assumed) shared the experience of a personal relationship with Jesus, and everyone understood the family rules and jargon. In such company it was considered safe and appropriate—it was expected, even—for one to speak freely of matters of the soul, to give "a word of testimony" of "what the Lord has been doing" in one's life, to share the insights and the struggles of one's daily walk of faith, and to offer or ask for prayer. To a large degree it is this strong sense of extended family that accounts for the personal bond that evangelicals often feel toward one another and for the considerable amount of cohesion within the movement itself. That dynamic, I sensed, was at work among the young people attending Creation.

Up on stage a sound crew was nearly finished setting up for the next group, the David Crowder Band, who would lead the audience in a sing-along of praise songs and set the mood for the evening's speaker. In the meantime slick commercials with booming soundtracks flashed across the video screens—a recruitment ad for Jerry Falwell's Liberty University, ads for a couple of Christian music Web sites, a trailer for a new Walt Disney animated movie based on C. S. Lewis's Christian allegory, *The Chronicles of Narnia*. Throughout the week the main-stage programs tended to be fast paced, with few moments of dead air. It was clear they had been designed for teenage attention spans.

Even so, three times each day at the festival—twice in the morning and once in the evening—the drums and guitars went silent and the main stage was given over to about forty-five minutes of gospel preaching. Speakers, for the most part, were seasoned pastors or Bible teachers who seemed accustomed to dealing with youthful audiences. They sprinkled their talks with levity and tried to keep things lively while delivering serious messages aimed at drawing their young listeners into a deeper faith. The opening-night speaker, Greg Laurie, was no exception.

A balding ex-hippie, Laurie is a crusade evangelist and megachurch pastor who has spent most of his career ministering to the MTV generation. He started out in the early 1970s preaching to surfers and Jesus Freaks in Southern California as a young protégé of Chuck Smith, founder of the Costa Mesa–based Calvary Chapel movement. Now in his fifties, Laurie is pastor of the Harvest Christian Fellowship, a fifteen-thousand-member congregation in Riverside, California, but still spends four or five weekends a year conducting stadium events that feature extreme sports, Christian rock music, and a youth-oriented evangelistic message. He seemed right at home on the Creation stage.

"How many of you have ever been stressed-out to the max? Raise your hands." Laurie paced the front of the stage, his own right hand uplifted as he scanned the audience. Hands went up all over the hillside. "Did you know that stress can actually harm you physically? Doctors tell us it can cause heart attacks, ulcers, depression, nervous breakdowns, and the list goes on...."

"Add to that the fact that we live in a scary world." Since the trauma of 9/11, he said, "America has not been the same place. We're afraid of terrorist attacks, we're afraid of nuclear weapons getting into the hands of terrorists." On the video screen a cutaway shot of the audience focused on a teenage couple sitting motionless, arm-in-arm, staring somberly at the stage.

"And then there are personal fears that concern us." Laurie slipped into a comedic riff on a list of phobias he said were gleaned from a *Time* magazine cover story. "I'm not making these up," he said. "There's ablutophobia: the fear of bathing—I hope you're not camping near someone with that; alektorophobia: the fear of chickens; and arachibutyrophobia: the fear of peanut butter sticking to the roof of your mouth.... And here's my personal favorite, phalacrophobia: the fear of baldness and bald people. What? What are you laughing at out there?"

Laurie was ready to make his point. "I'm here today to tell you that you don't need to be stressed-out or live in fear, because God has a cure for heart trouble." The cure, he said, could be found in the fourteenth chapter of the Gospel of John, which he read aloud. It's a passage in which Jesus tells his disciples:

> "*Let not your hearts be troubled. You believe in God. Believe also in me. In my father's house are many mansions.... I go to prepare a place for you. And if I go ... I will come again and receive you unto myself, that where*

*I am there you may be also. And where I go you know,*
*and the way you know." Thomas said to him, "Lord, we*
*know not where you go, so how can we know the way?"*
*Jesus answered him, "I am the way, the truth and the life.*
*No one comes to the Father except by me."*

For the next half hour or so he alternated between lighthearted banter and sober admonition as he sought to coax the young audience into embracing Jesus as the ultimate stress buster and the only source of eternal life. They needed to read and heed the Bible, he said, because "it tells us how to live forever, and what is right and wrong." If they would "take Jesus at his word" and repent and believe in Him, they could be assured of going to heaven when they die—or when Jesus returns at the Second Coming, whichever happened to come first. "It could happen tonight," he said.

Laurie was delivering what amounted to a basic salvation message, an explication of the evangelical version of the Christian gospel that presumably most of the young people at Creation had heard many times before and probably had already embraced. To me it seemed Laurie was preaching to the choir. But in a crowd this large, how could a preacher be sure? He wound up with a classic crusade-style altar call.

"Are you right with God? If Jesus were to come back tonight, would you be ready? You may be wondering, 'How can I be sure I won't be left behind? How do I get right with God?' "

Laurie quickly rattled off six steps. "You must recognize that you are a sinner.... Recognize that Jesus Christ died on the cross for you.... Repent of your sins.... Receive Christ into your life.... You must do it publicly.... And you must do it now."

He offered a brief prayer, asking God to "speak to those who need you tonight and bring them to yourself," and then, without pausing, addressed his audience once again. "Now, with our heads still bowed, if you want to get right with God, if you want Christ to forgive you of your sins, if you want to know you'll go to heaven when you die, I want you to stand to your feet wherever you are. Just stand up."

A gangly teenage boy sitting directly in front of me slowly unfolded his legs and pulled himself up.

"It may not seem like a big deal," Laurie continued, looking out over the crowd, "but you're confessing to him before people. You're making a stand"—off to my right, a young father sitting with his wife and toddler climbed to his feet—"you're saying, 'I mean it, and I don't care who sees it.' Stand up. Stand up."

All over the hillside, hundreds of people were coming to their feet, most of them teenagers, some wearing T-shirts with assorted Christian messages printed on the back. Many were standing alone, while others stood with arms wrapped around friends standing next to them.

Laurie was not quite finished.

"Some of you out there may need to come *back* to the Lord. You are a prodigal son or daughter. You need to return to Christ. You stand up, too." Dozens more started popping up all around me. "Don't be embarrassed. You're among friends and family here tonight. We love you. This is a big spiritual hospital right now, a place to get right with God."

Laurie paused for a moment and took in the sight of the young multitude standing before him. A few were still coming to their feet. He waited a few more seconds until he could detect no additional movement.

"Now," he finally resumed, "all of you who are standing, I want you to pray this prayer out loud after me, and if you mean it, God will hear it and answer your prayer."

He squeezed his eyes shut and began to speak in short phrases; the crowd echoed his words and inflections. "Lord Jesus ... I know I'm a sinner ... but you died on the cross ... and paid the price for every sin ... I have ever committed.... I turn from that sin now ... I put my faith in you ... I want to follow you ... from this moment forward.... Be my savior.... Be my Lord.... Be my God.... Be my

friend.... Thank you that you've forgiven me ... and that I'm going to heaven ... and I'm now ready for your return.... In Jesus'
name I pray.... Amen."

Years ago an evangelical pastor I knew shared a story that struck
me at the time as quite comical. It was the late 1970s and, largely
as a result of Jimmy Carter's rise to prominence, the nation's news
media had discovered a strange and fascinating phenomenon called
"born-again Christianity." The pastor recalled how a TV reporter
called him one day and asked permission to bring a camera crew
to his church in order to film someone being born again. The journalist, my pastor friend surmised, had hoped to come away with
dramatic footage of some exotic ritual or strange manifestation of
religious ecstasy. The pastor, of course, found the idea delightfully
absurd, and as he told the story we shared a good laugh. We both
understood what the misguided journalist apparently did not:
Christian conversion was something internal and largely invisible. It was a quiet and personal spiritual transaction. There was
nothing in the least visually dramatic about becoming born
again.

Watching the episode unfolding before me in front of the Creation stage, it occurred to me that perhaps I had been mistaken.

As Laurie and the crowd concluded their prayer, a cheer went
up. It reminded me of the sort of cheer one hears at sporting events
at the conclusion of the singing of the national anthem—the cheering begins quietly, overlapping the final phrases of the song, and
then spreads and swells until it envelops the entire stadium or
arena in a sustained expression of mass emotion. The entire hillside was on its feet and applauding. The young man in front of me
who had been among the first to stand was encircled by other teens
offering hugs and smiles. The young father to my right was whispering to his wife. Before the applause completely subsided Pastor
Harry came to the microphone to thank Laurie and to offer one
last piece of instruction.

"If you prayed that prayer with Greg tonight, we ask that you take just a few minutes and go over to our prayer tent." He pointed to a large white tent top just to the right of the stage seating area. "We won't keep you long, but we want to pray with you and give you a New Testament and just a have a brief word with you about the decision you made here tonight. Father—" he began to pray, "we thank you for each life committing themselves to you. Lord, continue to move by your spirit, that we might see a mighty harvest throughout this festival, in Jesus' name. Amen."

There was still more music to come, and as the TV screens switched over to commercials, the dusty aisles intersecting the seating area quickly became clogged with young people on the move. Many were headed in the opposite direction, toward concession stands to the left of the stage. But hundreds appeared to be making their way to the prayer tent, as Pastor Harry had instructed.

Going to the prayer tent at Creation was the equivalent of going forward at a Billy Graham crusade. It was a time to seal the deal, to publicly affirm a personal decision and arrange for follow-up contact. It also was a way for organizers to keep track of the numbers of "decisions for Christ"—traditionally the gold standard in gauging the effectiveness of evangelical ministries. (Laurie's Web site claims more than twelve thousand decisions were made during his 2003 crusades.)[3] The practice has been so widely used for so long that it is practically down to a science.

Just outside the crowded tent dozens of teens milled about waiting to be admitted by one of several greeters, who also served as gatekeepers. Once inside they were divided by gender into small groups and introduced to counselors, who would pray with them, give them a packet of literature, and have them fill out a "decision" card. I edged close to one group standing near a table in a far corner. A stocky man in an orange athletic shirt and khaki shorts, who introduced himself as Michael, was talking with two curly-haired high school boys from New Jersey.

"What are your names?" the man asked.

"Anthony."

"Aaron."

"And what decisions did you make tonight?"

"I rededicated my life to Christ," Anthony said, "and Aaron accepted Christ for the first time." Aaron nodded.

"That's fantastic. You've taken a life-changing step. You've given yourselves to Christ, and he's saved you, and he's promised that he'll never leave you. Do you guys know each other? Are you friends?"

"We're *best* friends," Anthony said.

"Then you can be Christian companions to each other. You know sometimes our friends can lead us into trouble. When I was a new Christian I had Christian friends, and they held me accountable. They wouldn't let me slide back. That's what you can do for each other. Are you plugged in to a good church?"

"Yeah," Anthony shrugged. "We're here with the youth group from our church."

"It's important that you go, and not just sometimes." The counselor punctuated his point by making eye contact with each boy. "Whenever you're at church, you're part of the body. You get nourished by the Word and by being with other Christians. When you don't go, things can get rough. So it's important you go every week. OK?" The boys looked at each other, and nodded.

He asked if they had any questions or specific prayer requests. They didn't. So they bowed their heads, and the counselor prayed, asking for God's "arm of protection around these two young men," that they would be "mighty warriors of the faith and companions who will encourage each other." Then he handed each of them a packet containing a copy of the Gospel of John, a leaflet offering instruction on next steps (read the Bible and pray daily, find Christian friends, attend church regularly, tell others of your decision), and a card requesting their name, address, church affiliation, and the nature of their decision.

The boys sat down on the grass and quickly filled out the cards and handed them back to the counselor. Then they shook his hand and left. The entire process had taken less than ten minutes.


Back at the main stage the program had resumed, and a popular punk-rock group called Relient K was finishing its set. The sun had disappeared behind the hills more than an hour before. The multicolored lights above the stage now pulsated against the darkened sky, illuminating the band and the dancing denizens of the mosh pit. The aisles still were heavily congested with people finding their way back from the prayer tent and the concession stands; the shuffling of thousands of teenage feet sent clouds of dust billowing into the still evening air.

All across the hillside excitement was beginning to build for the evening's headline act, Switchfoot. The quartet of California rockers was arguably the hottest group in contemporary Christian music at the moment. During the preceding year they had collected four Dove awards (Christian music's equivalent of the Grammys), including artist of the year and song of the year in the rock/contemporary category. Their fourth album, *The Beautiful Letdown,* had gone double platinum (over two million copies sold) and two singles from the album had made it onto *Billboard* magazine's top 50 alternative-rock and pop music lists—i.e., not in Christian music categories.

With their melodic rock sound and introspective but not overtly religious lyrics—not to mention their boyish good looks—Switchfoot had extended their fan base far beyond an exclusively Christian audience. They had played sold-out concerts all over the country, made a guest appearance on the *Tonight Show with Jay Leno,* and seen their music videos air regularly on MTV. The four

San Diego surfers were riding an impressive wave of crossover success.

And the Creation crowd loved them. As the band took the stage the audience came to its feet and exploded in a cheering ovation. Foot traffic around the dusty hillside quickly came to a halt. At the front of the mosh pit a cluster of teens wearing black Switchfoot T-shirts began batting the air in synch with the drumbeat and the opening riffs of electric guitar, and thousands behind them joined in the gesture. For the next hour all attention was focused on the giant TV screens and the energetic performers onstage.

Through most of the set the cameras stayed fixed on the band's blond-tressed lead vocalist, Jon Foreman, as he strutted and jumped about the stage in true Mick Jagger fashion during the friskier numbers, and deftly immersed himself in the emotive lyrics of the band's more musing songs. As they had during the BarlowGirl performance, and as they would with almost every group appearing on the main stage, the audience sang along as the band performed several of its hits: "More Than Fine" ("I want more than just a good time, I want more than just OK"); "The Beautiful Letdown" ("I was trying so hard to fit in, until I found out I don't belong here"); and "Dare You to Move" ("Where can you run to escape from yourself? Where you gonna go? Salvation is here").

For all of his talent, Foreman was not given to much between song chatter, especially of the Christian variety. Most bands performing at Creation, I would find, would pause at some point to give a brief testimony of their own faith in Jesus, to relate how a song had evolved from some personal crisis or a session of Bible reading, or simply to exclaim "praise the Lord!" in response to a particularly enthusiastic ovation. Not so with Switchfoot. "Thanks for listening to our music. It means a lot to us," Foreman managed at one point. After another song he looked into the audience and observed rather obliquely: "I see a lot of light out there. I see it in your eyes. It's good for the light to be together." He may have been alluding to the words of Jesus to his disciples, that they would be "the light of the world." But that would only be hazarding a guess. For whatever reason the young musician apparently felt constrained to keep it ambiguous.

But judging from the crowd's reaction, Switchfoot's fans didn't seem to mind the absence of God talk. Perhaps they found it gratifying enough just knowing that these young rock musicians who had also gained the accolades of the secular music world were born-again Christians just like them, even if they didn't always wear it on their sleeves. The band, after all, had delivered a dazzling demonstration of musical proficiency and professional showmanship. Even the camera work, flashing onstage images to the giant TV screens, was artful. It was a knockout performance that seemed to lack nothing—except for any direct acknowledgment of God. And therein lies something of an ongoing controversy within the Christian music world.

About a month before the Creation festival an aging and ailing rocker named Larry Norman gave what was billed as his last U.S. concert. It received relatively little national notice. He played in a small theater in his adopted hometown of Salem, Oregon, to a Christian audience of mostly baby boomers like himself, performing many of the songs he had written during the sixties, seventies, and eighties. It is unlikely that many of the young people at Creation would have recognized Norman's name, let alone his music, which they probably would have thought old-fashioned anyway. Which is a shame.

Perhaps more than any other single artist Norman was responsible for the rise of Christian rock. Although he didn't invent the genre, which came out of the Jesus Movement of the late sixties and early seventies, he was the first to achieve commercial success putting gospel lyrics to rock 'n' roll music. In doing so he led the way for other musicians, who expanded the genre into what subsequently would become the gold mine known as contemporary

Christian music. The breakthrough also would spark debates that persist to this day in some quarters over the definition and role of Christian music and musicians.

A born-again Christian since he was a child in San Francisco in the 1950s, Norman established his rock music credentials as a member of a moderately successful sixties band called People, which shared concert billings with such rock icons as The Doors, Janis Joplin, and the Grateful Dead. In 1969 Norman set out on his own, writing and performing rock songs that explicitly expressed his evangelical faith. Later that year Capitol Records released his first solo album, *Upon This Rock.*

Norman's initial success came at a time when few influential folks in either the evangelical world or the music business thought much of the idea of Christian rock. Christians tended to think of rock 'n' roll as the devil's music. Secular musicians questioned whether so-called Christian rock could really be considered rock at all. But Norman persisted. Three years after his first album he followed up with a more successful release, *Only Visiting This Planet,* on the MGM/Verve label. It included a piano-pounding rockabilly number that seemed to both summarize Norman's musical philosophy and answer the rising chorus of critics: "Why Should the Devil Have All the Good Music?"

Christian rock found an eager young audience well beyond the niche of the Jesus Freaks in Southern California, where it all began. It wasn't long before other artists and record labels started to recognize the potential of this new music market.

The 1970s saw an explosion of Christian musicians trying out a variety of contemporary styles. Among the early pioneers were groups such as Andrae Crouch and the Disciples, 2nd Chapter of Acts, and Love Song, and soloists like Mylon LeFevre, Carman, Keith Green, and Barry McGuire, the gravelly voiced former lead singer of the New Christy Minstrels, who scored a number-one solo hit in 1965 with "Eve of Destruction" before crossing over to Christian music. The field continued to expand in the 1980s with hard-rock bands like Petra, Stryper, and Whiteheart, and with the pop sounds of a young singer-songwriter named Amy Grant who, in 1981, became the first inspirational singer to earn a gold record. Two years later she won a Grammy, and was on her way to becoming the uncontested queen of contemporary Christian music.[4]

That decade also saw controversies surrounding this increasingly popular musical genre multiply, as some Christians continued to criticize its character, while others questioned its quality.

In 1985 Jimmy Swaggart, who was still a popular televangelist at the time, wrote a blistering attack on "so-called Christian rock," which he described as "a diabolical force undermining Christianity from within.... I turn on my television set. I see a young lady who goes under the guise of being a Christian, known all over the nation, dressed in skintight leather pants, shaking and wiggling her hips to the beat and rhythm of the music as the strobe lights beat their patterns across the stage and the band plays the contemporary rock sound which cannot be differentiated from songs by the Grateful Dead, the Beatles, or anyone else. And you may try to tell me this is of God and that it is leading people to Christ, but I know better."[5] (Three years after writing this Swaggart was caught in the company of a prostitute outside a Baton Rouge motel. He eventually confessed that he was guilty of an unspecified sin, and would temporarily leave the pulpit. He lost much of his audience as a result of the episode.)

Meanwhile, *Contemporary Christian Music* magazine, which debuted in 1978, and other new publications covering the fledgling industry began offering up a steady diet of music reviews—and not all of them were flattering. Some artists were panned by Christian reviewers for producing simplistic lyrics and mediocre tunes. In a *CCM* profile in 1987 singer-songwriter Michael Card complained that too many Christian songs were shallow and failed to deal with serious themes. "It's more like, 'Oh, here's a song on the Cross. What rhymes with cross? How about boss.'"[6]

But as the quality and consistency of the music improved, so did its commercial appeal, and some Christian artists began finding an audience outside the evangelical fold. Amy Grant opened the door in 1985 when her single "Find a Way" became Christian music's first top 40 hit. Grant's fans were thrilled to hear secular radio stations playing her overtly Christian lyrics: "If our God His Son not sparing / Came to rescue you / Is there any circumstance / That He can't see you through?" They were less thrilled a few years later when her crossover appeal resulted in another top 40 hit, "Baby Baby"—a wholesome but decidedly secular love song. Some Christian radio stations accused her of selling out, and pulled her music from their playlists.

Although others would follow Grant's crossover success, not all have faced the same backlash. "I'd like to think Christian fans today are more open-minded and not as possessive," Deborah Evans Price, who covers Christian music for *Billboard,* once told me. "Amy took the brunt of it. I don't know if it was because she was first, or because she's a woman, or both. But crossover artists still have to walk a fine line so they don't alienate their [Christian] fan base."[7]

It has been suggested that the backlash against Grant probably reflected the fact that she began to transcend what until then was a fairly limited notion of what Christian popular art had to be. In part it was an artifact of the evangelical subculture, intended for the edification of Christians who wanted to avoid the taint of worldly entertainment. In part it was a medium for ministry, a tool for advancing the Christian message. Grant's success raised bothersome questions. Why must Christian music always be explicit? What ultimately was the role of a Christian in the arts?

Grant addressed those questions when I interviewed her in Nashville in 2004 for *Religion & Ethics NewsWeekly.* "When I write a song and it talks about faith," she said, "my intent is not to put a sermon in a song. My intent is to either capture a truth or look for a truth, and I'm usually speaking to myself first.... One lover of art might be most profoundly affected by a painting of a crucifix. Another lover of art might be moved to tears to the point of falling on their knees and seeing God for the first time by looking at a landscape.... For an artist, how you express your wonder at life and your hope and your faith and all of that—there are no rules to it." T-Bone Burnett—a successful record producer and a born-again Christian whose musical credits include the highly acclaimed soundtrack to the 2000 film *O Brother, Where Art Thou?*—has put it more succinctly: "You can sing about the Light, or you can sing about what you see because of the Light. I prefer the latter."[8]

That may well be Switchfoot's philosophy. But we may never know. While the band appears to have successfully avoided the pitfalls that Grant and some other crossover artists have faced, success has not been entirely without a price. Prior to its signing with Columbia records in 2003, the band members spoke openly about their faith, both at concerts and in media interviews. Since going with the mainstream label, all such talk has ceased. Industry insiders say it is no coincidence—that the company insisted that the group downplay its faith in public to avoid being pegged a Christian band. If that's so, they certainly lived up to the agreement at Creation.

The rest of the week at the festival pretty much followed the pattern set on the first day. Squeezed between the morning and evening main-stage programs was a busy schedule of afternoon concerts at the fringe stage and small-group seminars held in the woods on topics ranging from personal evangelism ("Sharing Christ When You Feel You Can't") to gay marriage ("What's Wrong With It?"). When they weren't taking in the concerts and speakers many of the young people were back at their camps sneaking afternoon naps or standing in long lines at the concession stands, a record store, a small grocery, a T-shirt shop, and the shower houses.

The prayer tent also was kept busy throughout the week. On the last day Pastor Harry announced that more than 1,400 had filled out cards indicating they had made decisions for Christ. In addition, some 500 people were baptized, and more than 1,800 had signed up to sponsor poor children in Asia, Africa, and Latin America through Compassion International, a Christian relief agency that had helped to sponsor the festival.

By the time the final night arrived the main-stage proceedings had begun to take on a sense of routine, and after four days of heat and dust, the crowd's youthful exuberance was beginning to show some signs of wear. Program planners had hoped the final evening's headline act, MercyMe, would bring the festival to a climactic conclusion. Like Switchfoot, the Texas-based band had scored major crossover hits, and had carried off numerous gospel music awards. Unlike Switchfoot, however, they did it by singing overtly religious lyrics and performing in a conventional worship band style that tended to appeal to an older demographic than the bulk of the population at Agape Farm.

Still, it was closing night, and the crowd turned out in force. A Christian alternative-rock band, Kutless, and a punk-rock group called Audio Adrenaline brought the mosh pit roaring back to life one last time. The evening's speaker, author and youth evangelist Ron Luce, exhorted Christians in the audience (could there be any unsaved left?) to "put on the armor of God" and become "warriors battling for the souls" of the nation's youth. He admonished the young people to "stop playing games" and to "rise up like a mighty army to rescue your generation." Then he gave an altar call, urging his listeners to commit to witnessing to the lost. He also urged them to buy his latest book and an accompanying video, and to visit his Web site. Several hundred young people stood in response to the invitation, and many of them went to the prayer tent.

Shortly after 11:00 P.M. the program and the festival came to a close. The hillside emptied quickly, as the fatigued throngs of young people headed back to their camps, many to begin the melancholy business of packing for the trip home in the morning. No sooner had the program ended but work crews began what would be an all-night task of dismantling the stage and packing its components onto flatbed trucks and moving vans. By sunrise matted grass and a mountain of plastic trash bags would be about all that remained of the bustling center of the Creation festival.

The July night air had turned unusually brisk, much cooler than it had been all week. It was nearly midnight, and all around Agape Farm campfires began to appear, sending thin columns of wood smoke mixed with the sounds of acoustic guitars and youthful laughter filtering through the trees. Around many of the fires the teens and their leaders were taking part in what has become a standard, almost obligatory, ritual at Christian camps and youth retreats. The late-night campfire, I knew from my own teenage years, was a time for singing and praying together, for gazing into the glowing embers and deep into one's own soul, and then, in the comforting warmth of the crackling fire and the circle of Christian friends, to give a personal accounting of one's walk with the Lord. It may be the closest thing young evangelicals have to a confessional.

On a grassy knoll not far from the stage a red-and-white banner strung between two artificial palm trees marked the campsite of Student Impact, a youth group from the Brentwood Community Church of Rochester, New York.[9] Derek Allen, the church's senior high youth pastor, was beckoning his group of about thirty junior and senior high teens and young adult chaperones to take their seats around a smoldering fire ringed by metal folding chairs. The group had met around the fire each night of the festival. Allen, who looked to be in his midthirties, had high hopes for this final gathering—that the kids would cement the bonds that had been slowly developing among them during the week, and that the one or two holdouts in the group would finally yield and accept Jesus.

With the circle complete Allen and a volunteer leader named Gary began strumming their guitars. For the next twenty minutes they led the group in a half dozen contemporary worship songs, some of which I recognized from performances at the main stage. The teens obviously enjoyed singing, and were quite good at it, weaving in mellow harmonies and counter melodies with practiced skill. A few sat quietly and just stared into the flames.

Then it was time for testimonies. Setting his guitar aside Allen invited the kids to "share what has most impacted your life about this week, whether it was the speakers, the music, youth leaders, other students, anything like that."

Without further prompting five or six young teens spoke up in succession to identify a particular speaker or artist who had impressed them. "This was my first time at Creation," said Toby, a pint-sized thirteen-year-old who was in his pajamas and sitting on the ground at the edge of the fire. "I don't know how it is every year, but I got a lot out of the speakers. I listened most of the time, because they really knew how to talk to kids." Tamika, also thirteen and the only African American in the group, agreed. "They didn't just shake the Bible and make it all boring. They made it real fun."

Across the circle a blonde sixteen-year-old named Jennifer recalled an afternoon speaker who had talked about witnessing to the unsaved. "He said if you share the gospel, even if they don't accept it, don't worry about it, because sometimes people need to hear it seven times before they actually accept it. We just need to do it and not worry what the world thinks." Sitting next to her, Ashley, a pixieish thirteen-year-old blonde, offered that what she liked most about the week was "the fact that there are so many other Christians here, and they're not judgmental or anything. Like they walk past you and they don't look you up and down, you know, and care what clothes you're wearing or anything about how you look or whatever. They just accept you for who you are."

After one or two more testimonies, it was time for another song. "We're going to sing," Allen said, slowly strumming his guitar, "and when we come back, I want you to think about something specific that the Lord has done in your life this week."

A chilly dew had begun to settle over the campground, and other campsites nearby had grown quieter. One of the adults tossed another log onto the fire, sending a swarm of sparks spiraling into the air. The group began to sing quietly, prayerfully, and in unison.

> *Holiness is what I long for, holiness is what I need,*
> *Holiness is what you want from me,*
> *Take my heart and form it; take my mind, transform it;*
> *Take my will, conform it to yours ... oh Lord.*

As the song faded some of the older teens were ready to speak. Megan, an attractive nineteen-year-old in a gray sweatshirt and a baseball cap, leaned forward in her chair. "I've had a really, really rough year," she said, staring into the flames. "I graduated from high school and went off to college, and I guess you'd say I got into the party scene. I'd come home at night just feeling empty inside. It doesn't make you happy. It's not fulfilling at all. I knew I was doing something wrong." She paused and touched the corner of her eye with the back of her hand. "And then one of my girlfriends died, and another one got pregnant. So then—" the words came in a rush, "I got really angry at God, like, 'Why are all these things happening to me?' And then," her voice grew more serene, "a Christian friend reminded me that God will only give you so much, that he won't give you more than you can handle. That made me feel better, because obviously I *can* take what's been happening to me. And I've actually learned from it." She settled back in her seat.

Before anyone else could speak, Allen stepped in to clarify a point. "The Bible verse she's talking about says that God will not let you be tempted beyond what you can bear. The idea there is that God won't let anything come into your life that you can't say no to. But it's always our decision. We can never blame sin on an addiction or anything like that, because every single time we are tempted we have a choice. But he'll never let us be tempted beyond what we can take. OK, who's next?"

Barry, an athletic-looking seventeen-year-old who was new to the group, cleared his throat. "I also had a very rough year," he began. "My mother was diagnosed with cancer around Christmas. She was at the hospital a lot and I was at home, and I started drinking. Just a little at first. But then I started drinking pretty heavy, where I'd drink myself to sleep so I wouldn't have to stay up all night just totally stressed-out. Sometimes I would wake up in the morning to go to work, and I'd still be drunk." But then, he said, "God sent some people into my life to turn that around. I'm still facing some issues—" his voice choked, "but I haven't had a drink in a month and a half." Someone in the circle applauded. "And coming here, you guys have been just awesome. You just let me hang out and chill and just *be,* you know? Sometimes you just need to get away and let God work you over."

Several nodded and murmured in agreement. By now the climate of confession clearly had taken hold.

Next up was Vivian. A petite brunette, she looked to be about eighteen. I would later learn that she was twenty-five and one of the chaperones. She spoke in a ringing voice with an admonishing tone. "I had a chance last night to talk to some of the girls about how we do things sometimes because we think it will be fun, and we don't really think about the future. I shared with them some things I struggle with now. Obviously, I've had sex, and I'm not married. For those of you who don't know, I have a little girl. I didn't realize then some of the issues I'd be dealing with now."

Without changing her didactic tone, she told how she recently met "a really good Christian guy," and that they seemed to hit it off. But while she is interested in him, "he isn't sure about what he wants to do, and my past is a big part of it. I'm a little older than he is, but if I didn't have a daughter it would be a different story. It wouldn't be as hard a decision to make, whether to be with me."

She switched over to full preaching mode, and her captive audience sat quiet and still. "I don't think a lot of you guys think about that now, when you're out there doing things, whether it be having sex or drinking and drugs and stuff. You don't think about how it may be ruining your testimony, or the fact that maybe one day you're going to meet a wonderful guy or girl who's not going to want to be with you because of what you've done. I just want you think about that now, that you could be ruining your time with your future husband or wife because of what feels good now."

After a brief pause, Allen picked up his guitar and led the group in singing a folk-rock version of "Amazing Grace." Then he looked around the circle. "Who's next? OK, Lieutenant Dan."

A young man in camouflage fatigues leaned forward. His real name was Bob, and he was fourteen, but he seemed comfortable with the nickname the group had given him. "When I was in the eighth and early ninth grade, I wasn't exactly what you'd call a good Christian," he said in a flat, almost inaudible voice. "I was hanging out with the wrong kids, and I started swearing a lot. I started going with a girl who was not a Christian, and for about four months we did things that were not exactly what I would call moral. I'm not very proud of it. I had to break that off, and it hurt more than anything I have felt in my life. I came here to make new choices and to be with new people. I know I haven't been a very friendly person, but you all have taken me in. You've accepted me for who I am, and that means a lot. You've been like Christ to me."

After a few more testimonies and a closing song, the teens came to their feet and wrapped their arms around each other in a group hug that encircled the fading fire. Allen called on the junior high youth pastor, Jerry Michaels, to close in prayer.

"Lord, this has been an awesome week," Michaels began. "We've just been blown away seeing so many Christians sing together and pray together and just lift up their arms to you. We know it's just a taste of what heaven is going to be like." He prayed for the young people around the fire, "that they will stay passionate about you when they get home. We know this is a time when Satan likes to attack—just when kids are on fire for you and want to grow closer to you. We know their party friends are going to call. Keep them strong." He prayed for a restful night and a safe trip home—and it was over.

As anyone who has raised a teenager—or who has ever been one— can attest, adolescence is an emotional roller-coaster ride. Psychologists tell us that emotions play a far greater role in influencing behavior during adolescence than in any other stage of life. Advertisers, of course, understand this quite clearly, and have shown themselves adept at manipulating teenage behavior. So, too, clothing designers, movie studios, soft-drink marketers, and those who make and sell records, just to name a few. Parents, on the other hand, tend to be less good at it, mainly because they can never be certain about whose buttons are being pushed by whom.

One would have had to be blind or totally naive not to have detected the signs of emotional manipulation at work around the campfire and in other phases of the Creation festival. The music, the spoken messages, nearly everything about the daily routine at Agape Farm had been carefully crafted to motivate young people to make or strengthen their faith commitments—to bring, as Pastor Harry had prayed the first night, "a mighty harvest" of decisions for Christ.

And yet it would be cynical to conclude that it was all manipulation and nothing more. The attitudes and behaviors I had seen demonstrated around the campfire and among thousands of other teenagers during the week, after all, had not originated here. Most of the young people had arrived already firmly committed to what can only be described as a radically countercultural worldview—one that rejects the hedonism and materialism of the dominant culture in favor of a higher calling and a more demanding set of standards.

To what extent these attitudes were truly their own, or had been thrust upon them by their parents or other adults, one can only speculate. I can only say that it seemed genuine. The road these young people had chosen to travel is not an easy one. The kind of discipleship they were practicing, it seemed to me, came at much too high a cost to be faked. Listening to the young people's testimonies, moreover, I sensed an unmistakable air of disillusionment, if not with their parents, then certainly with their parents' world, which they perceived had forfeited Paradise and turned its back on God. They, on the other hand, had chosen to live as citizens of a heavenly kingdom.

Leaving the campfire I couldn't help thinking of an earlier gathering of idealistic young people. Like the kids from Rochester, and like BarlowGirl and their two young fans whom I had met on the first night, they had awakened to find themselves living in a world they were convinced had lost its way and that sought to lure them down a destructive path. They, too, had been inspired by the rock anthems of prophet musicians who called them to stand fast against the hypocrisy and deception of the dominant culture, and to reclaim their spiritual birthright by connecting to something greater than themselves.

As I headed for my tent in the quiet cool of the early morning darkness I felt that maybe I had misjudged the Creation gathering. Maybe it had been a lot like Woodstock after all.

# EIGHT

# Capital Crusaders

Washington, D.C.

It was 8:42 A.M. on Friday, January 28, 2005, and the Reverend Richard Cizik, vice president for governmental affairs of the National Association of Evangelicals, stood outside the coffee shop in the lower lobby of the Grand Hyatt Hotel holding a cell phone tight to his ear but saying not a word.

Reaching inside his rumpled overcoat, he pulled out a ballpoint pen and began clicking it open and closed as he listened to the voicemail messages relayed from his Capitol Hill office: an afternoon appointment at the Hart Senate Office Building had been moved ahead a half hour (there would be no time for lunch) ... a reporter from *Time* magazine asking for a return call ... a midmorning meeting with the White House liaison confirmed. He snapped the phone shut and scribbled a note on the back of a wrinkled manila envelope then, glancing at his watch, turned quickly to rejoin his companions waiting in the coffee shop.

The day was shaping up as an exceptionally busy one for the NAE's Washington representative, capping what had been an exceptionally busy week. Cizik's day had begun nearly two hours earlier with breakfast at the hotel with a group of college students attending a Christian Student Leadership Conference, an annual NAE event designed to expose evangelical young people to official

Washington in hopes that some will choose careers in government and politics. As in previous years the four-day conference had been Cizik's baby. He had planned it, recruited speakers from Congress, the White House, federal agencies, Washington think-tanks, and the media, and had presided over each session. About 125 students had attended, and, if previous years were any indication, roughly 10 percent of them could be expected eventually to land careers in public service. Among the program's alumni were former U.S. Senator Dan Coats (R-Indiana), the late Representative Paul Henry (R-Michigan), at least two federal judges, a former ambassador, and several congressional staffers. With the conference behind him it was time to get back to his normal routine as the chief lobbyist and Washington voice for the NAE and its thirty million constituents.

These were hectic days in the nation's capital. The second Bush inauguration was over and Congress was back in session, its Republican majority strengthened thanks in part to a heavy turnout of evangelical voters in November. The religious right, whose influence in Washington had ebbed and flowed over the years, had reached what was widely considered to be a new zenith with the 2004 election. Its political operatives were busy girding for battle over a handful of hotly contested judicial appointments, including one or two anticipated vacancies on the U.S. Supreme Court that, judging from the frail appearance of ailing Chief Justice William Rehnquist at the Bush swearing in, could not now be far off. Renewed fighting was expected over same-sex marriage, the president's "faith-based initiative" to permit religious groups to provide government-funded social services, and a host of other issues on which, in Cizik's words, "we evangelicals have a horse to ride." His appointment book was filling rapidly, and he had invited me along as he made his daily rounds.

Cizik is a tall and slender man in his midfifties, with angular facial features and graying blond hair swept across a receding hairline. He is an ordained minister in the Evangelical Presbyterian

Church, a small conservative offshoot of the mainline Presbyterian Church (USA), and although he has never led a congregation, he has the lanky appearance and homespun manner of a country preacher—traits that betray his rural upbringing in central Washington state. Yet by no means is he a rustic. A cum laude graduate in political science from Whitworth College in Spokane, he earned graduate degrees in public affairs from George Washington University in Washington, D.C., and in divinity from Denver Seminary. He studied international affairs at the National Political Science University in Taipei, Taiwan, where he also learned to speak Mandarin Chinese. And he has spent his entire career in the nation's capital, moving comfortably among policy makers and power brokers of both parties and on both ends of Pennsylvania Avenue.

I first met Cizik in the early 1980s, when I was covering Congress for *U.S. News & World Report* and he was a young legislative assistant at the NAE and a relative newcomer to Washington. He struck me then as an amiable but earnest student of the Washington political scene who was eager to learn the ropes in order to make a difference on behalf of the conservative Christians who had helped put Ronald Reagan in the White House.

It was clear now that his on-the-job training had paid off. Though he lacks the celebrity of a Jerry Falwell or a Pat Robertson, Cizik is well known inside the Beltway as a seasoned professional who gets things done the old-fashioned way: by doing his homework and cultivating relationships with decision makers and key staff members, who often are the real architects of government policy. Working quietly behind the scenes he had helped convince Congress to pass laws combating religious persecution, international sex-slave trafficking, and human rights abuses in North Korea and Sudan. He also helped nudge the Bush administration deeper into the fight against AIDS in Africa.

He is known, too, as a consistent voice of civility and moderation—qualities too often neglected by religious partisans in the heat of political battle. "It's easy to say to a member of Congress, 'You're going to pay in the next election if you don't carry out our agenda,'" Cizik had explained to me in an earlier conversation. "But that's not very smart, and I don't think it really works in the long run." Rather, he said he has learned during his twenty-five years in Washington that "you can accomplish far more by building bipartisan bridges" than by resorting to threats and narrow partisan rants.

To me it seemed that Cizik and the NAE exemplified what a writer for *USA Today* has described as the "growing maturity and sophistication" of the Christian right.[1] I was eager to see how that maturity might begin to play out in the politically charged aftermath of a close national election in which evangelicals had gained an undisputed place in the inner circle of the ruling Republican Party. How would they comport themselves now that they were Washington insiders? How adept would they prove to be as players in the Washington power game? How much influence had they really gained with the White House and Congress? And which of the varied and sometimes competing voices purporting to speak for evangelicals in Washington would be regarded as authentic and authoritative? I had fond hopes that the day ahead would begin to bring some answers.

Back inside the coffee shop Cizik slipped into a booth to finish a conversation with two political science professors he had introduced me to a few moments earlier. Both taught at small Christian colleges in the Midwest and had brought students to the NAE conference. For the past several minutes they had been ruminating over how to get the more than one hundred evangelical colleges in the United States to do a better job of preparing students for careers in public service.

"The problem," said one of the professors, "is that too many of our schools still seem to equate Christian service with being a pastor or a missionary. They don't see public service as a Christian calling. That's got to change." The 2004 election, he noted, had demonstrated what evangelicals can accomplish when they get involved in the political process. Some thirty-one million of them had showed up at the polls, about four million more than in 2000, and 78 percent of them voted for Bush.[2] "Voting is a good start," the professor said. "But if we're really going to maintain a moral basis in our society, we need more candidates and more office-holders who have a biblically informed worldview."

The solution, the two professors agreed, was to coax more Christian colleges to offer prelaw and political science programs deliberately designed to point students toward careers in government and politics. It would help also if evangelical academicians and theologians were to articulate a "public theology of cultural engagement"—heretofore lacking—to provide a philosophical framework for evangelical political involvement.

Cizik nodded. That, of course, had been the whole point of his just concluded conference. "We need more Christians in Washington, no question," he said. "But it's just as important that we encourage people to take a broader view of what it means to be a Christian in the public square. We can't be defined just by our involvement with two or three hot-button issues. That's the stereotype, but that's not all we are about."

Indeed, a few months earlier Cizik and other NAE leaders had produced a sweeping and, in some ways, historic document entitled "For the Health of the Nation: An Evangelical Call to Civic Responsibility," which laid out a surprisingly broad public policy agenda and rationale for political action. For the first time it put evangelicals on record supporting environmental protection ("care for the creation") along with helping the poor, defending human rights and religious freedom, working for peace, protecting families and children, and opposing abortion and embryonic stem cell research.[3] Except for the last two, these were not the sorts of issues that people tended to associate with Christian conservatives. Cizik and other signers of the document intended for that to change.

Not everyone in the movement shared their enthusiasm. While

James Dobson of Focus on the Family had been among the nearly one hundred original signers, Tom Minnery, Dobson's chief political operative and Focus's vice president for public policy, had questioned rather pointedly whether concern for the environment really reflected mainstream evangelical thought. "The movement to preserve marriage characterizes evangelicalism," Minnery insisted to a reporter shortly after the document's debut. "The issue of global warming does not."[4] And Oklahoma Senator James Inhofe, Republican chairman of the Environment and Public Works Committee and himself a born-again Christian, had warned that by putting environmental concerns high on their agenda, evangelicals risked being "led down a liberal path" by radical tree huggers, and distracted from family issues.[5]

Still, the NAE's leaders were convinced that civic responsibility on their part demanded a more balanced agenda. "We're in a position now to make a difference," Cizik explained to the professors, "and the way you do that is by building alliances and finding common ground. We have to do it that way if we're going to win here in Washington." His tablemates agreed.

Cizik checked his watch. It was time to move on to his next appointment. He excused himself from the table and shook hands with the two educators. A few minutes later he was behind the wheel of his blue Volkswagen Beetle, edging into the busy downtown traffic.

We were headed for a 10:00 A.M. meeting near the White House with Tim Goeglein, an assistant to President Bush and deputy director of the White House Office of Public Liaison. Goeglein worked for Bush's chief political strategist, Karl Rove, and functioned as middleman between the White House and conservative groups including the Christian right. It was Goeglein's job, as the *Washington Post* had put it, "to make sure conservatives are happy, in the loop, and getting their best ideas before the president and turned into laws."[6] One way he kept evangelicals in the loop, or at least feeling that they were, was by hosting weekly conference calls with a handful of religious and social conservatives—people like Minnery, Richard Land of the Southern Baptist Convention's Ethics & Religious Liberty Commission, former Dobson protégé Gary Bauer of the conservative think-tank American Values, the Reverend Donald Wildmon of the American Family Association, and Cizik's boss, NAE president and Colorado Springs megachurch pastor, Ted Haggard.

Goeglein had asked for today's meeting, Cizik explained, apparently after hearing that Haggard had been telling reporters that evangelicals had more influence at the White House during the Clinton presidency than during Bush's first term. (Haggard told the *Irish Times,* for example, that Clinton "gave us everything we asked for. We had total access to the White House." He had made a similar comment to me when I visited his church in Colorado Springs a few months earlier.)[7] "I guess Tim questions whether that's really the case," Cizik said with a chuckle. "Anyway, he and I have been wanting to get together for some time. We've talked over the phone, and have been in meetings together, but we've never had a one-on-one." There was no real agenda for the forty-five-minute informal conversation. It would be a chance to discuss "a wide range of issues and, mainly, just keep the lines of communication open." They had agreed to meet at a restaurant a block from the White House.

As we wound our way through the congested downtown streets I asked Cizik about his working relationship with other prominent religious right organizations in Washington—Dobson's political-action group Focus on the Family Action, for example, and the Christian Coalition, a much-vaunted grassroots organization founded by Pat Robertson in the early 1990s that recently had fallen on hard times. I was aware that in 2003 representatives of some seventy evangelical groups had begun meeting periodically across the Potomac River in Arlington, Virginia, to strategize on fighting same-sex marriage. Now that the inauguration was over, Washington was crawling with lobbyists and spokespeople from conservative religious groups all claiming a share of responsibility for reelecting the president and strengthening his hand in Congress, and all looking to maximize their influence during Bush's second term. I wondered just how closely they were coordinating their agendas and to what effect.

"First of all," he began, "you need to understand that to the average man on the street, and to much of the media, evangelical Christians and the religious right are one and the same—we're all just one big happy family." It was clear he wanted to disabuse me of that notion. "They are fine people, and they have some fine leaders, and we work with them whenever we can." His use of the third-person pronoun here was conspicuous. "I sit in on the Arlington Group every now and then. But a number of those organizations have a narrow range of interests, and have chosen to identify with one party, the Republican Party, to a degree I believe many evangelicals are not comfortable with."

He reminded me that the NAE is a network made up of 52 denominations representing some 45,000 congregations and roughly 30 million people. Member churches range from the Assemblies of God—a fast-growing conservative Pentecostal denomination—to the pacifist Mennonite Brethren. It also includes a number of parachurch groups such the International Bible Society, Compassion International, and Campus Crusade for Christ. "That's quite a wide tent," he said, "and as an organization it's our job to speak for all of them. So here in Washington we try to take a broader view than some of the family-values groups, for example, who are focused on abortion, homosexuality, and those kinds of issues to the exclusion of almost everything else.

"Now—would some of our members consider themselves part of the religious right? Of course. Do they tend to vote Republican? Yes, by a significant margin, I'd say. But it's a mistake to think of us as exclusively the religious right and exclusively Republican. The evangelical movement has always been larger and more diverse than that."

I knew there was plenty of polling data to back up what Cizik was saying. One survey conducted by *U.S. News & World Report* and *Religion & Ethics NewsWeekly* early in 2004, for example, had found that about a quarter of white evangelicals identify themselves as Democrats or as leaning Democrat, and subsequent polls found that about half of that number voted for John Kerry.[8] John Green, director of the Ray C. Bliss Center for Applied Politics at the University of Akron in Ohio, and probably the nation's top authority on evangelical voting patterns, has estimated that about a third of evangelicals are political moderates and swing voters who tend to be critical of Bush's policies on poverty, the economy, and the environment. Roughly 55 percent of that group voted for Bill Clinton both in 1992 and 1996. Were it not for issues like abortion and same-sex marriage, which tend to galvanize conservative Christians, says Green, evangelicals "would not be a strong constituency of the Republican Party. There'd be many more Democrats among them."[9]

Those findings were consistent with an earlier study by Christian Smith, a University of North Carolina sociologist who has made a career of studying evangelicals. In nationwide polling and in hundreds of extensive interviews in the late 1990s, Smith found evangelical political views to be "replete with diversity, complexity, ambivalence, and incongruities." Even more to Cizik's point, Smith discovered that "for every one evangelical we interviewed who expressed support for a Christian Right leader or organization there was another who expressed outright opposition."[10]

So the religious right, as Cizik sees it, is a subset of evangelicalism—an important one to be sure, but one apparently in which he saw neither himself nor the NAE fitting comfortably. Nor did he identify with the so-called evangelical left, a relatively small but vocal segment composed of people like Jim Wallis, a longtime peace and antipoverty activist and editor of *Sojourners* magazine; Ron Sider, head of Evangelicals for Social Action; and Tony Campolo, a now retired sociology professor and Baptist minister who counseled President Clinton during the Monica Lewinsky scandal.

It was not so much that Cizik and the religious right differed in basic political ideology. Cizik is, after all, by his own admission, a conservative Republican—although he confesses to some youthful indiscretions: In his college days he opposed the Vietnam War and supported George McGovern for president. He even ran for local office unsuccessfully as a Democrat. As a result of those experiences, he says, "I can appreciate what it's like to be a liberal, because I once was one."

Where Cizik and the NAE differ most from the religious right is on focus and style. "What portion of our time are we going to devote to sanctity of human life and the judicial appointments and what portion to human rights and creation care? All of these issues are important to us, and we deal with them almost on a daily basis. I say we have to try to be biblical, inclusive, comprehensive, and bipartisan"—qualities that, in Cizik's estimation, apparently did not reflect the modus operandi of much of the religious right.

"The problem," he continued, "is that there is this huge perception out there, among the press especially, regarding evangelicals, that if you're going to talk politics you talk to the religious right— so the same few groups get mentioned, and their leaders get quoted as if they represent 'the evangelical view' on matters political."

Why, I asked, did he suppose that perception existed?

"For one simple reason: They have the biggest megaphones. They make the most noise and attract the most attention. But do they speak for most evangelicals?" He left the question hanging.

The megaphones Cizik was referring to, of course, were the nation's broadcast airwaves. Some of the best known names and faces of the religious right—Falwell, Robertson, Dobson, and Florida pastor D. James Kennedy—were media celebrities, with nationwide TV and radio audiences and expansive mailing lists. Many others who were less well-known to the general public— people like Bauer of American Values, Wildmon of the American

Family Association, and Tony Perkins of the Family Research Council—also were savvy communicators with ready access to Christian media outlets. Together they had the capability of reaching millions of evangelical households almost on a daily basis. It was widely assumed, therefore, in Washington and in the secular media that whenever they barked out political orders, which presumably was often, millions of obedient followers snapped to attention—an undoubtedly simplistic assessment of the religious right's influence. And yet there was no denying the interconnection between the two enterprises: The rise of the religious right was inexorably linked to the ethos and machinery of Christian broadcasting.

For nearly half a century after the Scopes trial in 1925 American evangelicals were essentially absent from the public square. They tended to steer clear of political involvement except for voting—and even that was frowned upon in some fundamentalist circles. Politics was widely regarded as a futile and worldly pursuit that could only distract from the more important business of winning souls to Christ. That was a radical departure from the nineteenth century, when socially conscious evangelicals were at the forefront of the abolition movement, and crusaded for prison reform, child labor laws, and other social causes. But by the early twentieth century evangelicalism had become steeped in premillennial theology that saw the world's problems as beyond human repair and destined to get worse until Jesus returned to establish his kingdom on earth. And so evangelicals poured their creative energies and financial resources into building their own churches and parachurch organizations and a supporting infrastructure of Bible colleges and seminaries, publishing houses, and broadcast ministries to disseminate the gospel.

The advent of commercial radio turned out to be a godsend for the evangelical subculture. Enterprising preachers who were adept at raising money to buy airtime quickly became masters of the medium. The 1930s saw flamboyant radio personalities like Pentecostal evangelist Aimee Semple McPherson and Charles E. Fuller, a revivalist Baptist preacher and Bible teacher, attract national audiences rivaling those of some of the period's most popular secular entertainers. By the end of the decade, observes Mark Noll, the eminent historian of evangelicalism, they were joined by "scores, if not hundreds, of imitators who blanketed North America with evangelical and fundamentalist broadcasts."[11] In 1944 the fledgling NAE launched a sister organization, the National Religious Broadcasters, to watch out for the legal and professional interests of evangelical radio ministries that, by then, had grown to more than 150.

When television came along at the end of the decade, evangelicals quickly embraced the new technology and expanded their reach even farther by offering a blend of gospel and entertainment uniquely suited to the new medium. Soon a new generation of media stars was born—faith healers Oral Roberts and Rex Humbard, preachers Jerry Falwell and Jimmy Swaggart, talk-show hosts Pat Robertson and Jim and Tammy Faye Bakker, and others. By the early 1970s Christian radio and TV broadcasts boasted a combined nationwide audience of tens of millions of listeners and viewers a week.

But like the evangelical movement itself at the time, the Christian airwaves still were largely devoid of politics, except for occasional tirades against godless communism and federal regulations that threatened to limit religious broadcasts. All of that was about to change dramatically.

By the mid-1970s the cultural upheaval of the previous decade—the civil rights movement, the Vietnam War, the sexual revolution, the rise of modern feminism—had begun to breach the defensive ramparts of the evangelical subculture. Supreme Court rulings banning school prayer and legalizing abortion were being assailed in evangelical pulpits as a frontal assault on faith and family, signaling to some that political quiescence was no longer an option. Falwell, who like many evangelical and fundamentalist ministers had long spoken out against clergy involvement in politics, began using his *Old-Time Gospel Hour* broadcast to preach against abortion, decrying "the killing of millions of unborn children [as] America's national sin," and comparing it to the Holocaust. He soon realized, however, that preaching alone would not be enough— along with abortion, Falwell would recall in his 1987 autobiography, there were "other crises facing the nation that required immediate political action from men and women of Christian faith."[12]

The 1976 presidential election proved to be a political coming out of sorts for evangelicals. The candidacy of Jimmy Carter, a devout Southern Baptist and political moderate, energized conservative Christian voters, who were delighted by the media attention lavished on Carter's born-again faith, and by the prospect of having one of their own in the White House. But as president, Carter disappointed many of his coreligionists with his refusal to support a constitutional ban on abortion, and with his Justice Department's attempts to enforce antidiscrimination laws at Bob Jones University, a fundamentalist school in Greenville, South Carolina— a move many of them saw as a direct government incursion into the evangelical subculture.[13] As the 1980 election approached, Falwell and other religious conservatives began looking for a new candidate, and for new ways to assert themselves in the public square. They quickly found both.

In 1979 Falwell borrowed $25,000 from a Texas businessman and launched the Moral Majority, a grassroots organization aimed at mobilizing Christian voters behind conservative candidates and causes. Billing the new organization as "pro-life, pro-family, pro-moral, and pro-American," Falwell sent fund-raising letters to his broadcast mailing list and raised more than $2 million in the first year. Within two years the Moral Majority would claim to have more than four million members (the number would later be disputed), a $10 million budget, and a chapter in every state. Most of its spending went for media activities, producing a monthly newsletter that was sent to more than 840,000 homes, and daily political commentaries carried by some three hundred radio stations around the country.[14] State chapters tended to concentrate on voter registration and local races involving "pro-family" candidates. While the Moral Majority had not been the first or only manifestation of the new religious right, with Falwell at the helm it succeeded in positioning itself to the media as the voice of an awakened giant—or what a writer for *The New Yorker* at the time would describe hyperbolically as "a disciplined, charging army"[15]—that would invigorate the Republican Party and help elect Ronald Reagan to the presidency.

Winning the white evangelical vote, especially in the South, was crucial to Reagan's hopes of unseating the incumbent president, and courting the new religious right became a top priority. Though divorced and remarried and not much of a churchgoer Reagan successfully wooed evangelicals with his unflinching conservatism and Norman Rockwell view of American ideals. He had learned to speak their language, even if it wasn't his native tongue, and had dutifully professed his fealty to faith, family, and "traditional Judeo-Christian values." At a gathering of televangelists and other religious right leaders in Dallas a few months before the election, Reagan spoke admiringly of the Bible, explaining that "all the complex questions facing us at home and abroad have their answer in that single book." At that same meeting he delivered the coup de grâce by declaring to the assembled clergy: "I know you can't endorse me ... but I want you to know that I endorse you."[16]

The preachers swooned. They went home invigorated, and in November Reagan swept the evangelical vote by nearly the same two-to-one margin that Carter had garnered four years before. The Moral Majority and the rest of the religious right had played a role by helping to register and mobilize their conservative Christian flocks, although subsequent analysis would show that Reagan probably would have won the presidency even without evangelical support.[17] But that did not stop Falwell from accepting much of the credit. Looking back later he would declare the 1980 election "my finest hour."[18]

Not everyone at the Dallas gathering was eager to climb aboard Reagan's bandwagon, or anyone else's for that matter. Pat Robertson, whose father had been a Democratic U.S. senator from Virginia, still was arguing in 1980 that "active partisan politics" was the wrong path for true evangelicals. The better way to bring about change, Robertson insisted, involved "fasting and praying ... appealing, in essence, to a higher power."[19]

Six years later, apparently having repented of such thinking, Robertson set the wheels in motion for his own run for the 1988 GOP presidential nomination. He left his on-air perch at *The 700 Club,* relinquished his ministerial credentials, and recruited a corps of grassroots volunteers—many of them Pentecostal and charismatic Christians gleaned from his television mailing list—to quietly stake out positions in Republican precinct caucuses in Iowa and Michigan. The early organizing paid off. Robertson showed surprising strength in Michigan, winning more than 40 percent of precinct delegates to a state nominating convention,[20] and finished second in the Iowa caucuses behind Bob Dole and ahead of George H. W. Bush, the eventual nominee. But after poor showings in the New Hampshire and South Carolina primaries—precipitated in part by media scrutiny of Robertson's outlandish on-air remarks and the intense opposition of party regulars—his campaign faltered. While he had succeeded in tapping a new source of political activists, Robertson's candidacy had failed to ignite much excitement among evangelical voters beyond his own Pentecostal base.

Robertson dropped out of the campaign and went back to hosting *The 700 Club,* which had seen donor revenues fall off sharply during his political adventure and in the aftermath of the televangelist scandals. About a year later Falwell disbanded the Moral Majority, saying he, too, needed to devote more time to his church and broadcast pulpits. After nearly a decade it appeared as though the religious right had run its course. Abortion still was legal. Prayer in public schools still was not. Pornography was as ubiquitous as ever.

But Robertson was merely catching his breath. In Washington for the Bush inauguration in January 1989, he met a twenty-seven-year-old political activist and recent born-again convert named Ralph Reed and asked for his ideas on how to keep Robertson's political organization intact. Reed responded with a lengthy memorandum that would become the blueprint for the Christian Coalition.[21] Both Robertson and Reed were convinced that the new Bush administration could not be counted on to deliver on the religious right's social agenda. Moreover, Reed believed that Christian conservatives had "missed the boat in the 1980s by focusing almost entirely on the White House and Congress," when most of the issues evangelicals cared about were "primarily determined in the city councils, school boards, and state legislatures."[22] What was needed, he argued, was a new grassroots organization to recruit, train, and mobilize Christians to wage political warfare at the local level.

Later that year Robertson launched the Christian Coalition to do just that, and he installed Reed as its executive director. Despite his boyish appearance Reed was a seasoned organizer with shrewd political instincts. He also proved to be a capable and telegenic spokesman, and within a year the Christian Coalition began to assert itself as a potent political force. Its growing network of state and local chapters lobbied city councils and school boards on faith-related issues, supported "pro-family" candidates for local offices, and distributed voter guides sizing up candidates for state and national office. In 1991 it launched an annual Road to Victory conference in Washington—a combination of speeches and work-shops that quickly became a media magnet and a command performance for Republicans with presidential ambitions. In 1994 the coalition helped Republicans win control of both houses of Congress for the first time in forty years—a feat that would move *Time* magazine to put Reed on its cover next to the headline "The Right Hand of God," and to declare the Christian Coalition "the most potent faction in the ascendant Republican Party."[23] With a reported membership of 1.5 million and a budget of $25 million, the Christian Coalition seemingly had arrived as the leading voice of a resurgent religious right.

Unbeknownst to anyone at the time, it also had reached its zenith. President Clinton's reelection and Democratic gains in the U.S. House of Representatives in 1996 sapped the religious right of some of its fervor. A few months after the election Reed quit the coalition to go into private political consulting, and almost immediately the organization began to falter. Within a year of his departure, declining revenues prompted layoffs and other retrenchments. In 2001 Robertson stepped down as the coalition's president, and by 2004 the organization had closed its Washington office, moved to South Carolina, and was struggling to pay its bills—its revenues had fallen to one twentieth of what they had been a decade before.[24] The Christian Coalition, in the estimation of one prominent Virginia political scientist, had become "a shell of its former self."[25]

Meanwhile, a chorus of conservative voices had emerged that purported to speak to and for evangelicals in the political arena: Dobson of Focus on the Family, Land of the Southern Baptist Convention and host of a nationally syndicated radio program, Perkins of the Family Research Council, Louis Sheldon of the Traditional Values Coalition, Haggard and Cizik of the NAE, and others. Each had his own constituency or audience, and they sometimes overlapped. But no one person or group could claim to speak for all.

And while several groups had worked hard to get conservative Christians to register and vote their values in 2004, no single religious organization could take credit for engineering the heavy evangelical turnout at the polls. Religious right activism had become much more decentralized—and more thoroughly Republican—than before.

The collapse of both the Moral Majority and the Christian Coalition had underscored the difficulty of building and maintaining a regimented political organization composed of evangelicals who, by and large, were not inclined toward political activism. It was one thing to energize Christian voters to reelect an evangelical president or to support a state ballot proposal banning gay marriage. It was quite another, as Falwell and Robertson discovered, to keep them engaged in the ranks of a full-time partisan army. "Groups like this are hard to sustain," observed Green of the University of Akron. "They tend to run on fervor, and fervor gets old."[26]

Without their broadcast pulpits and their claims to vast audiences, there was little doubt that neither Robertson and Falwell, nor their religious right successors, would have gotten as far as they did in the political world. Real or not, their presumed ability to rally Christian activists via the airwaves was a source of power—power that, to a significant degree, had been credited to them by credulous outsiders. As Rice University political sociologist William Martin observed: "After years of having regarded television preachers as some kind of aberrant novelty act, the mainstream media not only began to give them unprecedented attention, but began to accord them even more influence than they apparently had." In 1979, for example, National Religious Broadcasters executive director Ben Armstrong asserted that 130 million people listened to religious radio and television programs every week. Subsequent studies, however, Martin noted, "showed the regular audience for religious programs to be about one-tenth that size [and yet], in their haste to be exciting, all manner of major media publicized Armstrong's exaggeration."[27]

Even the religious right's ideological adversaries, groups like People for the America Way and Americans United for Separation of Church and State, did not challenge the numbers. "The greater the audience size of the right-wing televangelists," after all, as University of Virginia professor Jeffrey Hadden explained, "the greater the threat and, hence, the greater the urgency to support countermovement organizations such as [theirs]."[28] A writer in the *Washington Monthly* insightfully summed up the apparent synergy at work at the time: "Falwell wants attention, liberals want an ogre, the press wants a good story. Whenever all parties want the same thing, they tend to get it whether they deserve it or not."[29]

It would come out later that the religious right's muscular image had been enhanced by other means. Cal Thomas, a nationally syndicated columnist who was one of Falwell's early lieutenants, confessed in 1999 that there was much less to the Moral Majority's grassroots machinery than met the eye. "We had the attention of the public because of heavy publicity," Thomas wrote, "but we won few converts outside of a small band of true believers.... The press didn't know that most of our 'state chapters' were little more than a separate telephone line in a pastor's office."[30] The Christian Coalition's organizational strength also had been overstated. In a year-end filing in 1995 the coalition reported that circulation of its *Christian American* magazine, which was sent to every dues-paying member, amounted to 353,000—not an insignificant number, but far short of the 1.5 million members the organization claimed at the time.[31] It was as Robertson had candidly observed more than a decade before: "Sometimes the perception of power is equal to the reality of it, and if people perceive it's there, maybe we can have some influence."[32]

After the 2004 election there could be no doubting the perception of evangelical power in Washington. Now firmly ensconced as a key constituency of the Republican Party, they had the ear of decision makers in Congress and the White House, and they were determined to have an influence on public policy. But whose voice would be heeded and which issues would be recognized as reflecting the priorities of the evangelical community? The megaphones of the religious right were anxious to be heard, and so was Cizik.

Cizik maneuvered his Volkswagen into a parking space in front of a restaurant just across 17th Street from the Old Executive Office Building, a massive and ornate granite structure built during the Ulysses Grant administration that houses most of the White House staff. We were a few minutes early for the appointment with Goeglein, so we went inside and took a table near the window and continued our conversation.

Cizik had brought along a copy of "For the Health of the Nation"—the outline of the NAE's public policy agenda—that he planned to give to Goeglein. "He already knows this, and so does the president," Cizik said, as he draped his coat over an empty chair, "but I just want to remind him that we evangelicals are interested in a range of important issues—not just those having to do with sex." He also wanted to ask Goeglein about the administration's plans to renew its push for the president's faith-based initiative, which had stalled in the last Congress but which Cizik thought had a better chance this year. "I think that one proposal, perhaps more than any other to come out of the Bush White House during the first term, really reflects the heart of the man. He really believes in the power of faith to change people's lives for the better, because it happened to him. And now he wants to unleash faith-based groups to do what they do best."

The president's religious faith had loomed large in the 2004 campaign, more so, even, than in 2000 when candidate Bush declared during a presidential debate in Iowa that Jesus Christ was his favorite philosopher "because he changed my heart." That one unrehearsed line delivered on national television had done for Bush what Reagan's "I endorse you" remark had accomplished for his candidacy twenty years earlier—it melted the hearts of conservative Christian voters and put them firmly in his camp.

It also guaranteed that for the next four years Bush's religion would be dissected repeatedly by the media as a curiosity and touted by his allies as a source of strength. For many evangelicals there was no doubting that Bush was an authentic man of faith. Like them he had a personal relationship with the Lord, and he was not afraid to say so. And as one of their own, he was deserving of their support.

I asked Cizik why Bush's faith was such an important part of the political equation for evangelicals. When Bush was seeking the GOP nomination in 2000, I recalled, there were other Republican candidates whose positions on abortion, gay rights, and other issues dear to evangelicals were clearer and stronger than Bush's. And yet he emerged as their favorite. Why did religious brand loyalty seem to take precedence?

"Do we support him just because he's an evangelical? The answer is no," Cizik said. He reminded me that two of Bush's 2000 primary opponents, Gary Bauer and Alan Keyes, also professed to be born-again Christians, as did Al Gore, the Democratic nominee. "We've come to recognize that there are some who claim a born-again experience who, nonetheless, don't share a majority of our political views. So simply identifying oneself as an evangelical is not enough.

"That being said, there is a real sense that when President Bush speaks about his faith, as he did in that debate and as he has so many times since then, that he's speaking from the heart. He is not just hewing to a checklist of issues, nor is he just following Karl Rove's political calculations. He's revealing something deeply personal that your average evangelical identifies with. You'll remember that in the debate Bush was asked in a follow-up question to explain *how* Jesus had changed his heart, and he said essentially that unless you've had the experience it's kind of hard to explain. My guess is that a lot of evangelicals listening to that were nodding in agreement. Here was a guy running for president with whom they shared not just a religious label, but a profound, personal, spiritual experience that most evangelicals would say is the most important thing in their lives, and sometimes words can't adequately explain it. Bush's language and his demeanor confirms to evangelicals that, yes, he is one of us."

I knew from my own experience that discerning who is "one of us" and who is not tends to be of more than passing interest to evangelical and fundamentalist Christians. In large part it has to do with the biblical imperative to evangelize, and with knowing whom to target with the gospel message. But in some Christian circles it is also considered a matter of spiritual vigilance to be able to discern "heartfelt Christians" from those who "merely profess" the faith but do not have an authentic relationship with Jesus, or hold to questionable doctrine, so as to avoid being led astray by nonbelievers. Of course, seldom would anyone admit to actually judging the authenticity of another's faith. The Bible, after all, was very clear on that: "Judge not that ye be not judged." On the other hand, as I was often reminded in my fundamentalist youth, the Bible also says, "by their fruits ye shall know them,"[33] which we took to mean that we were free to make reasonable assumptions about others based on their behavior. And to our way of thinking there was no surer sign of a counterfeit Christian than failing to uphold strict standards of personal piety. It was for that reason that some conservative evangelicals I knew were offended seeing news photos of President Carter drinking champagne and dancing at state dinners. How, they wondered, could he do those things and call himself a born-again Christian?

By the 2004 election the story of Bush's conversion was widely known. He and others had written about it, and he had talked about it on numerous occasions. And it was a story that resonated with evangelicals. Bush had always been a regular churchgoer. He was raised an Episcopalian, taught Sunday school at a Presbyterian church in Midland, Texas, and became a mainline Methodist when he and Laura Bush married in 1977. But it wasn't until the 1980s, at the age of forty, after talking with Billy Graham at the family's summer home in Kennebunkport, Maine, that he began what he called "a new walk where I would recommit my heart to Jesus Christ." He gave up drinking and adopted a daily regimen of prayer and Bible reading. "It was the beginning of a change in my life," Bush wrote in his 1999 autobiography. "I was humbled to learn that God sent His Son to die for a sinner like me. I was comforted to know that through the Son, I could find God's amazing grace, a grace that crosses every border, every barrier and is open to everyone. Through the love of Christ's life, I could understand the life-changing powers of faith."[34] Although he has never used the term "born again" to describe his experience, it was clear to evangelicals that Bush had come to know the Lord in an authentic way.

But how did being an authentic "heartfelt" Christian make Bush a better president, or at least a preferred one, for evangelicals? I directed Cizik's attention back to my initial question.

"For two reasons," he said, leaning on his folded arms and hunching over the table between us. "Our presidents, by their words and actions, have sort of become the symbol of the nation's self-understanding. They provide the vision and the energy that exemplify who we are as a nation. From a man of faith we would expect a vision that acknowledges God and is accountable to God. We would expect him to foster morality and to govern on the basis of biblical ethics—not in a sectarian way, but in a way that seeks justice for all and the betterment of society. That's the way it should be, anyway. And if he does well, the nation is well served, and it reflects positively on the Christian faith.

"Secondly, we know that George Bush is a man of prayer. He reads the Bible daily and seeks the wisdom and guidance of God. As evangelicals we believe that's essential to living a faithful Christian life. It's what all of us endeavor to do." He leaned back in his chair, and his eyes widened. "And here we have the leader of our country who does the very same thing! We take comfort in that. Frankly, I sleep better at night knowing we have a president who prays and seeks God's will and, very importantly, who believes that he is accountable to a higher authority. Now—" he shifted in his seat, "does he always get it right? Obviously not. No one does. And we disagree with him on some things. But at least we know that he is seeking God's will and that he wants to do what is right. And that is important to us.

"We also recognize that there are those around the president who would take this affinity we feel for him as a fellow evangelical and exploit it for political purposes, and we need to be careful not to allow that to happen. There is a temptation to give the benefit of the doubt sometimes where it shouldn't be given, just because he is one of us."

Although neither of us knew it at the time, just such a test of evangelical affinity would arise a few months later, with Bush's ill-fated nomination of White House counsel Harriet Miers to the U.S. Supreme Court. Like most Americans, evangelicals were surprised, and some were dismayed, when Bush announced on October 3, 2005, that he was naming his longtime aide and fellow Texan to replace retiring justice Sandra Day O'Connor. Social conservatives had been hoping for someone with the intellectual heft and ideological pedigree of an Antonin Scalia, and they did not perceive those qualities in Miers. White House operatives tried hard to dispel doubts about her judicial qualifications and the depth of her prolife commitment by quietly reassuring religious right leaders that they had nothing to worry about, because Miers was, after all, an evangelical Christian. The implication—and it was never more than that—was that if a case involving abortion or same-sex marriage were to arise, her evangelical faith would guide her to do the right thing.

It apparently was enough to mollify James Dobson who, after taking a phone call from Karl Rove, reported rather tentatively to his radio audience that he thought Miers would "make a good justice." It also seemed to satisfy Jay Sekulow, head of the American Center for Law and Justice, a Christian legal advocacy group founded by Pat Robertson. Interviewed on Robertson's television show, Sekulow called Miers's nomination "a big opportunity for those of us who share an evangelical faith ... to see someone with our positions put on a court"—even though he conceded that he did not know Miers's specific views on abortion.[35]

But other right-leaning activists would demand much more explicit assurances. "Just saying, 'I'm an evangelical Christian,' really doesn't go very far with us, because we know that for some people it's just a label," Cheryl Sullenger, a spokesperson for the antiabortion group Operation Rescue, told me in a telephone interview. "We want to know the specifics—what does a nominee believe about abortion?"[36] Cathie Adams, president of the Texas branch of the conservative Eagle Forum, put it in biblical terms. "President Bush is asking us to have faith in things unseen," she told the *Washington Post*. "We only have that kind of faith in God."[37]

Three weeks later, in the face of a widening conservative insurrection, the White House withdrew the Miers nomination, and almost without exception, Christian right leaders applauded the move. Her evangelical ties had not proved sufficient to carry the day.


I checked my watch. We had been sitting in the restaurant for nearly twenty minutes and Goeglein had yet to arrive.

Cizik glanced at his watch, and then out the window and down the street. He took out his cell phone and checked it for messages—nothing—and snapped it closed. We talked for a few more minutes, about the presidential inauguration a week earlier, and about the political climate in the new Congress.

At 10:30 A.M., Cizik called Goeglein's office and left a voice-mail message that he was waiting at the restaurant. Two minutes later he made another call, this time to retrieve his own office messages. As he listened he looked at me and shook his head. Something had come up at the last minute, and Goeglein had canceled.

"Well," he said, slipping his phone back into his pocket, "I guess you can look at this a couple of ways—either he blew us off because he knows we're in his pocket, or something in fact did come up." He chose to believe the latter. "His office *did* leave a message. But he has my cell phone number. He could have reached me." So much for keeping open the lines of communication, I thought.

As we got up to leave I could sense that Cizik was a bit embarrassed, but he shrugged it off. He had been around Washington long enough to understand how easily schedules can go awry, and he knew there would be plenty of other opportunities for a meeting. Yet if one were looking for early signs of what James Dobson and others had disdainfully described as "a return to business as usual"—the perennial postelection neglect of religious conservatives and their agenda by Republican officeholders—this certainly had the markings. I was inclined to chalk it up as an occupational hazard of being a political operative rather than a media celebrity. It was hard to imagine Dobson or Pat Robertson being stood up by a midlevel White House functionary or—even more unimaginable—abiding such a slight with as much equanimity. If Cizik felt snubbed he was doing a good job of hiding it.


Back in the car we headed for Cizik's next appointment: a prayer vigil at the Iraqi Embassy near Dupont Circle just a few blocks away. In two days Iraqi voters would go to the polls, braving the threats of a murderous insurgency to cast their ballots in the country's first free election in fifty years. It was a pivotal moment that would test whether democracy could take root in a post-Saddam

Iraq torn by sectarian religious strife and almost daily terrorist bombings. It also seemed then like a make-or-break moment for President Bush's embattled agenda in Iraq. The administration was counting on a strong voter turnout to shore up flagging support at home for a war that seemed to have lost its focus, and had no foreseeable end. Cizik had agreed to join with a group of evangelical ministers and laity outside the embassy to pray for the election's success, and for the safety of Iraqi voters.

When we arrived at the three-story brick Romanesque building at the corner of 18th and P streets about thirty people were milling about on the sidewalk beneath a flagpole bearing the red-white-and-black Iraqi flag, while two uniformed security guards watched from inside a low wrought-iron gate a few yards away. On the periphery a knot of reporters and photographers encircled a man in a dark overcoat and fedora and a bright red scarf, who was talking animatedly into their microphones. Over the din of midday traffic I could pick up just a few disjointed phrases—"a great outpouring ... solidarity with the Iraqi people ... dramatic step for democracy."

Addressing the assembled press was the Reverend Rob Schenck, president of the National Clergy Council and one of the event's organizers. I had run into Schenck on several previous occasions and knew him to be a passionate voice on conservative social issues, and one of dozens of religious entrepreneurs in the nation's capital. He was known also as something of a gadfly and self-promoter. As the founder of a Christian advocacy group called Faith and Action, which he operates out of a townhouse behind the Supreme Court Building, Schenk bills himself on his Web site as a "missionary to Capitol Hill ... bringing the Word of God to bear on the hearts and minds of those who make public policy."

Just how influential he is or how much actual ministering he does among top government officials, however, is not at all clear. One Capitol Hill staffer who has seen him in action once told me that Schenck spends little time doing the kind of legislative work that Cizik and others engage in on an almost daily basis. What he is most known for is his ability to attract media attention and his knack for showing up wherever and whenever there are new public eruptions of the culture wars. Outside the Alabama courtroom of "Ten Commandments" judge Roy Moore, on the Supreme Court steps during oral arguments over the Pledge of Allegiance, near a Florida hospital where brain-damaged Terri Schiavo lay dying of starvation—Schenck would be there, delivering biblical sound bites and admonishing evildoers as the TV cameras rolled. I had come to think of him as the religious right's answer to the Reverend Jesse Jackson.

Here on the sidewalk on the eve of the Iraqi vote, Schenck once again was in his element, basking in the media limelight. A local radio reporter wanted to know how large of a turnout it would take for the Iraqi election to be deemed a success. "The Iraqis are a brave and freedom-loving people," Schenck said, not about to be pulled into the numbers game, "and I'm confident that you will see them turning out in numbers sufficient to show beyond a shadow of a doubt that the spirit of democracy is alive in that troubled land. We are here today to support them"—and if he just happened to pick up a little personal publicity in the process, so much the better.

It was time to get the prayer vigil underway. Schenck thanked the reporters for coming and called on the Reverend Patrick Mahoney, head of the Washington-based Christian Defense Coalition and coorganizer of the event, to open the brief ceremony that would mark the beginning of a seventy-two-hour period of prayer and fasting to coincide with the Iraqi vote. For about twenty minutes the small, mostly young crowd recited scripture together and offered prayers on behalf of Iraq's citizens and the U.S. troops and Iraqi security forces who would be guarding the polling places. Cizik read a passage from the Gospel of Matthew that contained the words of Jesus from the Sermon on the Mount:

*Blessed are the peacemakers, for they will be called sons of God. Blessed are those who are persecuted because of righteousness, for theirs is the kingdom of heaven. Blessed are you when people insult you, persecute you and falsely say all kinds of evil against you because of me. Rejoice and be glad, because great is your reward in heaven.*

Then the entire crowd knelt in a huddle on the cold concrete sidewalk and, as the cameras rolled, Schenck prayed a concluding prayer, thanking God for the "tremendous courage of the Iraqi people" and calling for divine protection over the voting process.

With that the service ended. Schenck announced that the group had been invited inside the embassy for coffee and doughnuts—the fast apparently would be put on hold for an hour or so. The crowd quickly filed through metal detectors and into a sparsely furnished first-floor reception room with dark wood-paneled walls and crystal chandeliers that were slightly askew, a reminder of the neglect that had befallen the once elegant mansion during the fourteen years since the first Persian Gulf War, when Iraq hurriedly withdrew its diplomats from Washington.

The Christians were greeted by Faiz Al-Gailani, a jovial man with thinning gray hair and a bushy mustache who recently had been installed by the interim Iraqi government as the embassy's chargé d'affaires. In heavily accented English Al-Gailani, a Sunni Muslim, thanked his visitors for their prayers and support. "We, of course, are very grateful for what your country has done to help bring democracy to our land," he said, noting that he was a young man when Iraq last held free elections. "Many of our people do not remember such a time. Our young people have never experienced freedom. They have to learn what democracy means."

For the next several minutes he entertained questions and posed for pictures with his guests. Someone asked if he thought Iraq's new constitution would permit Christians and members of other religions to worship freely and participate fully in the majority Muslim nation. Al-Gailani chuckled and reminded the questioner that Christians have lived in Iraq "for many centuries, much longer than they have lived here in the United States." Indeed, at the outbreak of the war, there were an estimated eight hundred thousand Iraqi Christians, roughly 3 percent of the total population of twenty-five million. Most of them were Chaldean Catholics, an Eastern-rite sect whose roots in Iraq purportedly go back to the second century. Included among them had been Saddam Hussein's second-in-command, Deputy Prime Minister Tariq Aziz. Unlike in some Muslim countries—U.S. ally Saudi Arabia was a prime example—Christians under Saddam's secular Baathist regime generally were permitted to worship openly and unmolested as long as they did nothing to vex Saddam or challenge his authority. Al-Gailani expressed confidence that the rights of non-Muslims would continue to be safeguarded under the new regime.

What he did not say, however, and what I suspected was the question behind the question, was whether Christian missionaries from other nations would be permitted to proselytize in the new Iraq—a subject of keen interest to many evangelicals but a potentially explosive issue among Muslims throughout the Middle East. Within days of the U.S. invasion reports had surfaced that some evangelical relief agencies were amassing supplies in Amman, Jordan, and were preparing to follow U.S. troops into Iraq as soon as it was safe to do so. Along with food, water, and medicine the Christians were eager to disseminate their faith, or, as one missionary agency put it at the time, to help Iraqis "have true freedom in Jesus Christ."[38] Predictably, such talk inflamed radical mullahs in Baghdad and elsewhere, who already were characterizing the U.S. invasion as a crusade against Islam, and the Bush administration moved quickly to distance itself from such efforts.[39] While it was not illegal in Iraq for a Muslim to convert to another faith, proselytizing by foreigners was strictly prohibited. Had they pressed him, there probably was little Al-Gailani could have told his evangelical visitors that would have given them reason to hope that their missionaries would have a freer hand in the new Iraq.

The conversation was winding down. Schenck asked how public morale was holding up during the insurgency and wondered aloud if things in Iraq perhaps were "not as bad as it is often portrayed" by the American news media. "This is not an easy time in Iraq," Al-Gailani responded, "but what you see"—the reported bombings and violent attacks—"is not happening everywhere. It does not represent the accurate situation of Iraqi society." Schenck nodded knowingly. "But for freedom," the diplomat went on, "you have to sacrifice, and what you are seeing is sacrifice. It is difficult, yes. But it is worth it."

Cizik thanked Al-Gailani for his hospitality, and shook his hand vigorously while the others in the room applauded. As they prepared to leave Schenck asked if he could offer a prayer. "Yes, of course," Al-Gailani responded, and bowed his head.

"Holy God," Schenck began, "we are thankful for this moment in history. We are thankful for our Iraqi neighbors, for our friends. Help us to be friends to the Iraqi people for a very long time to come. We do pray today that in your compassion, in your mercy, in your grace, that you will grant the Iraqi people good success in this election, and that there will be cause for rejoicing in this land, and that hope will endure. We ask this in the name of *our* savior, Jesus Christ. Amen."

As we left the building a reporter for a Japanese television network pulled Cizik aside and asked whether American evangelicals supported the war in Iraq, and if that had been the real motive for coming to the embassy: to demonstrate support for President Bush's Iraq policy. Cizik shook his head. "The National Association of Evangelicals, which I work for, has not taken a position on the war," Cizik explained to the television camera. "But I think evangelical Christians as a whole want to pray for Iraq, want to be supportive in any way they can, because we know a lot's at stake.

If this effort in Iraq were to fail—I don't believe it will—but if our efforts fail, then millions of people around the world will lose, not just the Iraqis, because the terrorists win. And this is one war which the people of the world cannot afford to lose, because it's fundamentally a war against terrorism." The reporter nodded, and the interview was over.

Clearly this had not been a pep rally for the president and his decision to go to war in Iraq. Cizik was right about that. Evangelicals were all over the map on the legitimacy of the war, and even though polls consistently showed them as a group to be more supportive than the rest of the population, the numbers were falling.[40] No evangelical organization I was aware of had taken an official stand in support of the war. Yet as the fighting continued, evangelicals, like most Americans, were hoping and praying for a good outcome. That, it seemed to me, was what the prayer vigil had been about.

Two weeks later, writing in a monthly newsletter to NAE members, Cizik would recall the embassy visit and declare that the prayers offered on the sidewalk and around the world on behalf of the Iraqis appeared to have been answered. More than 8.5 million Iraqi voters had turned out that weekend and elected 275 representatives to a transitional National Assembly that would begin drafting a permanent constitution. The participation rate—some 58 percent of registered voters—had topped that of recent U.S. presidential elections. And while at least fifty Iraqis were killed in sporadic terror attacks over the weekend, election-related violence had been far less than anticipated. "The election," Cizik concluded in the letter, "was a heroic success."[41]

It was half past noon when we climbed back into Cizik's car and headed to Capitol Hill for two afternoon appointments. Our first stop was the office of Senator Joseph Lieberman. The Connecticut

Democrat and 2000 vice presidential candidate was cosponsor, along with Arizona Republican Senator John McCain, of a bill to combat global warming by reducing industrial emissions of greenhouse gases. The Senate had rejected a similar proposal in 2003, and it faced White House opposition and an uphill fight in the current Congress. It was not exactly the kind of issue one would expect evangelicals to get excited about. But Cizik recently had become a believer in the global warming threat, and now was doing his best to convert his fellow evangelicals. He had asked for a meeting with Lieberman's chief legislative aide on the environment, Tim Profeta, to see how they might help each other out.

In the outer lobby of Lieberman's office in the modern nine-story Hart Senate Office Building, we met up with the Reverend Jim Ball, executive director of the Evangelical Environmental Network, who would be joining us in the meeting. A Baptist minister in his early forties, Ball was a leading evangelical voice on climate change and other environmental issues. His group had gained national notoriety two years earlier with its "What Would Jesus Drive?" media campaign against gas-guzzling cars—"because transportation is a moral issue"—and more recently had launched a crusade against mercury poisoning of the unborn. Ball had met with Lieberman's aide on a number of previous occasions and had suggested the meeting to Cizik.

We had arrived right on time, and were immediately ushered into a conference room, where Ball introduced us to Profeta, an athletic-looking man with thinning brown hair who looked to be in his midthirties. Profeta had worked for Lieberman since 2000, representing him in legislative negotiations on environment and energy issues and directing the staff of the Senate Subcommittee on Clean Air, Wetlands, and Climate Change during Lieberman's term as chair in the 107th Congress. He had degrees in political science from Yale and environmental management and law from Duke, and had clerked briefly for a federal judge in Washington, D.C. In his relatively short tenure on Lieberman's staff he had attained the status of one of the chief architects of environmental policy on Capitol Hill.

We took our seats around a rectangular wooden conference table, and Cizik began the conversation by explaining rather apologetically the general neglect of environmental issues—and of global warming in particular—by evangelicals. "As a group," he said, "evangelicals just haven't taken the threat seriously, despite overwhelming evidence, in our view, that it is real." He handed Profeta a copy of the NAE's public policy statement, and pointed out the section on creation care. "Our position is that there are principles laid out in scripture that clearly teach us that we should be good stewards of the environment, and that's why we're here today. We have enormous respect for you and the senator and for what you're doing. We may be Johnny-come-latelies on the environment, but we want you to know we're with you."

"You are welcome," Profeta responded. "You are very welcome."

Ball interjected that "without Rich's leadership, we wouldn't be where we are now on this. He's really been at the forefront on this issue." Ball, in fact, was thrilled to have gained Cizik as an ally. Ball had been laboring for years to mobilize evangelicals on the environment but with minimal success. In 2002 Cizik had reluctantly agreed to accompany him to a conference of Christian environmentalists in Oxford, England, and it was there that Cizik shed his skepticism and became convinced of the evidence for global warming. Almost immediately he had begun speaking out on the issue and working against the odds to make it a priority on the NAE's agenda.

"When I saw the evidence laid out, and saw that it was not contested as much as some evangelicals had been saying," Cizik explained, "I became a believer, and I decided I would put my oar in the water, no matter who tried to take my head off." Now he was looking to Profeta and Lieberman for help in "making the moral, theological, and political arguments that will help us to see where we as evangelicals can stand—knowing that our friend in the White House opposes us on this."

Indeed, the president had signaled his own skepticism on global warming early on. Shortly after taking office in 2001 he had pulled the United States out of the 178-nation Kyoto Protocol on global climate change, arguing that science had not yet spoken conclusively on the subject, and that the treaty's proposed mandatory limits on carbon dioxide emissions would hurt the U.S. economy. Later he had offered a substitute proposal calling for voluntary limits, but it attracted little support. With the president opposed to mandatory measures to combat global warming, as Lieberman and McCain were calling for, it was not surprising that many of his religious right allies were content to ignore the issue entirely.

The history of neglect notwithstanding, Cizik explained, he, Ball, and others were hoping to get evangelical leaders to sign a prescriptive statement on global warming that would go beyond the generalities—important as they were—contained in the NAE's position on creation care. "We'd like for it to say that the Lieberman-McCain bill is a good first step," he said. "Evangelicals have tremendous regard for Senator Lieberman and his moral clarity. They appreciate that he is guided in his policy positions by his Orthodox Jewish faith, and that will help a lot."

Profeta had been listening carefully and jotting notes on a yellow legal pad. "But how do you get from a statement by your leaders to the support of evangelical voters?" he asked. "I don't understand the process."

"We don't either," Cizik deadpanned, and all three laughed. Then he ventured an answer. "You put the issue on your agenda—we've done that. You include it in all your public-policy briefings—we're doing that. Then people hopefully begin to cogitate, and we continue to build and educate. If we can get a few of the megachurch pastors on board it will help." He mentioned Saddleback pastor Rick Warren, a strong advocate for HIV/AIDS relief, and

Jack Hayford, president of the International Church of the Four-square Gospel, as good bets. "And Ted Haggard, our president, already is very strong on the environment. If we get the big guys, I think the medium- and smaller-size churches will follow."

While it would take some work to get ordinary evangelicals politically motivated on climate change, at least Cizik and the others would not be starting from scratch. The Pew Forum on Religion and Public Life had found in a survey a few months earlier that 52 percent of evangelicals said they would support strict rules to protect the environment, even if it cost jobs or resulted in higher prices.[42] That was about the same level of support as in the general population, and it suggested that ordinary evangelical churchgoers were probably more favorably inclined toward environmental causes than many of their most vocal leaders, even if it wasn't a high priority.

Cizik and Ball hoped that once mobilized, evangelicals could act as a bridge between pro-environment and pro-business antagonists in Congress, and perhaps nudge the president in a more environment-friendly direction. "With our Republican connections," Cizik concluded, "I think we're in a unique position to take the lead on this and make some real headway."

Profeta agreed. "Somehow it has become a partisan issue, and I don't know why," he said. "We see climate change as a poverty issue and a moral issue. The poor are hurt disproportionately by the kinds of natural disasters—the droughts and coastal flooding and intensified weather patterns—that are brought on by global warming." Both Cizik and Ball nodded in agreement. Within a few months Hurricane Katrina would provide a dramatic case in point, ravaging some of the poorest sections of New Orleans and the Gulf Coast in what would be one of the busiest hurricane seasons on record. "Part of our working with you," Profeta continued, "is to try and broaden the view that this is a global issue. It's not Democrats versus Republicans or environmentalists versus business. We need to find ways to communicate at a different level—to address the moral imperative."

The next twenty minutes or so were spent strategizing on what each could do in the coming months to advance their common cause. The NAE would invite Lieberman to address its leaders at a Washington meeting in March, providing the senator both personal exposure and a chance to plug his proposal in front of an admiring and potentially supportive crowd. Lieberman and McCain were considering plans to conduct town meetings around the country to explain and build public support for their proposal. Profeta suggested that the sessions might help convince doubting evangelicals about the reality of the global-warming threat. Cizik thought it was a great idea, and urged Profeta to include Colorado Springs on the itinerary. "Ted Haggard would jump at the chance to participate," he said.

With their tentative plans set, the meeting came to an end, and Cizik, Ball, and Profeta shook hands and parted company.

Two months later Lieberman appeared before the NAE leaders as agreed and recited the evidence for global warming, urging the evangelicals to "join us in this profoundly religious cause." His remarks were well received. He and McCain, meanwhile, had decided against holding town meetings on their proposal. On June 22, it came up for a Senate vote and was rejected 38–60—a worse defeat than in 2003, when it lost by a vote of 43–55. Unable to get a consensus from the NAE board in time, both Cizik and the NAE had remained officially neutral on the bill. But eight months later, in February 2006, more than seventy-five evangelical leaders, including Cizik, Pastors Warren and Hayford, and several members of the NAE board would sign a historic statement declaring for the first time that "our commitment to Jesus Christ compels us to solve the global warming crisis," and urging government and business to "act boldly and set the course." Predictably absent from the list of signers were Dobson and Minnery of Focus on the Family, Land of the Southern Baptist Convention, and others of the religious right, who considered environmental issues a distraction. Still, it was the breakthrough Cizik and Ball had been hoping for. The evangelical agenda had been broadened, and the seeds of a bipartisan alliance on global warming had been planted.


There was one last appointment on Cizik's schedule, and we didn't have far to go to keep it. Connected to the Hart Building to the west is the Dirksen Building, a seven-story white-marble structure that houses senators' offices along with several of the Senate's committees and their staffs. Cizik had arranged to meet there with Frank Jannuzi, a member of the Democratic staff of the Senate Foreign Relations Committee and a specialist on East Asia.

Before coming to work for the committee in 1997, Jannuzi had been a military and political analyst for the State Department, focusing on China-Taiwan relations and affairs on the Korean peninsula. Those areas were of particular interest to Cizik, who had studied in Taipei, and to a growing number of evangelicals, who had become increasingly concerned about religious persecution and other human-rights abuses in China and North Korea, and about security threats posed by the two communist nations.

Consequently, Cizik and Jannuzi had become frequent conversation partners. "I like to use him as a sounding board," Cizik explained, as we made our way to Jannuzi's fourth-floor office. Largely as a result of their relationship, Jannuzi had persuaded the committee's ranking Democrat, Senator Joseph Biden of Delaware, to support the North Korea Human Rights Act, a Republican-sponsored and NAE-backed measure linking increased humanitarian aid to human-rights improvements by the repressive Pyongyang government. President Bush signed it into law in October 2004. Cizik had asked for this day's meeting with Jannuzi "just to keep him abreast of what we're up to and to ask his advice on a couple of things."

We arrived at Jannuzi's office and were invited into the small cluttered work space he shares with another staffer. On the walls were detailed maps of the Caribbean, Asia, and the Korean peninsula. An old leather couch in the middle of the room was covered with books and bulging file folders. In his early forties, with dark hair and dark-rimmed glasses, Jannuzi bore a striking resemblance to the comedy actor Eugene Levy. He was affable and talkative, and for about an hour, we sat around a small wooden table, and he and Cizik traded political gossip and explored a range of foreign policy issues on which both saw opportunities for bipartisanship. This time, unlike the previous conversation, Cizik did most of the listening and note taking.

"The impression a lot of Democrats have of evangelicals," Jannuzi volunteered, "is that they are focused on a few hot-button issues, like abortion and gay marriage, which I suppose is understandable given the political traction that those issues have. But a lot of Democrats think, 'Gee, isn't homelessness a moral issue on which people of faith have been deeply involved in the past, and on which Democrats have a stronger track record than Republicans?' There are a bunch of issues like that, moral issues, that either are nonpartisan or would be more attuned to the Democrats' platform. And I think foreign aid is one of those issues."

Traditionally, he continued, Christians, "especially those with missionary experience, have been among the strongest advocates for foreign aid and international development," but their voices in the Republican Party are "drowned out by fiscal conservatives who see it primarily as a budget issue. We're spending less than three tenths of one percent of our Gross Domestic Product on foreign aid. At the height after World War II we were spending two percent. We're not talking about matching that or doubling or tripling what we're spending now. But we can do better. At the current level critical needs are not being met."

Cizik nodded and reported that a week earlier he had sent a

letter to the White House, signed by thirty evangelical leaders, urging the president to seek full funding of his Millennium Challenge Account, a $3-billion-a-year foreign-aid program Bush initiated in 2002 to provide aid bonuses to needy countries that demonstrate progress on human rights. So far the program had been funded at only about half that level.

"That's a great place to start," Jannuzi responded, "because this was the brainchild of the Bush White House and Secretary of State Powell, and Republicans in Congress have failed to deliver. It's not like we're trying to get them to do something they don't believe in. But keep in mind that this is supposed to be bonus money, in addition to traditional needs-based foreign aid, not in place of it. You've got hungry people living in countries that happen to be ruled by corrupt governments. We can't just ignore them."

He also urged Cizik to push for full funding of the president's Global AIDS Initiative, intended to provide $3 billion a year for medical care, education, and research in Africa and elsewhere, but which also had been underfunded.

"We've already weighed in on that one," Cizik said. "Some of our churches and member organizations have really begun to step up on HIV/AIDS, but there is so much more that the government can and should be doing. This is going to be a real priority for us."

Jannuzi was gratified to hear that. It was evident that he and Cizik saw eye to eye on a number of issues, and the more they talked the clearer it became that they had developed a useful rapport and a measure of personal trust. They talked about recent events in North Korea and commiserated over the slow implementation of the North Korea Human Rights Act. They talked about China and what leverage might be applied to encourage progress on human rights there. And Cizik concluded by asking for Jannuzi's advice regarding an NAE delegation's upcoming trip to Morocco. A recently appointed member of the U.S. Commission on International Religious Freedom had asked to come along. Did he think it was a good idea? "Not if you don't want the Moroccans to ignore the rest of you," Jannuzi said. "He would be seen as a representative of the government, as the important one." Cizik grinned and jotted a note. This was exactly the kind of candor he had come to expect from his sounding board.

When we left Jannuzi's office it was after 4:00 P.M., and Cizik still had some business to attend to at his own office, located in a modern townhouse a few blocks south of the Capitol. I tagged along to ask a few more questions.

As expected, the day had been a busy one and, for me, it had been eminently instructive. I felt I had, indeed, caught a glimpse of what others had described as the maturation of evangelical political involvement—a broadened agenda, a heightened professionalism and civility, a willingness to compromise and cooperate with erstwhile adversaries for a common good—reflected in the conduct of at least this one important evangelical organization and its Washington representative.

And I knew that there were others of like mind. A couple of weeks later I would spend some time with Richard Land of the Southern Baptist Convention and his associate, Barrett Duke, and would see much of the same dedication to old-fashioned legwork and effective coalition building, though with a decidedly more partisan edge. Land, an Oxford-educated Texan with a booming voice and a televangelist's pompadour, makes no apologies for his close personal ties to President Bush, whom he describes as "the greatest president of my lifetime," or for his own decidedly Republican leanings. But when it comes to pursuing a Washington agenda, he, like Cizik, rejects the "all-or-nothing" approach that still characterizes some on the religious right. "We understand the game much better than we did in the 1980s," Land would tell me. "You don't make the perfect the enemy of the good."

Yet whether or not the day with Cizik had been typical, I knew it had yielded but a limited snapshot. The environment, human rights, and bipartisanship had been the dominant themes, highlighting a seldom recognized progressive streak in evangelical politics. But had I accompanied Cizik four days earlier I would have found him carrying a banner in an antiabortion march near the White House and strategizing with Republicans on the Unborn Child Pain Awareness Act. A month later I might have listened in as he lobbied members of Congress to oppose a bill easing restrictions on embryonic stem cell research. Those issues, too, were unmistakably part of the NAE's Washington agenda, and reflected the traditional conservative bent of modern evangelicalism.

Indeed, those were the very kinds of issues that had drawn Christian conservatives back into the political game in the first place. But now that they were in, evangelicals were branching out in sometimes surprising ways and forging the least likely of alliances— working with feminists on sex-trafficking legislation, with gay-rights activists on the Global AIDS Initiative, with Tibetan Buddhists on the International Religious Freedom Act, with the ACLU on a prison-rape bill, and so on. "We evangelicals have learned to collaborate, to cross the aisles and religious barriers or whatever, in order to pass bills," Cizik explained. "This is what we have to do if we're going to win in Washington."

To win in Washington. Yes, that was the point. It is what Cizik had told the two professors earlier in the day. Evangelicals were learning to adapt, to play by the rules of the game, because they had discovered that that is what it takes to win.

But what, for them, would constitute winning? What ultimate objective did they have in mind as they crafted their legislative agendas, mobilized voters, and trained college students for government careers? This, for many nonevangelical Americans, was the scary part in watching Christian conservatives accumulate power in Washington. What did they intend to do with it?

"Are we out to turn this into a Christian nation? The answer is no," Cizik said as he settled onto a sofa in his sparsely furnished office. "Some of our members may think that way—Dr. Kennedy talks about 'reclaiming America for Christ,' and some others use that kind of language—but we at the NAE do not. We recognize that this is a pluralistic and religiously diverse nation, and that's just not what we're about.

"When I say we want to win, I mean we want to win legislatively. But I don't believe politics is a zero-sum game—that in order for me to win somebody's got to lose. Winning for us means establishing a common agreement about what we ought to do as a country about its most pressing problems. Sure there are issues on which we want to bring our values to bear. Look, we're evangelicals. We have an evangelistic impulse, and we don't apologize for it. Jesus gave us the Great Commission, to preach the gospel and make disciples of all nations by changing hearts one at a time. But we also have a biblical mandate to try and transform the culture for the common good. And when we talk about transforming culture, it doesn't mean we want to shove it down people's throats or that we're going to legislate our Christian convictions on non-Christians. We want to communicate our values in ways that appeal to all, whether they are Christians or not. And if we can't articulate a vision that someone who is not an evangelical can buy, we're never going to sell it."

Transforming culture, whether by political or more spiritual means, had been the subject of a rancorous debate in the evangelical world a few years earlier. Two former lieutenants in the Moral Majority, political columnist Cal Thomas and Michigan pastor Ed Dobson (no relation to James), had declared the religious right a failure and that politics was the wrong arena for Christians trying to transform America. "A change in people's behavior comes from a change of heart, and only the gospel can bring about that change," they wrote in their 1999 book, *Blinded By Might: Why the Religious Right Can't Save America*.[43] Drawing from their own experience, Thomas and Dobson cautioned against the seduction of political power, and warned that partisan entanglements could only compromise the church's authority, turning it into "just another lobbying group to which politicians can toss an occasional bone to ensure loyalty."[44]

But their arguments were shouted down by other leading evangelical voices. Writing in *Christianity Today* at the time, Christian commentator and former Watergate figure Charles Colson warned that if Christians were to withdraw from the political fray, "we would simply ride a pendulum swing back to the isolationism of the fundamentalist era." Instead, he argued, "we should learn from our mistakes and develop a biblically grounded political philosophy that gets us off the pendulum and provides a basis for acting 'Christianly' in politics."[45]

That, as I had come to learn, was precisely what Cizik and other evangelical activists had been trying to achieve. By broadening their agenda and drawing others of like faith into a productive and reasoned political engagement, they hoped to transcend the belligerent rhetoric of the culture wars and, in the name of heaven, to accomplish some earthly good. For them turning back was not an acceptable option. They had been thrust by circumstance and their own success onto center stage. They were in a position of influence in Washington with friends at both ends of Pennsylvania Avenue. How would they use it? It was, in Cizik's words, a "*kairos* moment"—a moment of decision and of truth.

"The world is watching to see what we as evangelical Christians will say and do," he said, glancing out his office window to the street below. "The question is, will we seize it? Will we seize the moment to act as biblical people?"

He returned his gaze to the window and to the congested city street as if somewhere in the bustling rush-hour traffic he would find his answer.

# NINE

# Redemption Road

New York City

I t was a sweltering June afternoon, the third and final day of Billy Graham's 417th crusade, and the crowd at Flushing Meadows Corona Park spilled far beyond the designated seating area in the shadow of the Unisphere, the landmark twelve-story globe from the 1964 New York World's Fair. The young and the old, parents with small children, seekers, true believers, and the merely curious—more than ninety thousand people in all had come to see and hear the world's most famous preacher in what was billed as his last crusade.

After nearly an hour of music and other preliminaries the frail eighty-six-year-old evangelist shuffled onto the stage to a standing ovation. Helped by his son, Franklin, he slowly made his way to the pulpit, where he would deliver the same simple message he had preached to more than 210 million people in over 185 countries over more than half a century: "Jesus Christ came, he died on the cross, he rose again, and he asks us to repent of our sins."

But as he started out on this historic day—his familiar chiseled face filling two giant video screens, his thick white mane of hair blowing in the humid breeze—Graham took longer than usual publicly thanking his coworkers for their hard work and for "putting up with me" for nearly sixty years. "I was asked in an interview if this was our last crusade, and I said it probably is—in New York," he said, in a slightly muffled voice with a lilting Carolina accent. And then, smiling, he quickly added: "But I also said, 'I never say never.'"

The crowd cheered wildly at the tantalizing prospect that perhaps this aging lion of God was not ready to be silenced after all, that there would be other crusades to come. And yet as Graham spoke wistfully about his own mortality—"Yes, I'm looking forward to death.... I know that it won't be long"—there was no escaping the melancholy reality that a historic era was drawing to a close.

For more than half a century Billy Graham has reigned as the single most visible and revered figure in American Protestantism, and as a unifying force among the nation's evangelicals. While his stature as a spiritual leader is more symbolic than real—there is no evangelical hierarchy over which Graham presides—his personal integrity and the simplicity of his message have kept him in a position of high national esteem. Of all the media stars and would-be leaders of the modern evangelical movement who have emerged since World War II, says historian Mark Noll, "none has come close to the visibility, influence, and sheer presence of William Franklin Graham."[1]

But with Graham's health failing—he suffers from Parkinson's disease, prostate cancer, and hydrocephalus—both the future of his ministry and the fate of the broader evangelical movement stand poised at a crucial moment. Graham's organization, the Billy Graham Evangelistic Association, has been preparing for years for the transition. Franklin Graham already is ensconced as its CEO and fills in whenever his father is too ill to preach. Yet no one, including the younger Graham himself, expects him to assume fully his father's mantle. "I can't be Billy Graham," he has often said. And while there are plenty of popular preachers who are capable of filling stadiums and sports arenas, and others have won national acclaim as successful pastors or broadcasters, no single individual is waiting in the wings to assume Graham's privileged place of personal influence.

That leadership vacuum, some experts believe, could mean difficult days ahead for the evangelical movement. With Graham's passing, says Noll, "the apparent unity that Graham's presence bequeathed to a diverse movement will be a thing of the past." Without a stabilizing center of gravity American evangelicalism, already prone to internecine squabbles over political, cultural, and theological issues, says Noll, "will no doubt continue to fragment because of differences in response to the demise of 'Christian America.'"[2] For those who wish for evangelicals to have a greater impact on the culture, or who simply value Christian unity, it is a bleak assessment to say the least.

Not surprisingly, given the historical moment, envisioning the future of American evangelicalism has become a popular pursuit among evangelical theorists and theologians. During the past decade Christian publishing houses have pumped out scores of books attempting to explore the uncharted waters with titles like *The Futures of Evangelicalism, Church Next, Ancient-Future Faith,* and *Evangelicalism: The Next Generation.* Academic journals, popular Christian magazines, and an ever proliferating number of Christian Web logs have weighed in in an attempt to spot revealing trends in worship and theology, and to document important shifts in evangelical attitudes on political and social issues.

While there is no shortage of opinion, there is little consensus about where the evangelical movement may or should be headed in the twenty-first century, and what it will take to get there. Some have sounded an alarm, cautioning against the insidious dangers of doctrinal laxity and cultural accommodation, while others warn conversely of a backward slide toward the belligerence and rigidity of the fundamentalist era. Still others are much more sanguine, expressing confidence that whatever lies ahead for America's evangelicals, it is in God's hands to be revealed in God's timing and for God's purposes.

Hoping to make sense of such a diversity of views, I sought out two leading voices in the emerging conversation. Both are presidents of leading evangelical seminaries and, as such, are responsible for preparing the next generation of evangelical leaders. And while they had much in common, they offered distinctly differing visions of the future of American evangelicalism.

R. Albert Mohler, Jr., was just twenty years old and freshly graduated from Southern Baptist–affiliated Samford University in Alabama in 1979 when conservatives in the Southern Baptist Convention won a crucial victory in their effort to capture control of the nation's largest Protestant denomination. At their annual convention in Houston, Texas, Baptist delegates—messengers, they are called—elected Adrian Rogers, a staunchly conservative pastor from Memphis, Tennessee, as their president.

The conservatives' plan was to use the power of presidential appointment to wrest control of the denomination's agencies and educational institutions away from more liberal churchmen who disagreed with them on theological issues such as "biblical inerrancy"—the belief that the Bible is free of errors—and social issues like abortion and homosexuality. Since the president had no authority to fire, only to appoint when vacancies occurred, consolidating what they called a "conservative resurgence"—their opponents called it a "fundamentalist takeover"—would take years to complete.

In 1983 Mohler graduated from Southern Baptist Theological Seminary in Louisville, Kentucky, but stayed on in various staff positions until 1989, when he became editor of the *Christian Index,* the official newspaper of the Georgia Baptist Convention. There he showed himself to be an incisive and aggressive crusader for biblical orthodoxy and conservative social policy. In 1993, at the age of thirty-three, he was appointed president of Southern

Seminary, his alma mater and the denomination's oldest and largest theological institution, and immediately set about purging liberals and moderates from its faculty.

From his influential perch at the seminary Mohler quickly established himself as a leader in the denomination and a hardline combatant in the culture wars. He was the chief author of a revised version of the Baptist Faith and Message, the denomination's confession of faith, which, among other things, called on women to "graciously submit" to their husbands, and banned them from the pastorate. In 2003 he exhorted Southern Seminary's trustees to assume a "wartime footing" in their mission to proclaim the gospel in a hostile culture. "Our assignment," he declared, "is not just to mobilize students. It's not just to build a seminary. You need to reconceive this seminary as a West Point or an Annapolis [whose purpose is] to train those who will go out and lead the church for the battle."[3]

Meanwhile, in his speeches and writings, and in daily commentaries on his nationwide radio program, Mohler increasingly turned his sights to what he perceived as a slide toward liberalism and laxity within the broader evangelical movement. "We need to launch a massive reeducation project with evangelical Christianity concerning our most basic beliefs," he told fellow Baptists in 2000.[4] Writing in *The Coming Evangelical Crisis* a few years earlier, he had warned of a heightening conflict between those in the movement who adhere to "theological conviction centered on core doctrinal essentials" and those promoting "a rather amorphous notion of religious experience as the evangelical essential. The collision of the two parties is taking place at virtually every level of evangelical life." Unless theological and spiritual integrity were restored, he had written, "evangelicalism is in danger of losing its soul."[5]

I sat down with Mohler in a coffee shop at the Marriott River Center in San Antonio, Texas, where he was attending the annual meeting of the Evangelical Theological Society, an association made up of some forty-two hundred biblical scholars and theologians from the nation's evangelical colleges and seminaries.

At the top of that meeting's agenda was a proposal backed by Mohler and other conservatives to sharpen the definition of biblical inerrancy as it appeared in the society's "doctrinal basis"— a brief statement of belief to which all ETS members must subscribe. The original statement, written when the society was organized in 1949, required members to affirm that "the Bible alone, and the Bible in its entirety, is the Word of God written and is therefore inerrant in the autographs." The need for clarification, in the conservatives' view, had become apparent a year earlier when two professors narrowly avoided expulsion from the society for espousing "open theism"—a belief that God can change his mind in response to human actions. Mohler and others had insisted that open theism was "absolutely incompatible" with biblical inerrancy, since the Bible teaches that God is omniscient and knows the future. The two scholars and those who opposed their expulsion argued otherwise. While the conservatives lost the vote on expulsion, they prevailed in clarifying the doctrinal statement in San Antonio.

The two debates had exposed a ragged fault line running through the organization and, perhaps by extension, through the wider evangelical movement. I had spoken with several ETS members who were not happy that either of the debates had occurred, and who felt that it reflected a rightward shift in the scholarly society. "It's sort of an effort by the Baptists and others, I think, to quash diversity," one college professor told me. "They're trying to do to the ETS what they did to the Southern Baptist Convention: narrow the lines, strengthen the boundaries, and leave no room for open discussion."

I mentioned the comment to Mohler as we began our conversation.

"I don't think it's 'sort of' an effort. I think it's an *explicit* effort," Mohler fired back. "I think there is some dishonesty in what you were told. If you go back twenty-five or thirty years, no one here would have been contending for what many of them are doing now in theology—this idea of the openness of God, or the idea of an incipient universalism and inclusivism [views suggesting that people can be saved without accepting Christ]. Some of these things are simply a denial of propositional truth. It isn't even slightly honest to suggest that there was a day when those things were openly discussed here. It's honest to say that the ETS, when it was formed, had a very loose, minimalist confessional requirement—that being the complete inerrancy of scripture. But the group was so small then, they knew each other. They didn't have to have much more than that. That's not the case today."

He reminded me that several years earlier the society had added a second statement to its doctrinal basis: "God is a Trinity, Father, Son, and Holy Spirit, each an uncreated person, one in essence, equal in power and glory." The reason, he said, was to block Jehovah's Witnesses—who believe in only God the Father, and that Jesus was God's creation—from gaining membership. "This society said, 'Hey, we're the *Evangelical* Theology Society. We're not a theological society that would include Jehovah's Witnesses, considering that their understanding of the gospel is aberrant."

It was one thing to set theological boundaries for membership in a voluntary organization. The ETS, after all, was an academic group. It had no ecclesial authority and did not bestow theological credentials or official recognition on behalf of evangelical colleges and seminaries. But what about the broader evangelical movement? How important was it, I asked, that evangelicals be of one mind—not only on major points of doctrine, but on political issues and on matters of social engagement? Was diversity of opinion somehow unacceptable?

"My main concern as a theologian is with the preservation of convictions that are right at the center of evangelical identity. The fact is, there are a lot of people who use the term who frankly don't fit within that group of commitments.

"As for the other issues, being of one mind is very important, and it's going to happen. Let me put it this way: I think we're going to see where the church stands and where it is headed by looking at who marries whom. The academics increasingly talk in a disapproving way about binaries—about a reductionism of everything into binaries. Well, that's one of the hard facts of life. You're either dead or alive. You're either male or female. And in a situation like gay marriage, either you're for it or you're not. Some people would like very much to live in the gray area of nondecision. But we're not living in that kind of world.

"And so there's much at stake in terms of where evangelicals are going to come down on this. I believe we're in a period where there will be a lot of sifting within the evangelical movement. And whatever emerges in the next ten years or so is going to be more specifically evangelical, because I think the cultural hostility against us is going to be greater, not lesser, and it's going to require that we define clearly who we are and where we stand."

Mohler was going for the whole package. He seemed to be making the case that not only must evangelicals, in order to rightfully wear that label, adhere to a clearly delineated set of biblical doctrines—and the more delineation the better—but that they also must subscribe to a common moral framework and, apparently, be willing to fight for it in the public square. I suggested to him that while he might well find a large segment of evangelicals willing to toe the line theologically, and who are eager to work in their communities evangelizing and discipling others, many conservative Christians I had met simply were not interested in enlisting in the culture wars or in becoming politically involved.

"Being involved in politics is no longer an option for us," he insisted. "We're in it, and there's no getting out—not unless you want to create some new kind of Amish or Mennonite community.

Life is political. And I think that's part of what evangelicals and other Americans rightly have understood, because these public policy issues are no longer debates over federalism, tax policy, the future of social security. It's now a battle over marriage, the dignity of human life, and some of the other issues. I don't think evangelical withdrawal is an option, because you can't get far enough away. I mean, where are you going to go?"

Is there a danger, I asked, that evangelicals will, and perhaps already have, become too identified with one political party?

"I end up talking about that a whole lot. Frankly, I'd like to be in a position where I had a hard time choosing between the parties—that both were committed to marriage, the preservation of human life, and so on. We're not there yet. In a fallen world I don't even expect that the people who agree with us agree with us for the right reasons, or will agree with us for long. On my radio program today one of the things I'm talking about is the fact that corporate America is very frustrated by the social issues. They want the Bush administration to focus on commerce, tax policy, etcetera, and they see this as a distraction.

"So, yes. I think there is a danger. I think the greater danger is that evangelicals will see politics as the way of solving our deepest problems. It isn't. It's a necessary issue of great importance. But Jesus Christ did not commission his church to be a political action committee."

On that point it sounded as if Mohler agreed with syndicated columnist Cal Thomas and Michigan pastor Ed Dobson. Partisan entanglements, they argued, could only compromise the church's authority and reduce it to "just another lobbying group."[6] It surprised me, frankly, I said to Mohler, that he was espousing that view, given the amount of energy and resources the Southern Baptists had thrown into the 2004 campaign.

"I think Cal Thomas has been wrong twice," he responded. "I have great admiration for him. But in his own words, he thought the Moral Majority was going to bring on revival. That was ridiculous.

But then to argue that politics isn't important is equally ridiculous. It's important, it's just not ultimate. There's no escaping the political responsibilities, any more than in Germany during the 1930s. You can't escape political responsibility.

"But we ought to have limited, finite goals for government. In other words, at its very best, government can do only some things relatively well, in terms of maintaining order and the commonweal, punishing the wrongdoer, and so on. In the biblical worldview there is a limited role for government. That's our main message in the political world, and that's what we're working toward."

Seeing so many evangelicals become politically engaged in the 2004 campaign, I reminded him, made some people nervous and suspicious about the ultimate agenda of religious conservatives. Even though it may have been overstated, and sometimes was based more on caricature than reality, many Americans were fearful about where evangelicals would take the country if they had their way. While evangelicals may espouse limited government involvement on economic and tax issues, their determination to take away a woman's right to an abortion, for example, or to amend the constitution to dictate who may and may not get married seemed to many Americans like a pretty major government incursion into personal matters. Were people justified in being fearful of the religious right and their agenda?

"Look, the only people who feel that way is a cultural academic elite that doesn't know what America looks like. Evangelicals are not oddities. They're your neighbors. They're the person who checks you out at the grocery store, the doctor you see at the clinic, the insurance salesman. I think you know this. Honestly, I feel like we're right back with the writer for the *New York Times* saying after Reagan won in 1980 that no one she knew voted for Reagan. It's like every four years, when conservatives win anything, the cultural elites—especially in the media world—all of a sudden discover people who have been there all along.

"Something happened in the 2004 election. But as an evangelical leader, whatever it was I'm not going to overblow it, because I think it was the marriage issue as much as anything else. It got people to the polls in Ohio and elsewhere. And I don't know what that means long term. But I believe you're going to see over the next ten years an enormous laboratory experiment being lived out in American society in terms of where we go. Evangelicals are going to be part of it.

"But taking away rights? As evangelicals we don't believe there is a right to abortion. It's certainly not in the Constitution. So yeah, you're looking at a real worldview collision there. Those of us on the conservative side see liberals as a threat. Again, we're dealing with actual policy decisions here. Abortion will be legal or not. Homosexual marriage will be a legal reality or not. Human cloning will happen or not. It's not like there is a lot of gray area in which to negotiate."

I had every reason to believe I would get an entirely different perspective from Richard J. Mouw, the president of Fuller Theological Seminary in Pasadena, California, and one of American evangelicalism's leading progressive voices. While some detractors have tried to depict him as an evangelical liberal—an oxymoron if there ever was one—the label hardly fits. Mouw's evangelical bona fides are beyond question.

Raised in a Dutch Calvinist family—his father was a minister in the Reformed Church in America—Mouw was active in Youth for Christ as a high schooler in the 1950s and worked summers at Bible conferences run by fundamentalist radio preacher Carl McIntire. He graduated from an evangelical college (Houghton, in New York), earned a divinity degree at an evangelical seminary (Western Theological, in Holland, Michigan), and after earning a doctorate at the University of Chicago taught philosophy at one of the nation's premier evangelical colleges (Calvin, in Grand Rapids, Michigan) for seventeen years. He joined Fuller's faculty in 1985 as a professor of Christian philosophy and ethics and served as Fuller's provost and senior vice president before becoming its president in 1993. He has written more than a dozen books on biblical, evangelical, and cultural themes, and is widely recognized as one of the leading figures in the reformed branch of American evangelicalism—not exactly a hotbed of theological liberalism.

What places Mouw squarely in the movement's more progressive wing—and outside the good graces of some of his more conservative coreligionists—is his demonstrated passion for social justice issues and his openness to interfaith dialogue. He was among the signers of the 1973 Chicago Declaration of Evangelical Social Concern, a Vietnam-era call for evangelical engagement against racism, sexism, militarism, materialism, and other forms of economic and social injustice—evils, according to the signers, about which evangelical Christians regrettably had "mostly remained silent."[7] Throughout his career he would continue to speak and write on those themes and work for their redress through such organizations as the International Justice Mission, the International Center for Religion and Diplomacy, and Christians for Biblical Equality, among others.

A firm believer in civil discourse, Mouw had been criticized by some evangelicals for warming up to Muslims and Mormons, and for a general advocacy of genial interfaith relations. And yet he remained solidly committed to traditional conservative social positions on issues like abortion and same-sex marriage, and to essential doctrines of the evangelical Christian faith. During an interview on National Public Radio a few years ago he recited some of the fundamentals he learned as a child: "That Jesus loves me, that there's a God in charge of history, that there's a book I can turn to for guidance. Now, I've nuanced those. But they're still the things I hold onto for dear life."[8]

I met with Mouw in Washington, D.C., where he had come to participate in the National Prayer Breakfast, an annual ecumenical gathering that drew thousands of leading evangelicals, along with the president and members of Congress, for a morning of public invocation on behalf of the nation. A record crowd had turned out, filling two ballrooms at the Washington Hilton Hotel. In a keynote address rock-star-turned-activist Bono called on the leaders of church and state to kick in more for the fight against poverty and AIDS. "This is not about charity in the end," Bono said. "It's about justice."

It was just the sort of speech that one would expect to bring Mouw cheering to his feet. "It was a *great* speech!" he announced afterward. "*Exactly* what we needed to hear!"

For the next hour or so, as we settled into a noisy lounge just outside the hotel ballroom, Mouw contemplated the future of evangelicalism. Like Mohler, he described a movement standing at a pivotal historical moment, facing inescapable challenges and consequential choices—and doing so in a post-Graham era with no one to sound a clear and certain trumpet.

"Some of us back in the sixties and seventies wished that Billy had been a little stronger on some of the issues of the day, like race, the Vietnam war, things of that nature," Mouw said, recalling his own early years as an activist. "But he was an amazing unifying figure. His simple gospel messages, the wonderful stories you'd read about people coming to Jesus Christ through his ministry—it was an inspiring vision that I think did bring a sense of unity to the movement. I'm not sure we'll ever see that again."

Like Mark Noll, however, Mouw considered evangelical unity under Graham to be more symbolic than real. The movement, after all, had always been fragmented, and that fragmentation, he said, was likely to continue.

"Almost immediately after Chicago in 1973 we saw it break up along cause lines. There we were signing the Chicago Declaration—blacks, whites, women, Reformed, Mennonites, different generations, different traditions. But soon afterward everyone sort of went in a different direction. The evangelical feminists did their own thing, the peace people did their thing, some of us went in a more Reformed direction. And, of course, by the end of the decade you had the Moral Majority and the new right, and they had an entirely different set of issues. So there's been such a fragmentation that I don't think any single figure could unite us now."

While he acknowledged some real theological differences—the kinds of issues that animated Mohler and his allies—"what I think really divides us more than anything right now is the political agenda. For most evangelicals the inerrancy of scripture is not an issue. We're not fighting about dispensationalism versus Reformed theology. We're not arguing about infant baptism versus adult baptism. It's not that we don't disagree on some of those things. We just don't spend much energy these days, most of us at least, arguing about it.

"If there are theological issues that divide us," he permitted himself a second thought, "it would be something like the question: 'What about a godly Muslim or a godly Jew?' None of us holds that God is going to save everybody in the end. We're not universalists. You know, I don't have much hope for Howard Stern, unless he makes a big about-face," he chuckled, "and certainly those folks who want to slaughter the Jews and all the rest, but—"

He completed his point with an illustration. "A few years back I was interviewed on CNN. And on the same program they had this home-schooled eight-year-old Southern Baptist girl, and they asked her, 'What happens to people who don't believe in Jesus?' And with a big smile on her face she said, 'They go to hell.' And then they asked me the same question, and I said something like, 'I think Jesus is the only way to heaven. But I think how he gets people there, there's a lot of mystery involved.'

"And that, in a way, symbolizes an important distinction in the evangelical movement between those who really want to take a hard line and divide the human race into two clear groups, and those of us who really do believe that there is only one name, that there is only one way to heaven, but we're willing to allow for a lot of mystery in how it works out. I think evangelicalism has matured in its willingness to accept some healthy messiness in its theology. It's just not something we fight over.

"But what really divides us are the political issues. Some of us thought bombing in Iraq was a mistake. Some of us thought some of the budget cuts were wrong and don't support down-the-line the kinds of policies that characterize the Republican administration. Those are divisive issues."

What Mouw was describing was the kind of polarization that in his view can, and often does, occur when preachers and other evangelical leaders become advocates in partisan politics. It wasn't that public policy issues were more important to evangelicals than doctrinal issues, in his judgment, but that political disagreements created estrangement where none otherwise would have existed. A fellow Nazarene, for example, may agree entirely with Focus on the Family leader James Dobson's religious beliefs while absolutely rejecting his passionate endorsement of Republican politicians. The resulting gap between the two would be difficult to bridge.

And yet Mouw would be the last to suggest that evangelicals withdraw from political and cultural engagement just to avoid potential rifts. He reminded me of the early years of the neo-evangelical movement in the 1950s when men like theologian Carl Henry and Boston pastor Harold Ockenga led their fellow conservatives out of fundamentalist isolationism. One of their projects had been the founding of Fuller Seminary.

"They really saw three kinds of engagement: One was intellectual. We've got to re-engage the academy and reject the anti-intellectualism that had become so prevalent in fundamentalism. The second was cultural. Both Henry and Ockenga talked about how we had been on the wrong side of the race issue, poverty issues, labor and management issues—and they said we needed to re-engage the culture. And finally they said, We've got to re-engage the body of Christ, the church, and reject the tendency to separate over relatively minor doctrinal issues. Henry even said we should be willing to partner with liberals, the social gospel people, if there were legitimate matters of shared concern. I think we've made progress on all of those, and I really don't hear anyone suggesting we should go back to the isolationism of the past."

Yet there were obviously different visions of what evangelical engagement should look like. Mouw's social justice agenda and Mohler's program of limited government and defense of the family seemed miles apart. I asked how he accounted for such vast differences.

"I think evangelicals have typically fluctuated, without always thinking about it, between a postmillennial optimism and a premillennial pessimism. During the fundamentalist era that translated into withdrawal and noninvolvement. And then came the seventies and eighties. The sexual revolution was a huge thing. People say to me, 'Why are you folks so hung up on biology and sex?' But it was really the sexual revolution as it posed a threat to our children—what was being taught in the schools, what our kids were seeing on the magazine rack at the grocery store, what was showing up on television that increasingly invaded our homes. So there was this real fear of what was happening.

"And then there was a tremendous upward mobility among evangelicals in the early 1970s. You used to go downtown and there was a Baptist and a Methodist and a Presbyterian and an Episcopal church. On the edge of town might be a little Assemblies of God, or a Wesleyan, or a Nazarene church. Today those churches own the best real estate in town. Over two decades, tremendous upward mobility. The Wesleyans, the Pentecostals, the Nazarenes emerged as the wealthy churches.

"So suddenly there was a sense that we've got something. We've got some new power. Let's take on this sexual revolution. And they did, but it didn't go well. And that was because there was no corresponding theological construct. There was no well thought-out theology to guide their political engagement. It was just this sudden reversion to 'Christian America' and 'let's go back to our founding fathers.' And that goes nowhere. So now if we give up, we move back to the margins, home-school our kids, do evangelism, stop voting, and wait for Jesus to come and rescue us. I'm not sure that's where we're headed. That's the worst-case scenario."

He recalled reading an article by Milwaukee's former Roman Catholic Archbishop Rembert Weakland a few years back that noted that many American Catholics were raised on a theology that prepared them to survive as immigrants on the margins of society. But as Catholics moved into positions of influence in business and government, Weakland observed, they suddenly found that they didn't have a theology or spirituality that provided guidance on how to exercise power.

"I think that's true of evangelicals today," Mouw said. "We're accustomed to thinking of ourselves as a beleaguered remnant. And the kind of theology we heard in sermons and read in magazines was designed to reinforce this sense that we are destined to be a people who are on the margins of cultural life. But now that we're in positions of influence we have nothing to guide us in the exercise of power—in how to negotiate compromise. If we had been willing to do what Europe did on abortion and say absolutely no abortions in the third trimester, we would have far fewer abortions today. Instead we have the most liberal abortion policy in the world. Why? Because it was all or nothing. We didn't believe Christians could negotiate on an issue like that.

"I think we need to do some serious thinking about a theology of engagement, because we really have no choice. The problem within evangelicalism is that there is a tendency to go for the slogan or the proof text, whether we are on the left or the right, and kind of look for the simplest of answers. I think a mature evangelicalism would be one that allows for debate about these things as a people, and that the debate itself is a good thing because we learn from it. Whether we'll ever get there ..." His voice trailed off.

We returned to the subject of unity. Was there anything on the horizon that might prevent the continuing fragmentation of the evangelical movement? Underlying his vision, it seemed to me, was a latent tone of pessimism. He had articulated a forward-looking vision but at the same time seemed doubtful that it would ever be realized. He disagreed with my assessment.

"You know what? I disagree with the Southern Baptists. I disagree with the fundamentalists. But there's a strong part of me that wants to say, At least they are bringing people to Jesus Christ in a way that most of the mainline denominations are not. I feel a kinship with them that I don't feel often with the more liberal leaders of my own denomination. I'm a Presbyterian, and the ways in which the mainline Protestants often play fast and loose with the Bible really bothers me. With the fundamentalists at least we know how to argue. If somebody says, 'But the Bible says ... ' you take it very seriously. But when I'm with a Presbyterian pastor, and we're arguing about homosexuality, and I say, 'But what do you do about Paul's teaching in Romans?' and he says 'I don't read it'—I don't know how to argue with that. So in that sense, even in our worst fights there's still a sense that we're fighting within a family. Pat Robertson, with whom I disagree on many things, there still is a kinship I feel with him.

"In the not too distant future," he continued, "I think we're going to see some denominations, as we have known them, either being destroyed or greatly wounded by the fractious debates over sexuality and things of that nature." He was talking about the mainline denominations. "And in their place we will see new configurations, new networks of congregations. We're seeing it already around people like Rick Warren at Saddleback and Bill Hybels at Willow Creek and what they are offering to churches around the country. If your average Fuller graduate who is a Presbyterian pastor gets to take time off and go to one meeting a year, it's going to be a conference at Willow Creek or Saddleback—not something the denomination puts together. For evangelicals denominational identity is no longer nearly as important as wanting to strengthen the local church and its ministry in a way that's faithful to the scriptures.

"I think what we saw today with Bono talking about AIDS offers another promising possibility. How we as evangelicals respond to the AIDS crisis in Africa, how we deal with children and orphans, how we deal with poverty-related issues could bring a new sense of mission and unity to the movement. That's something I can begin to feel very optimistic about."

I had heard two strikingly different prescriptive visions for the future of American evangelicalism. One had been a rousing battle cry—a call, in the words of the Apostle Paul, to "put on the whole armor of God" and defend the doctrinal ramparts against the enemies of faith and family gathering outside the gates. The other echoed the prophet Micah, reminding his people that the Lord requires that they "do justice, love mercy, and walk humbly with your God." Yet underlying both, easy to miss in the din of debate, was a shared vision of the evangel itself—the redemptive message of the gospel that always has been at the core of evangelical existence.

It was a vision that Mouw poignantly touched on near the end of our conversation.

"We were preparing for our fiftieth anniversary at Fuller in 1997," he said, "and I pulled a group together to talk about what it means to be an evangelical institution. For three hours we talked about, what exactly is our evangelical identity? And these people were everything from Presbyterian to Anglican to Pentecostal to Mennonite. We covered a lot of ground in that discussion. But you know what we discovered? It isn't just about doctrine. It isn't inerrancy. It isn't our political views. One of our church historians spoke up, and he said, 'You know what it really is? It's having a heart for the lost.' And we all looked at each other and said, 'Yeah, that's what it is.'

"Being an evangelical means that there is only one name under heaven by which we are saved, that Jesus alone is the savior, and without Jesus people are in deep trouble. As evangelicals we have to have a passion for bringing people to Jesus Christ. All the other issues—the doctrinal issues, the political issues, the social justice issues, and all the rest—are terribly important. But at the heart of it, truth and justice and peace and righteousness without a saving knowledge of Jesus Christ do not have the eternal consequence that the gospel has.

"And because of that we're going to keep on wrestling—like Jacob with the angel—with our more fundamentalist brothers and sisters. We're not going to walk away from them, because we feel a kinship with them. We share that passion to proclaim the gospel of Christ."

# Epilogue

Grand Rapids, Michigan

From the outside the building appeared pretty much as I had remembered it. A one-story wing and gymnasium had been added to one side, roughly doubling the overall floor space, and a new glass-and-brick entryway now faced the parking lot on the opposite side. But the main brick structure with its high-pitched roof and white concrete cross built into the facade was just as it had been in the early 1960s, when I first walked through the doors of Maplelawn Baptist Church.

It seemed fitting that I conclude my journey into evangelical America at the place where it began. This, after all, was mile-marker 0 in my own faith journey. It was here that I was introduced to evangelical Christianity and to the precepts and promises of God-breathed scripture. Here I had had my first experience of Christian community and the care and nurture that goes with being part of an extended family. Here, too, I encountered and embraced—and eventually discarded—a fundamentalist ethos that would become the baseline for the remainder of my personal religious quest. So my return to Maplelawn would be a homecoming of sorts and the final stop on my journalistic excursion.

I was not aware of it at the time, but my years at the church had coincided with a period when the evangelical movement was just stirring itself awake after decades of cultural hibernation. The neo-evangelicals led by Billy Graham, Carl F. H. Henry, Harold Ockenga, and others were slowly emerging from the isolated dens of a fundamentalist subculture that not everyone was eager to abandon. The people at Maplelawn, for instance, disdained the kinds of worldly associations that the neo-evangelicals were pursuing. Their leader, Pastor Smith, as I recalled, had not been a fan of Billy Graham. As a "second-degree separationist" he refused to associate with liberal churches or with anyone, like Graham, who did. He and his flock were proud to wear the fundamentalist label, and they were not about to change.

I had often wondered over the years how Maplelawn had fared in fending off the incursions of modernity. Since the mid-1960s the country and the world had gone through convulsive changes, and many evangelical churches I knew, some of them no less conservative than Maplelawn, had adapted reasonably well by forging new alliances and adopting new styles of worship and ministry without sacrificing their core biblical commitments. During the same period, "fundamentalist" had become a disparaging term associated with Islamic terrorists or just about any type of fanatic. Even the country's most famous fundamentalist, Jerry Falwell, had ceased using the label. Was it possible that the Baptist church of my youth had somehow managed to withstand the pressure and remained locked in a time warp? Or had it, too, adapted its message and methods to changing times? I wondered where it now fit within the broader evangelical movement, and whether it even considered itself a part of it.

Those were some of the questions that brought me back to Maplelawn on a summer Sunday morning—that and a chance, perhaps, to see some old familiar faces.

I arrived just a minute or two before the start of the service and slipped quietly into a seat near the back. The sanctuary, for the most part, looked the same: white cement-block walls with plain frosted windows along the sides; brass-colored cylinder-shaped lights with cross cutouts suspended from a high wood-plank ceiling; wooden theater-type chairs fastened in rows with aisles in the center and on both sides. The front of the church had a surprising modification: a plain wooden cross, which I remembered had hung on the wall above the baptistry, was gone, and in its place was a large white projection screen. Apparently Maplelawn had adopted the Saddleback seeker-style motif of contemporary praise, with song lyrics flashed on the screen. Chalk up one accommodation to modern cultural fashion. I wondered what Pastor Smith would have thought of it.

The sanctuary was a little more than half full—maybe a hundred people, most of them middle-aged or older, with a smattering of younger couples. The children, I guessed, were in a separate service somewhere out of sight. Except for one African American man seated near the front it was a white crowd. I would learn later that the church also had a service in Spanish that typically drew between 100 and 140 people from the neighborhood, many of them immigrants from Central America. This was a huge change. In the early sixties you would not have found anyone of color at Maplelawn—or living in the neighborhood, for that matter.

I scanned the crowd looking for familiar faces. One of the ushers I recognized as a young deacon from the old days. I couldn't remember his name, but he looked now to be well into his seventies. To my left seated a few rows ahead of me on the opposite side of the church I recognized the mother of a friend. She and her husband, who I knew had passed away several years before, had taken special interest in me and always made sure I had rides to church activities. She looked tiny and frail. I looked forward to speaking with her after the service.

The service was just about to begin when an elderly man in a yellow linen blazer walked up the center aisle and took a seat near the front. His wavy hair looked strikingly familiar, and when he turned to sit down I recognized him immediately. It was Pastor Smith. I was astounded. He had to be close to ninety by now. I had no idea he was still around. I checked the worship folder and saw that he was listed as "Pastor Emeritus." I knew that he had left Maplelawn shortly after I did, and had moved to a church in Iowa, but I had lost track of him after that. I was amazed at my good fortune. There were so many questions I wanted to ask this man who had been so influential in my early years as a Christian. I wondered if he had mellowed at all in the past forty years, if he had changed his mind on things like Christian political involvement and confrontational soul winning. I wondered what he thought about the religious right, and if he had ever warmed up to Billy Graham. We had so much to talk about.

A young associate pastor started the service off with a scripture reading and an opening prayer, and then led the congregation in a couple of contemporary praise choruses with the words projected on the screen. So far it was a typical modern evangelical service— not at all like the Maplelawn of old, with hymns, choir anthems, and organ music. After the offering he turned the service over to a visiting minister from Louisiana and his large musical family, who performed several twangy southern gospel numbers accompanied by a tape-recorded sound track. The highlight of their performance was a peppy rendition of "Are You Washed in the Blood of the Lamb?" cheerfully sung by the minister's blonde eight-year-old daughter. It was a definite throwback to the revival-meeting music of the 1950s and 1960s, and seemed eerily out of synch with the first part of the service.

The reversion to an earlier era continued when it came time for the sermon. The Louisiana minister, a handsome man in his early forties, was a pugnacious preacher who prowled back and forth on the platform, waving his Bible with one hand and beating the air with the other. It was a style reminiscent of a better known Louisiana preacher, Jimmy Swaggart.

He had titled his sermon "A Saint's Duty," and he reminded his listeners that "if you are washed in the blood, if you know the Lord as your savior, then you are a saint, not a sinner," and that it is a saint's duty to "continue steadfast in doctrine and in the fear of God. Now some people say doctrine is not important. Well, I'm here to tell you that if you don't think doctrine is important then you don't think the Bible is important, and you are not part of who we are. Amen?" A few male voices from the front echoed his "amen."

For the next twenty minutes the preacher continued in that vein, repeatedly drawing contrasts between "what some people say," and what Bible believers know to be true. In an almost taunting tone he chided "some churches" for failing to instill "godly fear" in people. "A godly fear motivates people to keep God's commandments.... It's not right for a church to have some who live holy and others who live hellish lives. If people live hellish lives the church is not to receive them. You need to get rid of those people! You don't break bread with them! Amen?"

When it came time for the invitation he exhorted his listeners to come forward and repent. "You know what your duty is. You need to come to the Lord and say 'Help me to fear you. I need that fear to keep me from sin.' You come now and get right with the Lord." Several made their way to the altar and prayed with the preacher, and after a closing chorus the service ended.

I could not recall when I had last heard such a combative and hounding sermon. I had no way of knowing whether it was typical of the current fare at Maplelawn. The Louisiana preacher, after all, was a guest speaker. Yet judging from the enthusiastic response, it had been well received. No one could possibly have mistaken this for a Saddleback-style seeker-sensitive service. It seemed exactly as it had been in the old days.

Now I was more anxious than ever to speak with Pastor Smith, and as soon as the service ended I made my way to find him.

When I caught up to my former pastor, he was downstairs in a Sunday school classroom, and had just taken a seat near the back next to his wife. It was an adult Bible class, and Pastor Smith was one of about a dozen students. The lesson had not yet begun, so I went in hoping we could chat for a least a few minutes. Seeing him up close I was amazed at how little he had changed. He was slightly stooped but otherwise looked in good shape for a man in his late eighties. His hair was full and only slightly gray. And when we shook hands, his grip was firm.

I introduced myself, repeating my name twice, but it didn't seem to register. He looked at me rather blankly.

You baptized me, I said, in 1963. I was a teenager then.

He didn't remember.

Well, that was a long time ago, I said.

Mrs. Smith spoke up. She thought she remembered me. "You lived in the neighborhood, didn't you?"

Yes, I said. I reminded them that I had been in the youth group with their daughter, and I mentioned the names of some of the others who were in the group in those days.

When I mentioned their daughter's name, the pastor looked at me and smiled but said nothing.

"I think I *do* remember you," Mrs. Smith said, and spent the next couple of minutes catching me up on the whereabouts of some of my teenage friends. The pastor, meanwhile, seemed to be tuning out.

I turned to him and asked how long they had been back in Grand Rapids and at Maplelawn. Mrs. Smith answered, and as she recounted their recent history she reached over and took her husband's hand and put it in her lap, and began patting it gently. He looked at her, smiled, and looked away.

I knew the conversation I had hoped for wasn't going to happen.

Mrs. Smith and I continued our small talk for a few more minutes. When I saw that the class was about to begin, I took both of their hands and told them how important Maplelawn and Pastor Smith's ministry had been in getting me started on my Christian walk, and how much I appreciated all that they had done. I told them I had thought about those days often over the years, and that I would never forget them.

The melancholy I felt when I left Maplelawn that day probably had less to do with my disappointing encounter with the Smiths or with the Louisiana preacher's belligerent sermon than with the sad realization that the accuracy of my memory of those years had been confirmed. I was grateful to have had the opportunity to revisit my fundamentalist past. And that was exactly what my visit to Maplelawn had been. If my boyhood church was not entirely locked in a time warp, in four decades it certainly had not ventured far. And yet, I could see that the church was wrestling with some of the same issues that I had observed other evangelicals confronting with greater or lesser degrees of success—issues that beg to ask how one is to live authentically as Christians in a changing world.

As I came to my journey's end I realized that there had been few real surprises along the way. In my travels around the country I had met many fascinating people, and some who were inspiring. A few I had found perplexing or tedious or simply annoying. For the most part, though, the evangelicals I had met were just extraordinarily normal. Al Mohler was right: Evangelicals are not oddities. They are your neighbor, your doctor, the insurance salesman, the person who checks you out at the grocery store. They are hard-working couples and single parents, callow college students and elderly widows—ordinary people who are trying hard, like the rest of us, to find their way in the world as best they can, caring for their families and serving their God.

Their distinctive faith obviously sets them apart from those who do not share it. But there is nothing alien or weird about evangelical Christianity. It is a faith well rooted in the cultural and theological traditions of the West. Some among them express crazy notions from time to time about how life works. But in a population of sixty million people that is to be expected. I still believe, as I did starting out, that evangelicals as a group do sometimes face unfair and inaccurate stereotypes, and some of us in the media are at fault for that. But they are not victims, at least not in the ways or as often as some would claim. Their distinctive faith aside, evangelicals are looking and acting more and more like the rest of America. They have found their way into the cultural mainstream, where they are both influencing and being influenced by the society around them.

For those within the movement who worry about its future, I will leave it for others to offer prescriptions. But my sense is that those who nervously wonder if anyone will rise up to fill the shoes of a fading generation of leaders worry needlessly. Leadership vacuums seldom last. More to the point, they should recognize that evangelicalism's most appealing asset has never been its leaders—as inspiring and enterprising as some have proven to be—but its message. The gospel proclamation is what millions are drawn to when they take up the evangelical banner. The real challenge that American evangelicalism must face is the same that Christians have confronted in every generation: to find within its scriptures and traditions the means of applying the gospel message to their times.

# Acknowledgments

I owe a tremendous debt of gratitude to a host of people whose help and co-operation have made this book possible.

First and foremost, I want to thank each of the individuals I encountered during my travels and whose stories fill these pages. I appreciate their generosity of spirit in allowing a nosy journalist to pry into personal matters of faith. I hope I have done them justice in these portraits. I especially want to thank Richard Cizik of the National Association of Evangelicals and historian Mark A. Noll, formerly of Wheaton College, now of the University of Notre Dame, for subjecting themselves repeatedly to my interrogations and for their patience and persistence in explaining matters in ways that even a journalist could understand.

I want to thank my editor at Viking, Carolyn Carlson, for her wisdom, patience, and deft editing skills and for her unfaltering enthusiasm for this project. Thanks, too, to her assistant Katherine Carlson (no relation) for keeping my feet to the fire. And special thanks to my agent, Gail Ross, and her associate, Howard Yoon, for helping me to develop the book concept and for making it happen.

I also want to give special thanks to my former employer, *U.S. News & World Report*, for granting permission to incorporate material I produced for its college guide, *America's Best Colleges 2004 Edition*, in my chapter on Wheaton College.

I am grateful to several of my friends, colleagues, and family members upon whom I thrust portions of unfinished manuscript and who were kind enough to offer constructive feedback: Mark Noll, Clyde Taylor, Joseph Caplan, Marcella Donnell, Amy Downes, and Doreen Sheler. Thanks to each of you for your helpful comments. Thanks, too, to my friend Roger

Woodward, whose generosity kept me from going blind during long hours at the computer.

As always, I am most deeply indebted to my wife, Doreen, who abided my many absences and long hours of self-imposed isolation with utmost grace and understanding. Her encouragement and support throughout made a world of difference.

# Notes

## PROLOGUE

1. Robertson's on-air gaffes would only get worse. In August 2005 he called for the assassination of Venezuela's leftist president, Hugo Chavez. In November 2005 he warned citizens of Dover, Pennsylvania, who had voted out of office school board members who supported the teaching of intelligent design in public schools that they should not be surprised if disaster struck their town. And in January 2006 he suggested that Israeli Prime Minister Ariel Sharon's massive stroke was divine retribution for ceding land to the Palestinians.

## 1. AWAKENING

1. Hosea 14:1 (New Revised Standard Version).
2. Gimenez asserted this during an interview with the author on February 4, 2005. The Reverend Ted Haggard, president of the National Association of Evangelicals, was reported to have made a similar remark. See Adelle M. Banks, "Thousands Rally for 'America for Jesus,'" Religion News Service, October 22, 2004.
3. See for example Ken Garfield, "Moral Values Highest Concern," *Charlotte Observer,* November 4, 2004.
4. Peter Wallsten, "Evangelicals Want Faith Rewarded," *Los Angeles Times,* November 12, 2004, A1.
5. Richard N. Ostling of the Associated Press, "Election Reinforces Religious, Moral Divide," *Telegraph-Herald,* November 6, 2004, D17.

6.  David Broder, "An Old Fashion Win," *Washington Post*, November 4, 2004.

7.  Lisa Anderson, "Faith Takes Key Role in Political Landscape," *Chicago Tribune*, November 4, 2004.

8.  See, for example, Cal Thomas and Ed Dobson, *Blinded By Might: Why the Religious Right Can't Save America* (Grand Rapids, MI: Zondervan, 1999), Chapters 5–7; and Tom Sine, *Cease Fire: Searching for Sanity in America's Culture Wars* (Grand Rapids, MI: Wm. B. Eerdmans, 1995), especially Chapter 7.

9.  Among many verses: Matthew 5:37, 6:13, 13:19; John 17:15; Ephesians 6:16; 2 Thessalonians 3:3.

10. John 12:31, 14:30, 16:11.

11. Ephesians 6:12 (King James Version)

12. James Dobson, "Why I Use 'Fighting Words,' " *Christianity Today*, June 19, 1995, 28. The concluding phrase in the quotation is taken from Revelation 12:9.

13. David D. Kirkpatrick, "Some Backers of Bush Say They Anticipate a 'Revolution,' " *New York Times*, November 4, 2004, 1.

14. Dan Gilgoff and Bret Schulte, "The Dobson Way," *U.S. News & World Report*, January 17, 2005, 62.

15. Karen Tumulty and Matthew Cooper, "What Does Bush Owe the Religious Right?" *Time,* February 7, 2005, 28.

16. Barry Lynn, "Bush Re-Election Means More Attacks On Church-State Wall," in a press release appearing on the Web site of Americans United for the Separation of Church and State, www.au.org, on November 3, 2004.

17. Dobson is quoted to this effect by Gilgoff and Schulte in *U.S. News & World Report*. Kennedy made similar comments in a statement reported by Dana Milbank, "For the President, a Vote of Full Faith and Credit," *Washington Post,* November 7, 2004, A7.

18. These estimates come from John Green of the Ray C. Bliss Institute of Applied Politics at the University of Akron in an e-mail exchange with the author.

## 2. ROOTS AND BRANCHES

1.  Shortly after our conversation Noll accepted an appointment to the history department at the University of Notre Dame, where he continues his study of Protestant origins.

2.  David Bebbington, *Evangelicalism in Britain: A History from the 1730s to the 1980s* (London: Unwin Hyman, 1989), 2–17, as summa-

rized by Mark A. Noll, *American Evangelical Christianity: An Intro-duction* (Oxford: Blackwell, 2001), 13.

3.  Cited in "Defining Evangelicalism," an article appearing on the Web site of the Institute for the Study of American Evangelicals at Wheaton College: www.wheaton.edu/isae/defining_evangelicalism.html.

4.  The survey, conducted in March 2004 by Greenberg Quinlan Rosner Research, may be viewed in its entirety at the Religion & Ethics NewsWeekly Web site: www.pbs.org/wnet/religionandethics/week733/release.html.

5.  George M. Marsden, *Fundamentalism and American Culture,* 2nd ed. (New York: Oxford University Press, 2006), 324n.11.

6.  I am deeply indebted to Noll, whose authoritative published works and generous personal communication inform much of the historical section that follows. Of particular help were Noll's *The Rise of Evangelicalism: The Age of Edwards, Whitefield, and the Wesleys* (Downers Grove, IL: InterVarsity Press, 2003), and *American Evangelical Christianity.* Other sources, including specific citations from these two works, will be noted where appropriate.

7.  Both Wesley quotations above appear in Wesley's journal, as quoted by Noll, *The Rise of Evangelicalism,* 84, 97.

8.  Romans 8:16.

9.  From Whitefield's journals, as cited by Noll, *The Rise of Evangelicalism,* 79.

10. Stuart C. Henry, *George Whitefield, Wayfaring Witness* (New York: Abingdon Press, 1957), 61, as cited by David T. Morgan, Jr., "The Great Awakening in North Carolina, 1740–1775: The Baptist Phase," *North Carolina Historical Review,* vol. 45 (1968), 264–83.

11. Jonathan Edwards, "Unpublished Letter of May 30, 1735," as cited by Noll, *The Rise of Evangelicalism,* 77.

12. Mark Galli, "George Whitefield: Sensational Evangelist of Britain and America," in Galli and Ted Olson, eds., *131 Christians Everyone Should Know* (Nashville: Broadman & Holman, 2000), 65.

13. Noll, *The Scandal of the Evangelical Mind* (Grand Rapids, MI: Eerdman's, 1994), 61.

14. Ibid.

15. Randall Balmer and Laura F. Winner, *Protestantism in America* (New York: Columbia University Press, 2002), 18.

16. From a telephone interview, January 5, 2006.

17. Balmer and Winner, *Protestantism in America,* 59.

18. Ibid., 18. While Baptists, Methodists, and Presbyterians all divided into separate northern and southern entities in the 1840s, probably the

most consequential and enduring split occurred among Baptists. The Southern Baptist Convention, organized in 1845, today is the largest Protestant denomination, with some sixteen million members.

19. Marsden, *Fundamentalism and American Culture*, 11.
20. Ibid.
21. Quoted by Marsden, 11.
22. Balmer, *Encyclopedia of Evangelicalism* (Waco, TX: Baylor University Press, 2004), 246.
23. Joel A. Carpenter, *Revive Us Again: The Reawakening of American Fundamentalism* (New York: Oxford University Press, 1997), 78.
24. Marsden, *Fundamentalism and American Culture*, 31.
25. Ibid., 91–92. See also Balmer and Winner, *Protestantism in America*, 62–63.
26. Quoted in Marsden, 113.
27. Ibid., 104.
28. See Balmer and Winner, *Protestantism in America*, 20, 64, 73, and Marsden, 118–19.
29. Marsden, 119.
30. Ibid., 158.
31. Ibid., 158–59.
32. From a sermon by the Reverend Oliver W. Van Osdel, *Baptist Temple News* IX (January 3, 1920), cited in Marsden, 157.
33. John C. Green, "Seeking a Place: Evangelical Protestants and Public Engagement in the Twentieth Century," in Ronald J. Sider and Diane Knippers, eds., *Toward an Evangelical Public Policy* (Grand Rapids, MI: Baker Books, 2005), 19.
34. The text of the Butler Act, enacted on March 21, 1925, appears in full at the Scopes Trial Homepage at the University of Missouri–Kansas City Web site: www.law.umkc.edu/faculty/projects/FTrials/scopes/tenn stat.htm.
35. Marsden, 185.
36. David Gushee and Dennis Hollinger, "Toward an Evangelical Ethical Methodology," in *Toward an Evangelical Public Policy*, 118.
37. Noll, *American Evangelical Christianity*, 16.
38. Christian Smith, *American Evangelicalism: Embattled and Thriving* (Chicago: University of Chicago Press, 1998), 9.
39. Carpenter, *Revive Us Again*, 144–54. Ockenga is quoted on 147.
40. Ibid., 145–48.
41. Ibid., 158.
42. Ibid., 159.
43. Ibid., 150.
44. Ibid.

45. See History of the NAE at the National Association of Evangelicals Web site: www.nae.net/index.cfm?FUSEACTION=nae.history.
46. Balmer, *Encyclopedia of Evangelicalism*, 276–77.
47. Quoted in Smith, *American Evangelicalism*, 11.
48. Billy Graham, *Just As I Am: The Autobiography of Billy Graham* (New York: HarperCollins, 1997), 286.
49. Noll, *American Evangelical Christianity*, 44.
50. From an interview with the author in Toronto, Ontario, November 23, 2002.
51. Graham, *Just As I Am*, 303.
52. Noll, *American Evangelical Christianity*, 53.
53. Marsden, 239.

## 3. GOD'S COUNTRY

1. James C. Dobson, *Dare to Discipline* (Carol Stream, IL: Tyndale House, 1970), 7.
2. The first part of this quote is from "The New Strong-Willed Child," an article appearing online at http://www.family.org/fofmag/pf/a0033440.cfm. The second part is from *Dare to Discipline*, 36.
3. The familiar form of the saying is derived from Proverbs 13:24: "Those who spare the rod hate their children, but those who love them are diligent to discipline them."
4. From *Focus on the Family: Celebrating Twenty-Five Years of God's Faithfulness* (San Diego, CA: Tehabi Books, 2002), 31–32.
5. Michael J. Gerson, Major Garrett, and Carolyn Kleiner, "A Righteous Indignation James Dobson—Psychologist, Radio Host, Family-Values Crusader—Is Set To Topple The Political Establishment," *U.S. News & World Report*, May 4, 1998, 20–24, 29. Dobson reportedly made similar remarks at a national meeting of Republican conservatives in Phoenix a month earlier.
6. These were estimates provided early in 2005 by Tom Minnery, Focus on the Family's vice president of public policy, in a telephone interview.
7. Randall Balmer, "Athletes in Action," *Encyclopedia of Evangelicalism* (Waco, TX: Baylor University Press, 2004), 41–42.
8. Clifford Putney, "Muscular Christianity," *The Encyclopedia of Informal Education*, www.infed.org/christianeducation/muscular_christianity.htm. Last updated: January 28, 2005. The article is excerpted from *Men and Masculinities: A Social, Cultural, and Historical Encyclopedia*, Michael Kimmel and Amy Aronson, eds. (Santa Barbara, CA: ABC-Clid, 2004).

9.  In January 2005, six months after my visit, White retired as the Navigators' international president and CEO, and was succeeded by Michael W. Treneer. White continues as chairman of the Navigators' board of directors.

10. Alan Cooperman, "Group Trains Air Force Cadets to Proselytize," *Washington Post*, November 12, 2005, A6.

11. Tom Roeder, "Academy: Group Treated Normally," *The Gazette* (Colorado Springs), November 15, 2005, B1.

12. Robertson's and Falwell's remarks, their later explanations, and the repudiations are reported by Laurie Goodstein in "After the Attacks: Finding Fault," *New York Times*, September 15, 2001, 15.

## 4. SADDLEBACK SEEKERS

1.  Michael Cromartie, "Salvation Inflation? A conversation with Alan Wolfe," *Books & Culture*, March 1, 2004.

2.  Peter F. Drucker, "Management's New Paradigms," *Forbes*, October 5, 1998, 152.

3.  See Scott Thumma, Dave Travis, and Warren Bird, "Megachurches Today 2005, Summary Research Findings," on the Hartford Seminary Web site: hirr.hartsem.edu/org/megastoday2005_summaryreport.html.

4.  From an April 5, 2004, survey for *U.S. News & World Report* and PBS's Religion & Ethics NewsWeekly, conducted by Greenberg Quinlan Rosner Research.

5.  Jonathan Mahler, "The Soul of the New Exurb," *New York Times Magazine*, March 27, 2005.

6.  Gary Thomas, *Sacred Marriage* (Grand Rapids, MI: Zondervan, 2000).

7.  Ibid., 202–4.

8.  Ibid., 204.

9.  Ibid., 206.

10. From the Wiccan Rede, usually attributed to Gerald Gardner (1884–1964), a British writer and occultist who is considered by many to be the founder of Wicca. See en.wikipedia.org/wiki/Wicca.

11. www.saddleback.com/flash/believe2.html.

## 5. WHEATON THUNDER

1.  This chapter is based on "A Place for Faith," an article I wrote for *U.S. News & World Report* and that appeared in the magazine's 2004 college guide, *America's Best Colleges*. It contains excerpts from that article as well as additional material.

2.  From a comparison of fall enrollment growth from 1990 to 2004, based on U.S. Department of Education numbers compiled by the National Association of Independent Colleges and Universities and made available by the Council for Christian Colleges and Universities. The report may be viewed online at www.cccu.org/news/newsID.396/news_detail.asp.

3.  Figures for the 2005–6 academic year supplied by Wheaton's media relations office.

4.  Malone, David B. "Jonathan Blanchard: Abolitionist," (an exhibit on the abolitionist career of Jonathan Blanchard), Buswell Memorial Library, September 2003–February 2004. Online exhibit created January 2004 at www.wheaton.edu/learnres/ARCSC/exhibits/jblanchard1/.

5.  Alan Wolfe, "The Opening of the Evangelical Mind," *Atlantic*, October 1, 2000, 55.

6.  Ibid.

7.  Ibid.

8.  Mark Noll, *The Scandal of the Evangelical Mind* (Grand Rapids, MI: Eerdmans, 1994 ), 3.

9.  Ibid., 16.

10. The Gallup Poll News Service, November 19, 2004. Meanwhile, an August 30, 2005, survey by the Pew Forum on Religion and Public Life found that 70 percent of white evangelicals believe that "humans and other living things have existed in their present form from the beginning of time." See pewforum.org/surveys/origins/#3.

11. Meg McSherry Breslin, "It'll Be Dancing By the Book," *Chicago Tribune,* October 24, 2003, 1.

12. Richard N. Ostling, "Rule Change Reflects New Challenges," *Chicago Tribune,* March 7, 2003, 10.

13. LeAnn Spencer, "Thunder of Approval Meets Mascot," *Chicago Tribune,* September 30, 2000, 5.

## 6. MAYAN MISSION

1.  Mark 16:15.

2.  Missionary statistics were provided by Johnson via e-mail and are derived from his "Missiometrics 2005: A Global Survey of World Mission," coauthored with David B. Barrett and Peter F. Crossing, and published by the International Bulletin of Missionary Research.

3.  From an unpublished paper, "The Changing Face of Evangelicals," presented to the Institute for the Study of American Evangelicals by George M. Marsden, history professor at the University of Notre Dame, October 13–14, 2005.

4.  Quotes from Johnson are from a telephone interview with the author, March 1, 2006.

5.  Philip Jenkins, *The Next Christendom: The Coming of Global Christianity* (Oxford: Oxford University Press, 2002), 2.

6.  Larry Rohter, "Searing Indictment," *New York Times*, February 27, 1999, A4.

## 7. BACK TO THE GARDEN

1.  See www.barlowgirl.com/bios/.

2.  The number of pledges is reported by Lifeway Christian Resources, a bookselling entity of the Southern Baptist Convention, sponsor of the True Love Waits campaign, and can be found on the Lifeway Web site: www.lifeway.com/tlw/media/news_justthefacts.asp. Preliminary studies of the effectiveness of such campaigns so far have produced mixed results.

3.  See www.harvest.org/news/index.php/1/8/25/68.html.

4.  *Encyclopedia of Evangelicalism* (Waco, TX: Baylor University Press, 2004), 303.

5.  Swaggart, Jimmy, "Two Points of View: 'Christian' Rock and Roll," *The Evangelist,* August 1985, 49–50.

6.  I am deeply indebted to freelance journalist Steve Rabey, whose comprehensive and highly readable history of contemporary Christian music appeared in the July 1998 issue of *CCM* magazine, 18–44. The article proved to be an invaluable resource in the preparation of this summary of key events, artists, and trends.

7.  From a telephone interview with the author in March 2004.

8.  As quoted by Donald Hughes, "Being T-Bone Burnett," on the Jesus Journal.com Web site: http://www.jesusjournal.com/content/view/120/85/

9.  Out of respect for the privacy of the young people, I have changed their names and those of their church, leaders, and hometown. However, all of the conversations and descriptions recorded here are accurate.

## 8. CAPITAL CRUSADERS

1.  Susan Page, "Christian Right's Alliances Bend Political Spectrum," *USA Today,* June 15, 2005, A1.

2.  According to a postelection survey by the University of Akron's Ray C. Bliss Center for Applied Politics, sponsored by the Pew Forum on Religion and Public Life, 63 percent of evangelicals turned out in 2004

and 78 percent of them voted for Bush. Voter turnout in the general population was 60.8 percent, with 51 percent for Bush.

3.  The document was approved by the NAE board on October 7, 2004, and appears in full on the NAE Web site: www.nae.net/images/civic_responsibility2.pdf.

4.  As reported by Adelle Banks of the Religion News Service, March 11, 2005.

5.  As reported by Michael Janofsky, "When Clean Air Is a Biblical Obligation," *New York Times,* November 7, 2005, A18.

6.  Jim VandeHei, "Pipeline to the President for GOP Conservatives," *Washington Post,* December 24, 2004, A15.

7.  Haggard is quoted by Lara Marlowe, "Born Again Bush Can Be Sure of Millions of Evangelical Votes," *Irish Times,* September 14, 2004, 11. Haggard made a similar comment to me during an interview in his Colorado Springs office on June 4, 2004: "We had more [White House influence] under the Clinton administration than we have under the Bush administration. The Clinton administration never denied us once. Never once."

8.  The USNews/PBS survey was conducted March 16–April 4, 2004, by Greenberg Quinlan Rosner Research, and the results were reported in part in Jeffrey L. Sheler, "Nearer My God to Thee," *U.S. News & World Report,* May 3, 2004, 59. The figures from Green were obtained during an e-mail exchange with the author in November 2005.

9.  Sheler, "Nearer My God to Thee," 59.

10. Christian Smith, *Christian America? What Evangelicals Really Want* (Berkeley and Los Angeles: University of California Press, 2000), 94, 122.

11. Mark A. Noll, *American Evangelical Christianity: An Introduction* (Oxford: Blackwell, 2001), 17.

12. Jerry Falwell, *Strength for the Journey: An Autobiography* (New York: Simon & Schuster, 1987), 334-341.

13. Randall Balmer, "Religious Right," *Encyclopedia of Evangelicalism* (Waco, TX: Baylor University Press, 2004), 575.

14. Falwell, 363–64; Sara Diamond, *Not By Politics Alone: The Enduring Influence of the Christian Right* (New York: Guilford Press, 1998), 67.

15. Frances Fitzgerald, "A Disciplined, Charging Army," *The New Yorker,* May 18, 1981, 54–63.

16. Allan J. Mayer, "A Tide of Born-Again Politics," *Newsweek,* September 15, 1980, 28.

17. See William Martin, *With God on Our Side: The Rise of the Religious Right in America* (New York: Broadway Books, 1996), 220.

18. Quoted in Frances Fitzgerald, *Cities on a Hill* (New York: Simon & Schuster, 1986), 189, and cited in Martin, *With God on Our Side*, 220.

19. Allan J. Mayer, "A Tide of Born-Again Politics," *Newsweek*, September 15, 1980, 28.

20. Under the convoluted system then in place in Michigan, Republican precinct caucuses elected delegates to a state convention that, in turn, elected delegates to the Republican National Convention. Robertson supporters claimed to have won 41 percent of some 9,000 state delegate slots in the August 1987 caucuses, about the same as Bush, while Jack Kemp was said to have finished a distant third. That should have translated into about 40 of Michigan's 77 delegates to the GOP national convention going to Robertson. But after a drawn-out process of procedural and court challenges, Bush ended up with 37 Michigan delegates, Kemp with 32, and Robertson with 8. After the 1988 election Michigan Republicans replaced the caucus system with a presidential primary.

21. Balmer, "Christian Coalition of America," *Encyclopedia of Evangelicalism*, 160–61.

22. Reed is quoted in "Robertson Regroups 'Invisible Army' Into New Coalition," *Christianity Today*, April 23, 1990, 35.

23. "The Gospel According to Ralph," *Time*, May 15, 1995, 28.

24. See Bill Sizemore, "Once Powerful Group Teeters on Insolvency," *Virginian-Pilot*, October 8, 2005, A1.

25. Ibid., quoting Mark J. Rozell, a professor of public policy at George Mason University in Fairfax, Virginia.

26. Green is quoted by Judy Kosterlitz in "Pious and Partisan," *The National Journal*, October 23, 2004.

27. Martin, 212–13.

28. Jeffrey Hadden and Anson Shupe, *Televangelism: Power and Politics on God's Frontier* (New York: Henry Holt, 1988), 147.

29. Tina Rosenberg, "How the Media Made the Moral Majority," *Washington Monthly*, May 1982.

30. In Cal Thomas and Ed Dobson, *Blinded By Might: Why the Religious Right Can't Save America* (Grand Rapids, MI: Zondervan, 1999), 91.

31. Diamond, 79–80.

32. Quoted by Martin, 212.

33. "Judge not ..." (Matthew 7:1); "By their fruits ..." (Matthew 7:20).

34. George W. Bush, *A Charge to Keep: My Journey to the White House* (New York: Perennial, 1999), 136.

35. Quoted by Steven G. Vegh, "Strategist's Bid for Miers Drowned Out by Critics," *Virginian-Pilot,* October 28, 2005, A1.

36. From a telephone interview on October 28, 2005.

37. Michael Grunwald, Jo Becker, and John Pomfret, "Strong Grounding in the Church Could Be a Clue to Miers's Priorities," *Washington Post,* October 5, 2005, A1. Adams was alluding to Hebrews 11:1: "Now faith is the substance of things hoped for, the evidence of things not seen" (King James Version).

38. As reported by Deborah Caldwell, "Should Christian Missionaries Heed the Call in Iraq?" *New York Times,* April 6, 2003, 14.

39. Ibid.

40. For the diversity of views see, for example, Bill Broadway, "Evangelicals' Voices Speak Softly About Iraq," *Washington Post,* January 25, 2003, B9. On polling data, a Pew Research Center for the People and the Press survey taken in March 2003, found that nearly 76.7 percent of white evangelicals "favored the U.S. taking military action to end Saddam Hussein's rule" compared to 64.8 percent of the general population. A similar Pew poll in October 2005 found 67.9 percent of evangelicals still thought going to war was the right decision, compared to 48.2 percent of the general population. See people-press.org/reports/.

41. For election results, see John F. Burns and James Glanz, "Iraqi Shiites Win, But Margin Is Less Than Projection," *New York Times,* February 13, 2005, A1. For Cizik's remarks, see "Praying for Democracy," *NAE Washington Insight,* February 2005.

42. John Cochran, "New Heaven, New Earth," *Congressional Quarterly Weekly,* October 14, 2005.

43. Thomas and Dobson, 73.

44. Ibid., 193.

45. Charles Colson, "What's Right about the Religious Right?" *Christianity Today,* September 6, 1999, 58.

## 9. REDEMPTION ROAD

1. Mark A. Noll, *American Evangelical Christianity: An Introduction* (Oxford: Blackwell, 2001), 44.

2. Ibid., 283.

3. Jeff Robinson, "SBTS Enrollment Gains Prompt Trustees to Revise Master Plan," *Baptist Press,* October 20, 2003.

4. Steve Kloehn, "Southern Baptists Lean More to the Right," *Chicago Tribune,* June 14, 2000, 5.

5. R. Albert Mohler, Jr., "Evangelical: What's In a Name?" *The Coming*

*Evangelical Crisis,* John H. Armstrong, ed. (Chicago: Moody Press, 1996), 31–32.

6.  Cal Thomas and Ed Dobson, *Blinded by Might: Why the Religious Right Can't Save America* (Grand Rapids, MI: Zondervan, 1999), 193.

7.  The text of the Chicago Declaration of Evangelical Social Concern may be found at the Web site of Evangelicals for Social Action: www .esa-online.org/conferences/chicago/chicago.html.

8.  Cited by Alan Rifkin, "Jesus with a Genius Grant," *Los Angeles Times Magazine,* November 23, 2003, Part I, 22.

# Suggested Reading

Armstrong, John H., ed. *The Coming Evangelical Crisis*. Chicago: Moody Press, 1996.

Balmer, Randall, and Lauren F. Winner. *Protestantism in America*. New York: Columbia University Press, 2002.

Bartholomew, Craig, Robin Parry, and Andrew West. *The Futures of Evangelicalism: Issues and Prospects*. Grand Rapids, MI: Kregel, 2003.

Carpenter, Joel A. *Revive Us Again: The Reawakening of American Fundamentalism*. New York: Oxford University Press, 1997.

Dayton, Donald W., and Robert K. Johnston. *The Variety of American Evangelicalism*. Knoxville: University of Tennessee Press, 1991.

Graham, Billy. *Just As I Am: The Autobiography of Billy Graham*. Grand Rapids, MI: Zondervan, 1997.

Henry, Carl F. H. *The Uneasy Conscience of Modern Fundamentalism*. Grand Rapids, MI: William B. Eerdmans, 1947.

Jenkins, Philip. *The Next Christendom: The Coming of Global Christianity*. Oxford: Oxford University Press, 2002.

Kantzer, Kenneth S., and Carl F. H. Henry, eds. *Evangelical Affirmations*. Grand Rapids, MI: Academie Books, 1990.

Marsden, George M. *Fundamentalism and American Culture*. New York: Oxford University Press, 2006.

Martin, William. *A Prophet With Honor: The Billy Graham Story*. New York: William Morrow and Company, 1991.

———. *With God on Our Side: The Rise of the Religious Right in America*. New York: Broadway Books, 1996.

Mouw, Richard J. *Calvinism in the Las Vegas Airport: Making Connections in Today's World*. Grand Rapids, MI: Zondervan, 2004.

————. *Uncommon Decency: Christian Civility in an Uncivil World*. Downers Grove, IL: InterVarsity Press, 1992.

Murray, Iain H. *Evangelicalism Divided: A Record of Crucial Change in the Years 1950 to 2000*. Carlisle, PA: The Banner of Truth Trust, 2000.

Noll, Mark A. *American Evangelical Christianity: An Introduction*. Malden, MA: Blackwell Publishers, Inc., 2001.

————. *The Rise of Evangelicalism: The Age of Edwards, Whitefield and the Wesleys*. Downers Grove, IL: InterVarsity Press, 2003.

————. *The Scandal of the Evangelical Mind*. Grand Rapids, MI: William B. Eerdmans, 1994.

Penning, James M., and Corwin E. Smidt. *Evangelicalism: The Next Generation*. Grand Rapids, MI: Baker Academic, 2002.

Sine, Tom. *Cease Fire: Searching for Sanity in America's Culture Wars*. Grand Rapids, MI: William B. Eerdmans, 1995.

Smith, Christian. *American Evangelicalism: Embattled and Thriving*. Chicago: University of Chicago Press, 1998.

————. *Christian America? What Evangelicals Really Want*. Berkeley: University of California Press, 2000.

Thomas, Cal, and Ed Dobson. *Blinded by Might: Why the Religious Right Can't Save America*. Grand Rapids, MI: Zondervan, 1999.

Webber, Robert E. *The Younger Evangelicals: Facing the Challenges of the New World*. Grand Rapids, MI: Baker Books, 2002.

Wolfe, Alan. *The Transformation of American Religion: How We Actually Live Our Faith*. New York: Free Press, 2003.

# Index